Office 2016 For Seniors For Dummies

A Wiley Brand

by Faithe Wempen

For Dummies
A Wiley Brand

Office 2016 For Seniors For Dummies®

Published by:
John Wiley & Sons, Inc.,
111 River Street,
Hoboken, NJ 07030-5774, www.wiley.com

Published simultaneously in Canada

Library of Congress Control Number: 2015950349

ISBN 978-1-119-07749-7 (pbk); ISBN 978-1-119-07752-7 (ebk); ISBN 978-1-119-07738-1 (ebk)

Manufactured in the United States of America

10 9 8 7 6 5 4 3 2 1

Contents at a Glance

Table of Contents

Introduction

Microsoft Office 2016 is by far the most popular suite of productivity applications in the world, and with good reason. Its applications are powerful enough for business and professional use, and yet easy enough that a beginner can catch on to the basics with just a few simple lessons.

If you're new to Office 2016, this book can help you separate the essential features you need from the obscure and more sophisticated ones you don't. For the four major Office applications I cover in this book — Word, Excel, Outlook, and PowerPoint — I walk you through the most important and common features, showing you how to put them to work for projects in your job, everyday life, and home.

About This Book

This book is written specifically for mature people like you, who are relatively new to using Office applications and want to master the basics. In this book, I tried to take into account the types of activities that might interest you, such as investment planning, personal finance, email, and documents and presentations that you might need to prepare for work, clubs, volunteer opportunities, or other organizations that you participate in.

Foolish Assumptions

This book assumes that you can start your computer and use the keyboard and mouse (or whatever device moves the pointer onscreen).

If you're using a computer for the first time, *Computers For Seniors For Dummies* shows you the essential skills that all computer applications use.

Office 2016 runs on Windows 10 (the newest version of Windows), Windows 8, and Windows 7 computer operating systems, so I assume you're using one of these. The examples in this book show Office 2016 running in Windows 10, but Office works mostly the same on all operating systems.

How This Book Is Organized

This book is divided into several handy parts to help you find what you need and skip stuff you don't use.

Part I: Getting Started with Office

In this first part of the book, I explain some basics that apply to all the Office 2016 applications generically, such as saving, opening, and printing files. I also show you some features that all Office 2016 applications have in common, such as selecting and formatting text, using the Clipboard, and applying formatting themes.

Part II: Word

This part explores the most popular application in the Office suite, Microsoft Word. This word processing program helps you create letters, reports, envelopes, and myriad other text-based documents. You'll see how to format text, change page size and orientation, insert graphics, and more.

Part III: Excel

In this part of the book, you can read about Excel, the Office spreadsheet application. See how to enter text and numbers in a worksheet, write formulas and functions that perform calculations, and format worksheets attractively. You can also find out how to create charts and use Excel to store simple databases.

Part IV: Outlook

Outlook is the email, contact management, and calendar application in Office. In this part of the book, discover how to send and receive email in Outlook, and also how to use Outlook to track appointments and store your personal address book.

Part V: PowerPoint

In this part of the book, I show you the basics of PowerPoint, the Office presentation application. You can read how to create presentations that include text and graphics; create cool animation and transition effects; add a musical soundtrack; and share your presentation with others, either in a live-action show or on CD.

The Appendix shows some simple ways to customize how Office applications work when you start them.

Conventions Used in This Book

This book uses certain conventions to help you find your way:

- Wherever possible, I use labels on figures to point out what you should notice on them. These labels reinforce something I say in the text or contain extra tips and hints.
- When you have to type something, I put it in **bold type**.
- For menu and Ribbon commands, I use the ➪ symbol to separate the steps. For example, if I say to choose Home➪Clipboard➪Copy, click the Home tab, find

the Clipboard group, and then click the Copy button in that group. In most cases, I provide the group name as part of the path to help you find the command more quickly. (Each tab has a lot of different commands on it.)

Tip icons point out extra features, special insights and helps, or things to look out for.

Warning icons indicate potential problems to avoid, problems that are difficult to fix or make bad things happen.

Time to Get Started!

This is your book; use it how you want. You can start at the beginning and read it straight through, or you can hop to whatever chapter or topic you want. For those of you who are pretty new to computers, you might want to start at the beginning. If you're new to Office, the beginning part will give you a good foundation on what features work similarly in all the programs.

Part I
Getting Started with Office 2016

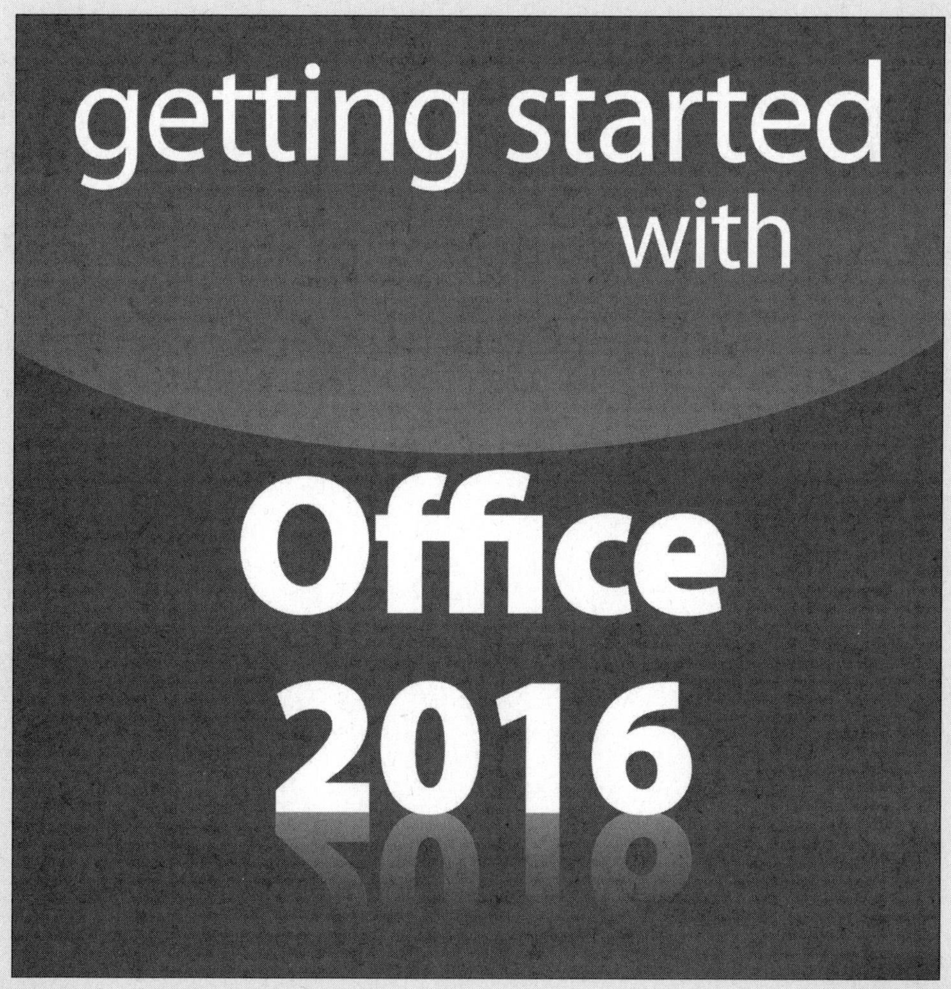

Visit www.dummies.com for more great content online.

The Two-Dollar Tour

Chapter 1

Step right up for a tour of Microsoft Office, the most popular suite of applications in the world!

Here are some of the things you can do with Office:

- Write letters, reports, and newsletters.
- Track bank account balances and investments.
- Create presentations to support speeches and meetings.
- Send and receive email.

The Office suite consists of several very powerful applications (programs), each with its own features and interface, but the applications also have a lot in common with one another. Learning about one application gives you a head start in learning the others.

In this chapter (and Chapter 2), I take you on a quick tour of some of the features that multiple Office applications have in common, including the tabbed Ribbon area. I also show you how to insert text and graphics in the various applications, and how to move around and zoom in and out.

Get ready to . . .

In these first few chapters, I use Microsoft Word, PowerPoint, and Excel as the example applications because all of them work more or less the same way: They let you open and save data files that contain your work on various projects. Microsoft Outlook works a bit differently, as I show you in Chapters 11 through 13.

This book shows Microsoft Office in the Windows 10 operating system. Office works the same way in Windows 7 and Windows 8 except for minor differences in opening the applications and working with files. I'll explain any differences as we go along.

Start an Office Application

The steps for starting an Office application differ depending on which version of Windows you have:

- **Windows 10:** Click the Start button, and then click All Apps. Scroll down to the M section, and click Microsoft Office 16. Then click the desired Office application.
- **Windows 8.1:** From the Start screen, click the down arrow at the bottom and then locate and click the application you want. Or, from the Start screen, begin typing the first few letter of the application's name and then click it in the search results.
- **Windows 7:** Click the Start button, and click All Programs. Click the Microsoft Office 2016 folder, and then click the Office application you want to start.

Start a New Document

When you open Word, Excel, or PowerPoint, a Start screen appears, containing a list of recently used documents and thumbnail images of templates you can use to start new documents. To start a new blank document (which you'll want to do in order to follow along with this chapter), you can press the Esc key, or you can click the Blank template. The template has a slightly different name depending on the application; in Word it is called *Blank document,* in Excel it's *Blank workbook,* and so on. **Figure 1-1** shows the Start screen for Microsoft Word, for example.

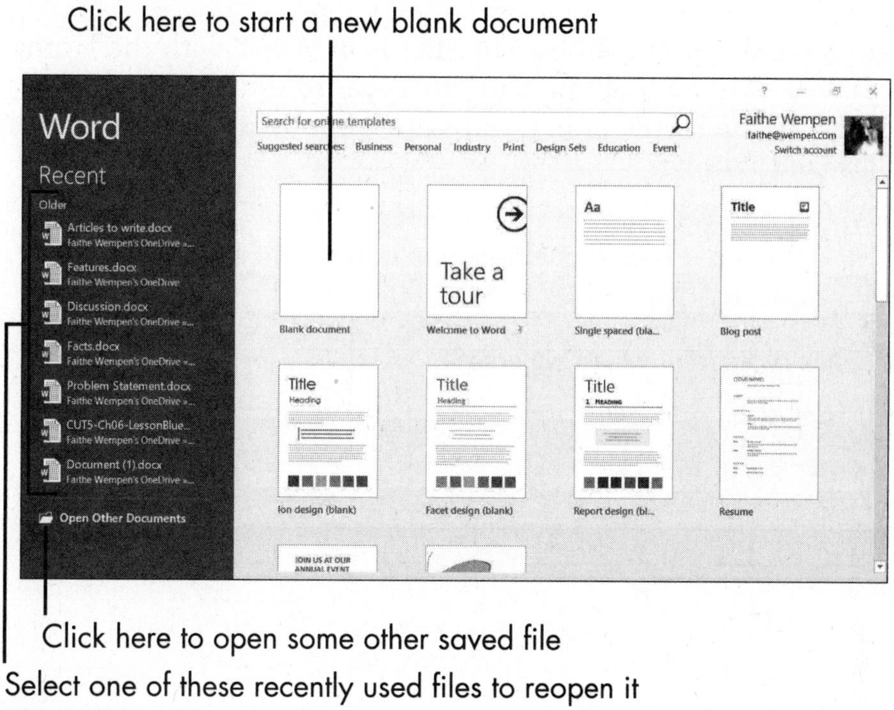

Figure 1-1

To create an additional new blank document after the application is already up-and-running, press Ctrl+N at any time.

Office 2010 and earlier started a blank document automatically in Word, Excel, and PowerPoint, without having to go through a Start screen. If you want that old-style behavior back, click File and then click Options. On the General page, scroll down to the bottom and clear the Show the Start Screen When This Application Starts check box.

Explore the Office Ribbon and Tabs

All Office 2016 applications have a common system of navigation called the *Ribbon,* which is a tabbed bar across the top of the application window. Each tab is like a page of buttons. You click different tabs to access different sets of buttons and features.

Figure 1-2 shows the Ribbon in Microsoft Word, with the Home tab displayed. Within a tab, buttons are organized into groups. In Figure 1-2, the Home tab's groups are Clipboard, Font, Paragraph, Styles, and Editing.

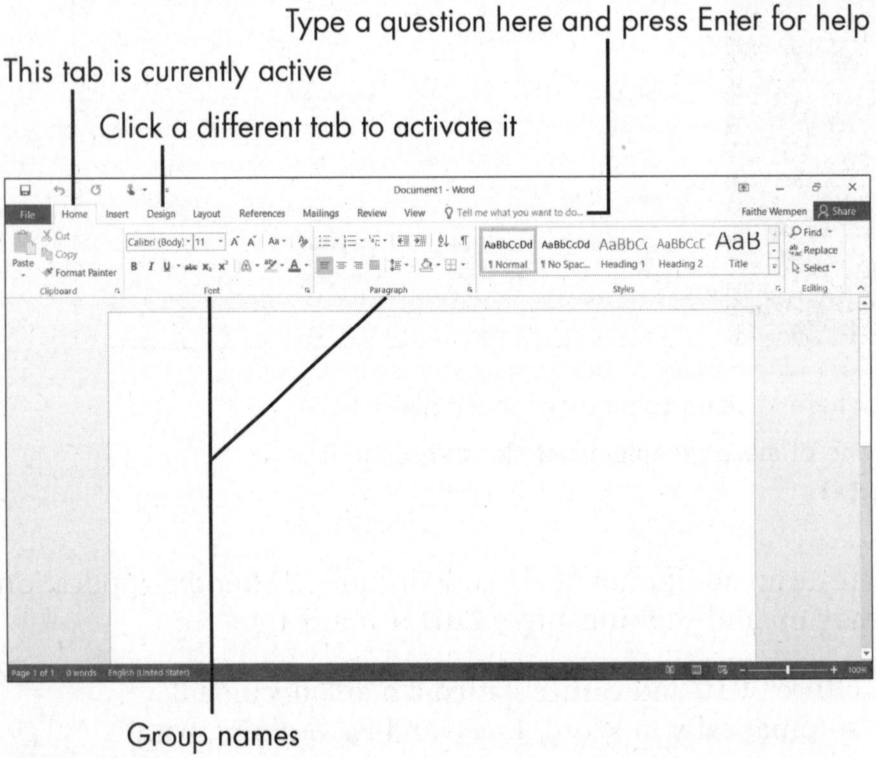

Figure 1-2

Each Office application has a set of tabs for the tasks it performs. For example, Word has a Mailings tab that holds the commands for doing mail merges. Excel has a Formulas tab that holds the commands for setting up calculations.

You might find tabs that were added by *third-party* (non-Microsoft) software. For example, if you have a program called Adobe Acrobat installed, you might have an Acrobat tab in each of the Office applications.

The buttons and controls on the tabs operate in different ways. **Figure 1-3** points out some examples on Word's Home tab.

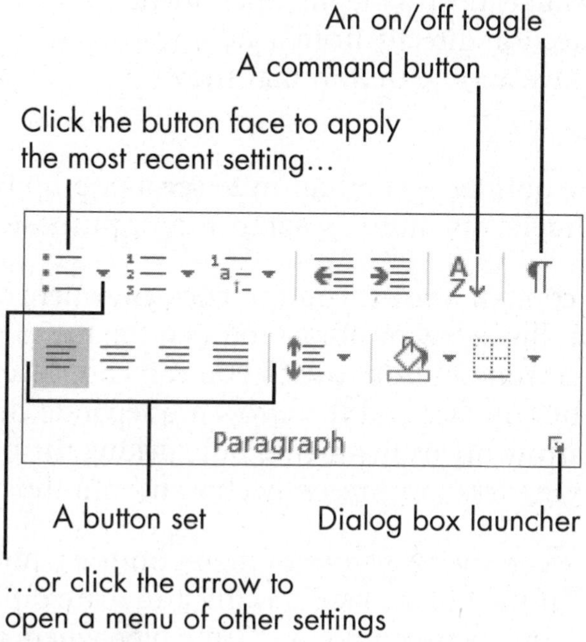

Figure 1-3

- **On/off toggles:** When the button is selected (it turns orange), the feature is on. Each time you click the button, it switches between on and off.
- **Command buttons:** When you click the button, the command executes. If you click a command button again, the command repeats.
- **Connected button sets:** In connected sets of buttons, selecting a button deselects (cancels) the previous selection in the set.

For example, Figure 1-3 has four buttons in the bottom row for paragraph alignment. The leftmost one is selected; if you click one of the others, it's automatically canceled.

- **Menu buttons:** Buttons with arrows on them open menus or color palettes.
- **Galleries:** A *gallery* is like a permanently open menu or palette; click a selection directly from a gallery. Most galleries also have a More button that shows more choices.

You can hover the mouse pointer over a button to see a pop-up box, called a ScreenTip, which tells the button's name and/or purpose.

With some buttons that contain arrows, you can click anywhere on the button face — directly on the arrow or not — to open the menu or *palette* (an array of colored squares from which you can choose a color). With others, the button face and the arrow are separate clickable areas. Clicking the arrow opens the menu, but clicking the button face applies whatever setting was most recently chosen from the menu.

To tell the difference between the two types of menu buttons, point the mouse at the button. If the button face and the arrow are different colors or if there is a thin line between them, it's the type where you have to click directly on the arrow to get the menu. If there's no separation, you can click anywhere on the button.

In the bottom-right corner of many of the groups is a small square with an arrow. Clicking this square (called a *dialog box launcher*) opens a dialog box related to that group. For example, the one for the Paragraph group in Figure 1-3 opens the Paragraph dialog box, which contains controls for every button in that group plus more options not available on the Ribbon.

Not sure which tab contains the command you want, or what the command is called? The Tell me what you want to do. . . box (shown in Figure 1-2) enables you to ask questions in plain English. Just type your question in the box and press Enter to see a list of relevant commands, and then click the one you want to issue that command.

When you resize the application's window so the window is narrower than normal, or when you run the application on a computer that has low-resolution video settings, the controls on the Ribbon *compress* (squeeze together). Some of the groups turn into single buttons with drop-down lists for accessing the individual controls within that group. For example, in **Figure 1-4**, most of the groups are compressed, and one of the groups has been opened as a drop-down list.

Above the main part of the Ribbon is a small toolbar called the Quick Access toolbar. You can add buttons for frequently used commands here (as many as you can fit). To add a button, right-click any control from any tab and choose Add to Quick Access Toolbar, as shown in **Figure 1-5**. To change the position of the Quick Access Toolbar, right-click it and choose Show the Quick Access Toolbar Below the Ribbon (or Above, if it's already below).

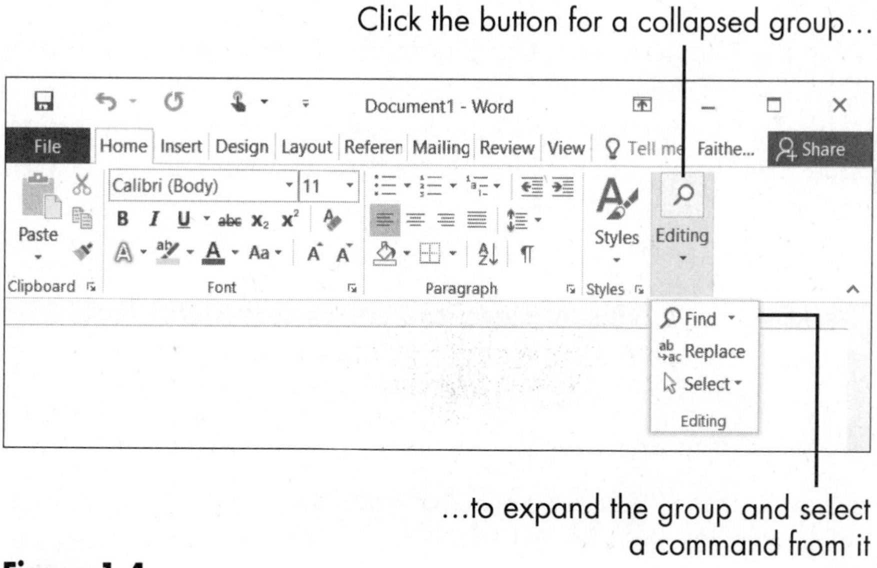

Figure 1-4

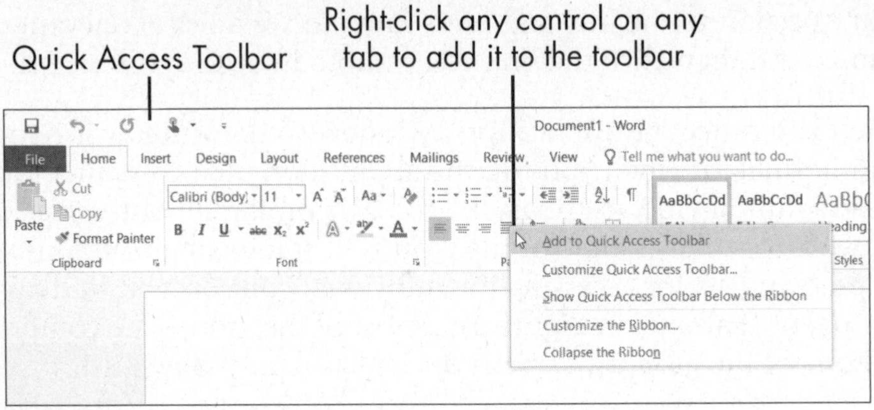

Figure 1-5

You can also customize the Ribbon itself, but that's beyond the scope of this book. If you want to experiment with it on your own, choose File⇨Options and click Customize Ribbon.

Understand the File Menu (Backstage View)

Clicking the File tab opens the File menu, also known as Backstage view. Backstage View provides access to commands that have to do with the data file you are working with — things like saving, opening, printing, mailing, and checking its properties. The File tab is a different color in each application. In Word, for example, it is blue. To leave Backstage view, click some other tab or press the Esc key.

Backstage View lists top-level categories at the left; click one to see the commands available. The content to the right of the category list depends on what you have chosen.

When a document is open and you enter Backstage View, the Info category appears. It provides information about the current document, and offers commands for protecting the document, checking for issues, and managing versions. In addition, if the document uses a different file format than Word 2016, a Convert button appears, enabling you to upgrade the document format. See **Figure 1-6**.

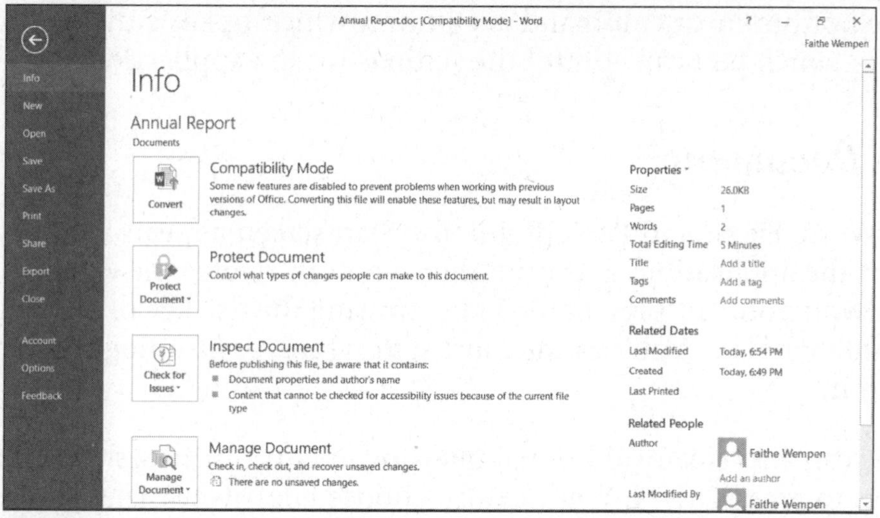

Figure 1-6

Some of the other categories, when selected, make additional commands or options appear to the right of the list. For example, in **Figure 1-7**, you can see that when Share is selected (in Word), a submenu of commands appears to the right, along with buttons for specific operations.

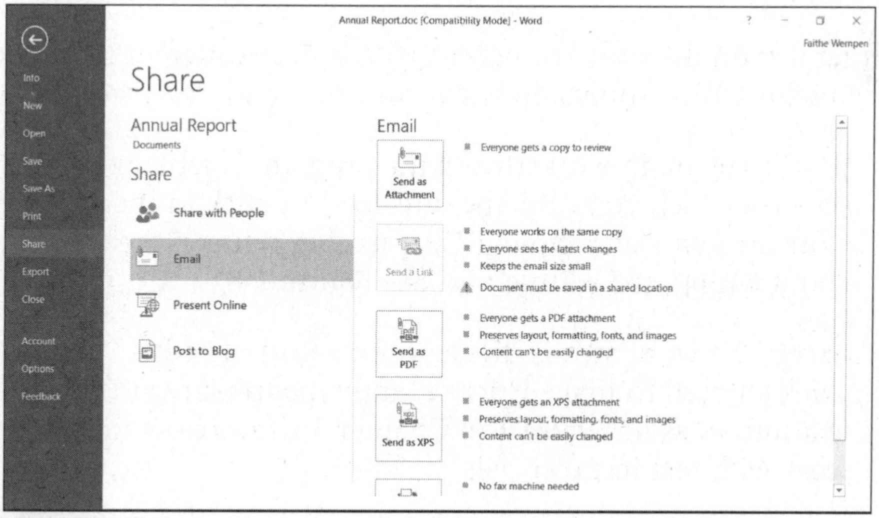

Figure 1-7

The bottom-most command is Options, which opens a dialog box from which you can control the settings for the application.

Create a Document

In Word, Excel, and PowerPoint, the Start screen appears when you start the application, and from there you can create a new document (or workbook, or presentation) by pressing the Esc key or clicking the Blank template. You can then just start typing or inserting content into it.

You can also create additional new documents. An easy shortcut to do so is to press Ctrl+N. You can also choose File⇨New. That latter method has the advantage of opening a selection of templates you can use to jumpstart your work if you don't want a totally blank document to start with. Choose one of the templates that appears, or click in the Search for online templates box, type a keyword, and press Enter to look for a certain kind of template. Let's forego the templates for now, though, and keep working in this chapter with a blank document.

Type Text

Putting text on the page (or onscreen) is a little different in each of the three major Office applications: Word, Excel, and PowerPoint.

- **Word:** The main work area of the program is a blank slate on which you can type directly. Just click in the work area and start typing! Chapter 2 explains more about typing and editing text. See **Figure 1-8**.
- **Excel:** The work area is divided into a grid of cells. Click any cell to make it active, and type to place text into it, as in **Figure 1-9**. Chapter 7 shows how to work with text in Excel cells.

In Word, there is a single work area

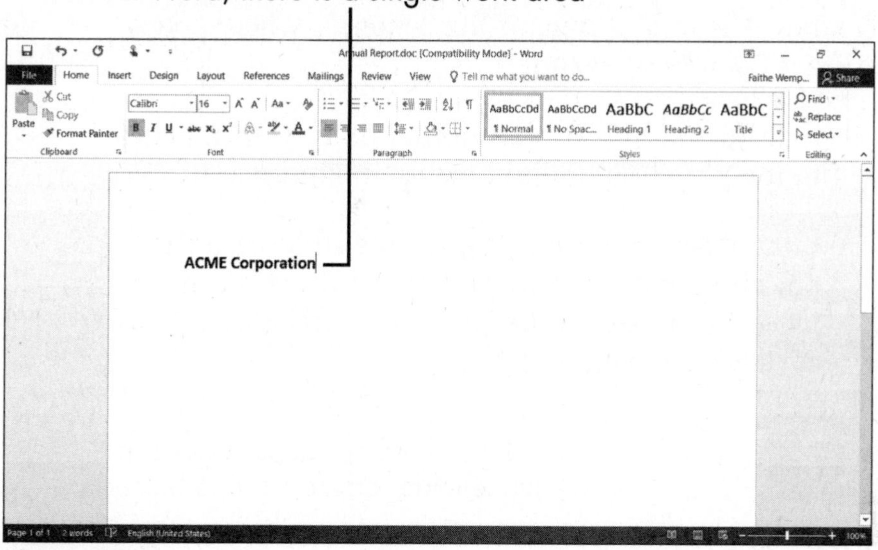

Figure 1-8

In Excel, text is entered into individual cells

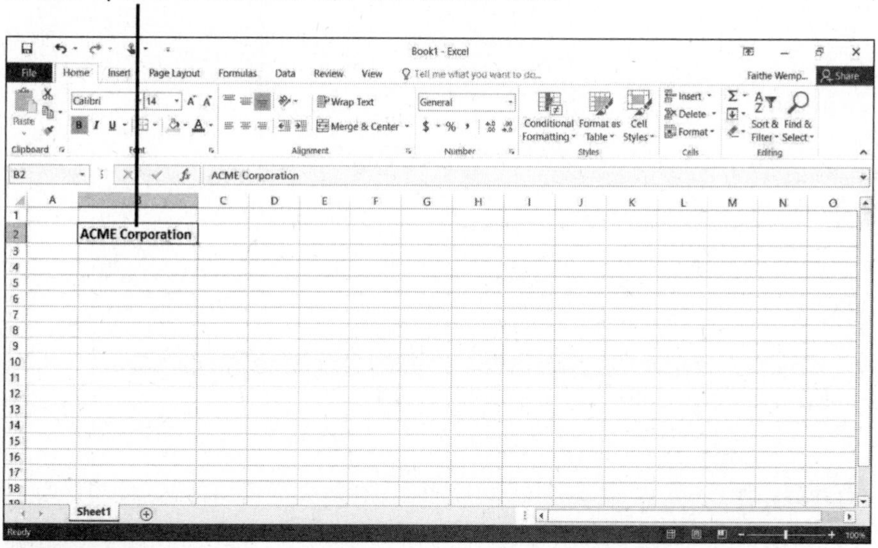

Figure 1-9

- **PowerPoint:** The work area is divided into three panes. The largest one, in the center, is where you insert content on a slide.
  - If a slide has a text placeholder on it, you can click in the placeholder and type, as in **Figure 1-10**.
  - If there isn't a placeholder on the slide, or if the placeholder doesn't meet your needs, you can place a text box on the slide manually. (That's covered in Chapter 11.)

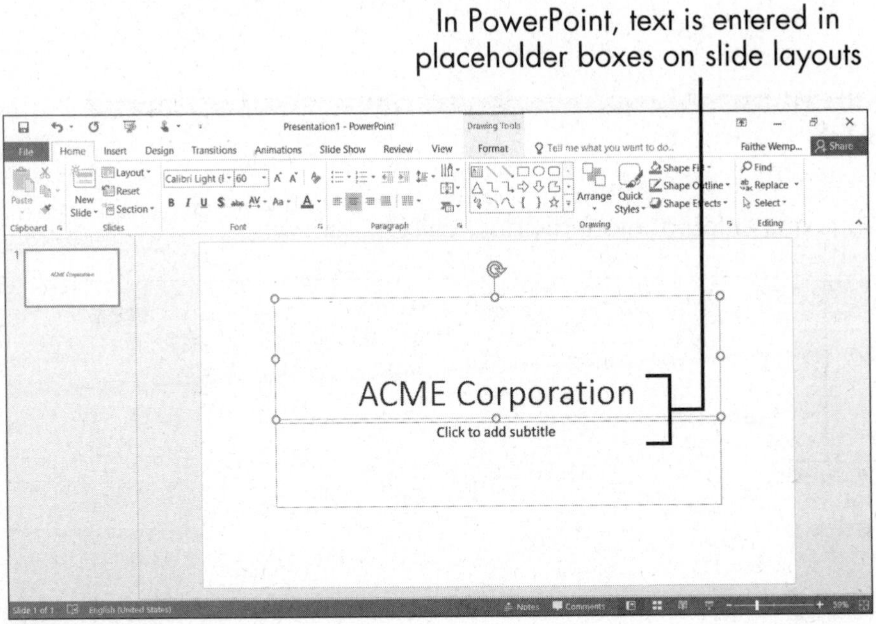

Figure 1-10

Insert a Picture

All Office applications accept various types of pictures. Here's how to insert a photo (or other graphic file) into Word, Excel, or PowerPoint:

1. Click the Insert tab.
2. Click the Pictures button. The Insert Picture dialog box opens. See **Figure 1-11**. The default location that opens is the Pictures folder for the user currently signed into Windows.

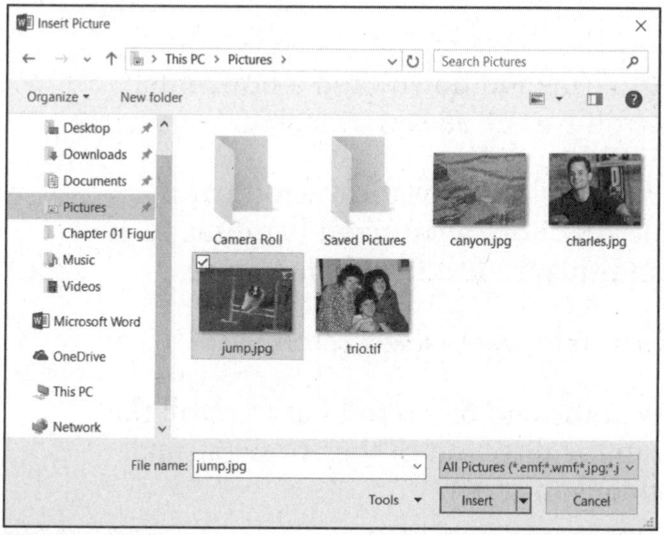

Figure 1-11

3. Select the picture you want to insert. (You might need to change to a different location. That's covered in Chapter 3.)
4. Click the Insert button.

The preceding steps apply to picture files, such as images from a digital camera or that you downloaded from the Internet. There are lots of other graphic types, such as online images, WordArt (stylized text), and drawn lines and shapes. Each of these has its own procedure for insertion. Later chapters discuss these in more detail.

You can drag and drop pictures directly from File Explorer into any document in an Office application.

Move Around in a Document

As you add content in one of the applications, there might be so much content that you can't see it all onscreen at once. You might need to scroll through the document to view different parts of it.

The simplest way to move around is by using the scroll bars with your mouse:

- In Excel, a vertical (up and down) and a horizontal (left to right) scroll bar are always available.
- In Word and PowerPoint, the vertical scroll bar is always available. The horizontal scroll bar disappears if there is no undisplayed text from side-to-side.

Figure 1-12 shows several ways to use a scroll bar:

- Click the arrow at the end of a scroll bar to scroll the display slowly in the direction of the arrow (a small amount each time you click).
- Drag the box in the scroll bar to scroll quickly.
- Click in the empty space on the bar to one side or the other of the scroll box to move one screenful at a time in that direction.

The size of the scroll box (the blank rectangle you drag in the scroll bar) indicates how much content you can't see at the moment. For example, in Figure 1-12, the scroll box occupies about one-half of the scroll bar; this means that there is about one screenful of undisplayed content. In a very large spreadsheet, the scroll box might be very small.

You can also move around by using keyboard shortcuts. As you gain experience with the applications, you might find using keyboard shortcuts more convenient than using the scroll bar. Chapter 4 lists shortcuts for Word, Chapter 7 lists shortcuts for Excel, and Chapter 14 lists shortcuts for PowerPoint.

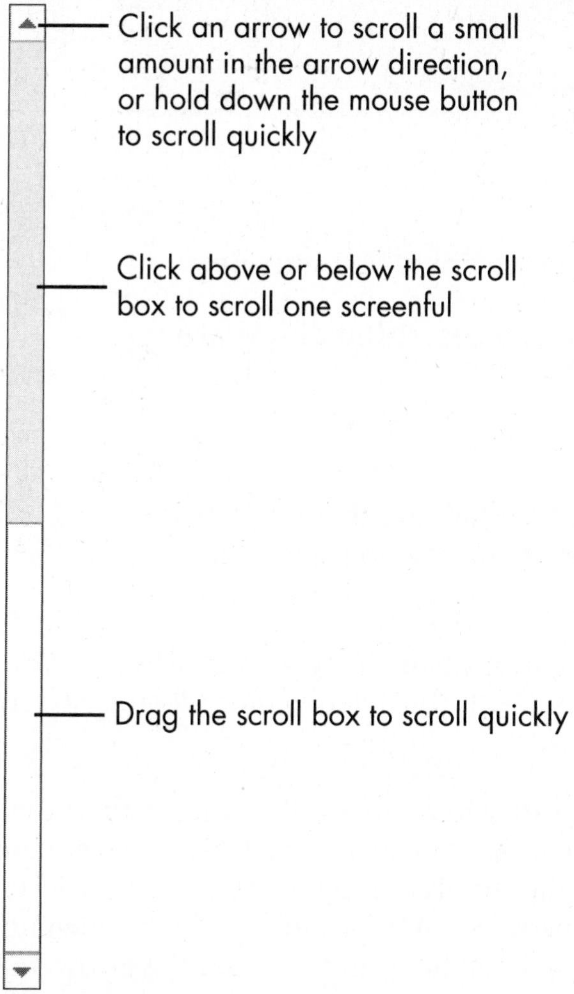

Figure 1-12

Select Content

Selecting content is an essential skill for any Office application. Many commands in Office applications apply to whatever text or graphics you select. For example, to make some text bold, select it first, and then click the Bold button. **Figure 1-13** shows some selected text.

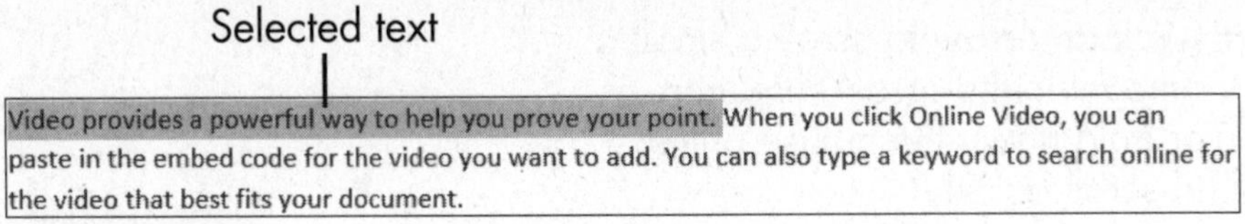

Figure 1-13

To select text in Word or PowerPoint, you can either

- Drag the mouse pointer across it (holding down the left mouse button)

  or

- Click where you want to start and then hold down Shift as you press the arrow keys to extend the selection.

When text is selected, its background changes color. The color depends on the color scheme in use; with the default color scheme, selected text is blue.

In Excel, you usually want to select entire cells rather than individual bits of text; when the cell is selected, any formatting or other commands that you issue applies to everything in that cell. To select a cell, click it. You can extend the selection to multiple cells by dragging across them or by holding down Shift and pressing the arrow keys.

You can also select text by using keyboard shortcuts. Chapter 4 lists shortcuts for Word, Chapter 7 lists shortcuts for Excel, and Chapter 14 lists shortcuts for PowerPoint.

To select a graphic, click it with the mouse. Selection handles (white squares) appear around the outside of it. **Figure 1-14** shows a selected graphic in Word.

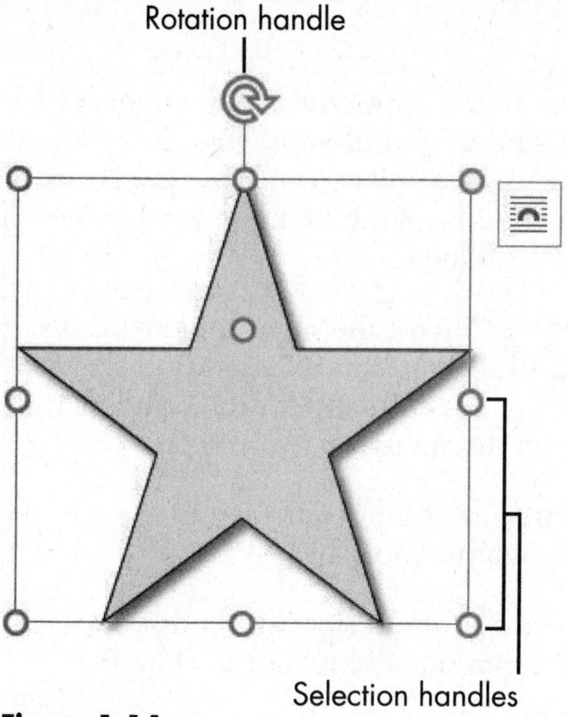

Figure 1-14

When a graphic is selected, you can do any of the following to it:

- **Move it.** Position the mouse pointer on the graphic (not on the border) and drag.
- **Copy it.** Hold down the Ctrl key while you move it.
- **Resize it**. Position the mouse pointer on one of the selection handles and drag.
- **Delete it.** Press the Delete key.
- **Rotate it.** Drag the rotation handle, which is the circular arrow above the graphic.

Zoom In and Out

While you're working in an Office application, you might want to zoom in to see a close-up view of part of your work, or zoom out to see a bird's-eye view of the whole project. The lower the zoom percentage, the smaller everything looks — and the more you can see onscreen at once, without scrolling.

Word, Excel, and PowerPoint all have the same zoom controls, located in the bottom right corner of the application window. (There are also zoom controls on the View tab in each application.) **Figure 1-15** shows the zoom controls on the status bar.

- Drag the slider to adjust the zoom (to the left to zoom out, and to the right to zoom in).
- Click the minus or plus button (at opposite ends of the slider) to slightly zoom out (minus) or in (plus).
- Clicking the number of the current zoom percentage opens a Zoom dialog box, which shows more zooming options.

Zooming doesn't affect the size of printouts. It is only an onscreen adjustment.

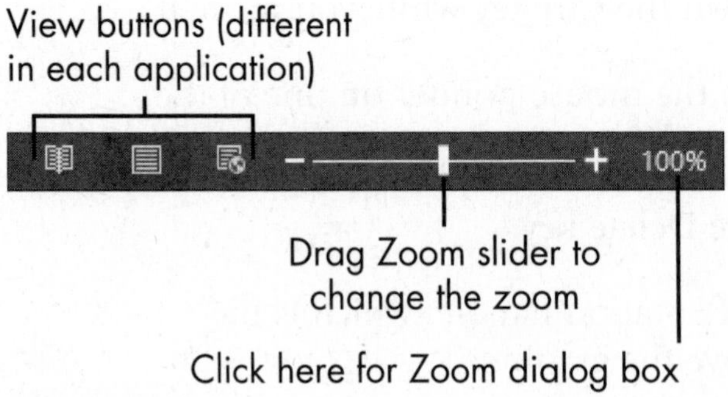

Figure 1-15

Change the View

Each Office application has a variety of viewing options available. Each view is suited for a certain type of activity in that application. For example, in Word, you can choose Draft view, which is speedy to work with and presents the text in a simple one-column layout. Or you can choose a Print Layout view, where you can see any special layout formatting you applied, such as multiple columns.

These views are available:

- **Excel**
  - *Normal:* Displays a regular row-and-column grid.
  - *Page Break Preview:* Shows a zoomed-out version of the worksheet with page break lines that you can drag to adjust where they fall.
  - *Page Layout:* Displays the content as it will appear on a printed page.
- **Word**
  - *Read Mode:* Optimizes the display for onscreen reading. You cannot edit the document in this view.
  - *Print Layout*: Shows the document approximately as it will be printed, including any layout features, such as multiple columns.
  - *Web Layout:* Displays the document as it will appear if saved as a Web page and published on a Web site.
  - *Outline:* Displays the document as an outline, with headings as outline levels.
  - *Draft:* Displays the document in simple text form, in a single column.

- PowerPoint
  - *Normal:* This default view provides multiple panes for working with the content.
  - *Outline:* The same as Normal view except instead of thumbnails of each slide you see a text outline of slide content.
  - *Slide Sorter:* All of the slides appear as thumbnail images, which is useful for rearranging the order of slides.
  - *Notes Page:* Each slide appears as a graphic on a page where notes are displayed.
  - *Reading View:* Similar to Slide Show view except in a floating window rather than full screen.
  - *Slide Show:* The presentation is shown to the audience, one slide at a time. The Slide Show view controls appear on the Slide Show tab, rather than on the View tab with the other views.

Each application has shortcut buttons to a few of the most common views. You can find these buttons to the left of the Zoom slider, as pointed out in Figure 1-15. Hover your mouse over a button to find out which view it selects.

Enjoying the tour so far? There's lots more ahead in Chapter 2, where I continue walking you through the important features that the Office apps have in common.

Exploring the Common Features of Office 2016

Chapter 2

Get ready to . . .

Text handling is quite standardized in Word, Excel, and PowerPoint. The same commands that you use to edit and format text in one program work almost exactly the same way in another. So, after you master them in one application, you'll be off and running in the others.

Some of these standardized features include

- **The Clipboard,** which lets you copy and move content seamlessly between applications
- **Text formatting,** which you use to format text with the same set of Font tools, no matter which application you're in
- **Themes,** which help you apply consistent formatting to documents created in different programs
- **The spell checker,** which you use to correct your spelling and grammar in all applications, and even maintain common custom dictionaries between them

This chapter looks at each of these tools plus a few other handy standardized tools.

Edit Text

In Word, Excel, and PowerPoint, you just click where you want the text to go, and begin typing. (Chapter 1 covers the basics.)

The *insertion point* is the flashing vertical marker (cursor) that shows where the text you type will appear. You can move the insertion point with the arrow keys, or you can click where you want to place it.

When the mouse pointer is over an area where you can place text, it turns into an I-shaped pointer called an *I-beam*. The shape of the I-beam makes it easy for you to precisely position it, even between two tiny characters of text. **Figure 2-1** shows the insertion point and the I-beam mouse pointer.

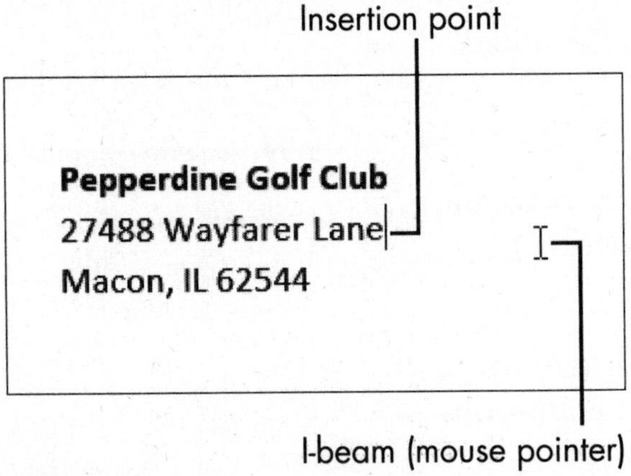

Figure 2-1

To insert new text, position the insertion point where you want to insert it, and then type the new text.

To remove text, you can use any of these methods:

- **Backspace it.** Position the insertion point and then press the Backspace key to delete text to the left of the insertion point.

- **Delete it.** Select the text and then press the Delete key, or position the insertion point and then press the Delete key to delete text to the right of the insertion point.
- **Type over it.** Select the text and then type new text to replace it. Whatever was selected is deleted.

In Word, you can't move the insertion point past the end of the document, so if you want to begin a document with the insertion point in the center of the document, for example, you would normally have to press Enter to create extra blank paragraphs until the insertion point arrives where you want it. Here's a way around that, however: Double-click the document at the location where you want the insertion point. Even if that location is beyond the end of the document, the insertion point moves there (and the end of the document moves down past the new location).

Move and Copy Content

For large-scale editing (such as whole paragraphs and pages of text), you can easily move or copy text and graphics within the same application (even between different data files) or from one application to another.

For example, suppose you want to create some slides for a presentation you're giving at a club meeting. You could write the outline in Word, and then copy the text over to PowerPoint to dress up with graphics and animation.

Here are two ways of moving and copying:

- **Drag and drop:** Use the mouse to drag selected text or graphics from one location to another.

To drag and drop between applications, both application windows must be visible onscreen at once. You may need to move and resize windows to make that happen. To move a window, drag its title bar. To resize a window, drag the bottom-right corner of the window. If it won't resize, it's probably maximized; click the Restore button to un-maximize it and make it resizable.

- **The Clipboard:** Cut or copy the content to the *Clipboard* (a temporary holding area in Windows), and then paste it into a different location. I tell you more about how to use the Clipboard later in this section.

To use the copy-by-dragging method, select the content to be dragged, and then hold down the left mouse button while you drag it to the new location. Then release the mouse button to drop it there.

- **Dragging and dropping within a document:** If you're dragging and dropping content within a document but the source and the destination locations are too far apart to see at the same time, you might want to open another window that contains the same file, and then scroll them to two different spots. To do this in Word, Excel, or PowerPoint, choose View⇨Windows⇨New Window. Because you need to be able to see both the starting and ending points at the same time, you might have to arrange and resize some windows onscreen.

If you open a new window with View⇨Window⇨New Window, the second window will have the same name but will have a number appended to it, such as `Budget.xlsx:2`. The second window is an alternate view of the first; any changes made in one are reflected in the other.

- **Dragging and dropping between documents:** Open both documents at the same time. You must be able to see both the starting and ending points at the same time, so you might have to arrange and resize some windows onscreen.

You aren't limited to copying content between documents in the same application. That is, you can copy from Word to Word, Word to PowerPoint, and so on. **Figure 2-2** shows an example where I copied content from a Word document to an Excel spreadsheet.

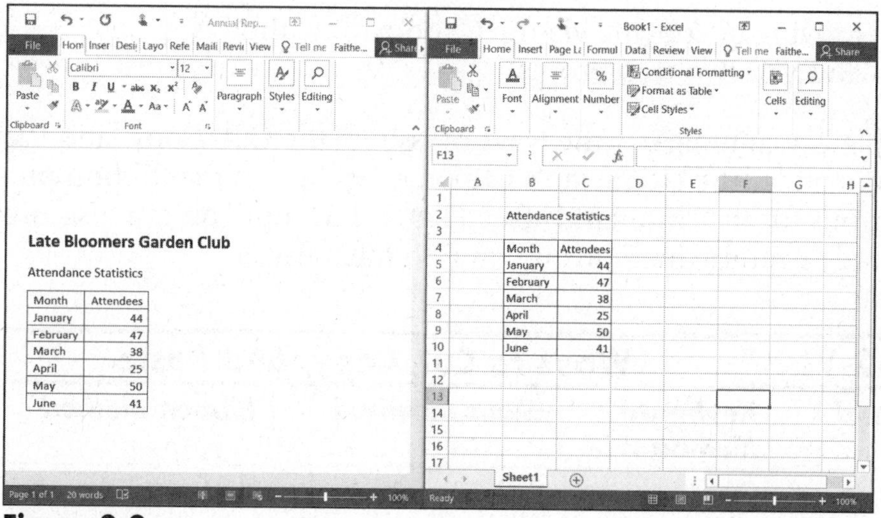

Figure 2-2

To make a copy of the selected text or graphic using drag-and-drop, hold down Ctrl while you drag. You'll notice as you drag that the mouse pointer shows a tiny plus sign, indicating that you're making a copy.

If setting up the display so that both the source and the destination appear onscreen at once is awkward, you're better off using the Clipboard method of moving content. This method places the source material in a hidden temporary storage area in Windows, and then pastes it from there into the destination location. Because the Clipboard is nearly universal, you can use it to move or copy data from (almost) any application to any other application, even non-Microsoft programs. For example, you could copy text from Word and paste it into a graphics program such as Photoshop, and it would appear there as a graphic. Or you could copy spreadsheet cells from Excel and paste them into a website–building application such as Dreamweaver, and the cells would appear there as a web table.

The three Clipboard operations are Cut, Copy, and Paste.

- **To move something:** Use Cut and then Paste.
- **To copy something:** Use Copy and then Paste.

Moving or copying via the Clipboard method is always a two-step process.

Table 2-1 summarizes the ways of issuing the Cut, Copy, and Paste commands. The Home tab's Clipboard group on the Ribbon provides buttons for the commands (see **Figure 2-3**), but you can also use keyboard or mouse methods if you find them easier.

Table 2-1 Ways to Cut, Copy, and Paste

Command	*Keyboard Method*	*Mouse Method*	*Ribbon Method*
Cut	Ctrl+X	Right-click and choose Cut	Home➪Clipboard➪Cut
Copy	Ctrl+C	Right-click and choose Copy	Home➪Clipboard➪Copy
Paste	Ctrl+V	Right-click and choose Paste	Home➪Clipboard➪Paste

If you use the Ribbon buttons frequently for Cut, Copy, and Paste, consider adding them to the Quick Access toolbar so you can get to them without having to switch to the Home tab. Read how to do this in Chapter 1.

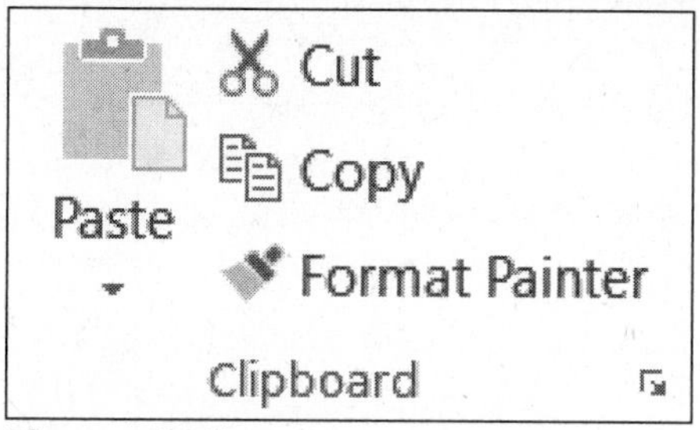

Figure 2-3

Choose Fonts and Font Sizes

Across all the Office programs, you can choose different fonts and font sizes for your work.

- A *font* is a standard way of making each letter. (It's also called a typeface.) Common fonts include Times New Roman, Courier New, and Arial.
- The *font size* controls the height of the letters. The letters in this paragraph are size 12.5, which usually is a good size for documents in Microsoft Office.

The font size is based on the distance from the top of the tallest letter to the bottom of the lowest letter, measured in points. One *point* (pt) is $\frac{1}{72}$ of an inch.

The default font and size in Word is Calibri 11-point. If that isn't what you want, you can choose a different font or size.

To choose a font or resize it, follow these steps:

1. Select the text to affect.
2. Open a drop-down list on the Home tab (in the Font group). You can select Font or Font Size.
3. Make your selection. See **Figure 2-4**.

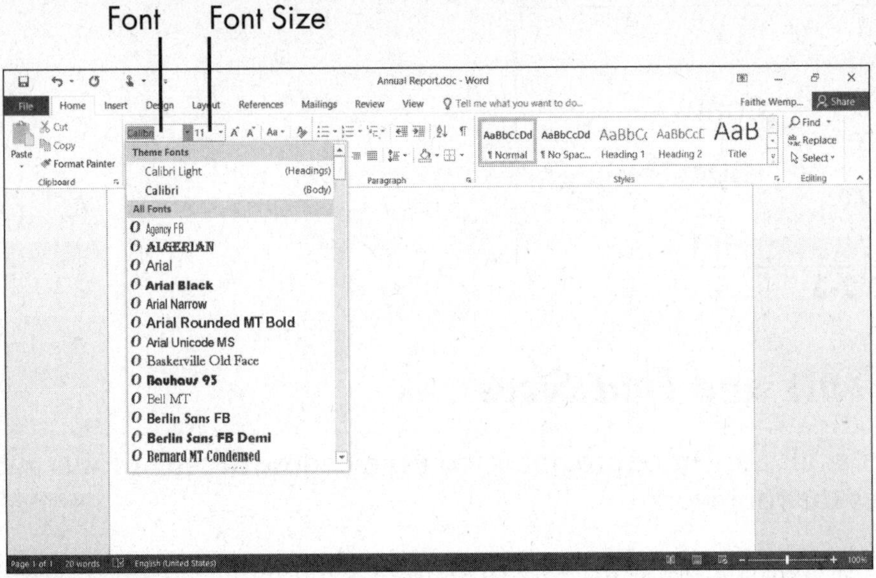

Figure 2-4

If you don't select any text to affect before you choose a font or size, the new setting applies to the spot where the insertion point is at the moment. Any new text you type there will have that new setting.

Different computers have different size monitors, so screen size isn't a reliable indicator of how large the text will be when it's printed. Also, adjusting the Zoom feature in the applications can affect how large the text looks onscreen. (Read about the Zoom tool in Chapter 1.)

To modify the default font and size for all new documents in the future, open the Font dialog box by pressing (Ctrl+D), choose a different font and size, and then click the Set as Default button. In the confirmation box that appears, click Yes.

The Font drop-down list contains a Theme Fonts section at the top. The fonts listed here are the fonts applied by the current theme. If you choose those fonts, rather than specific fonts from the lower part of the list, the fonts will update automatically when you change themes.

(That's a plus if you aren't sure what look you want for the document.) I explain more about themes later in this chapter.

Word, Excel, and PowerPoint all have Grow Font and Shrink Font buttons on the Home tab (Font group) immediately to the right of the Font Size drop-down list (**Figure 2-5**). As you might expect, the Grow Font button increases the font size each time you click it, and the Shrink Font button decreases the font size.

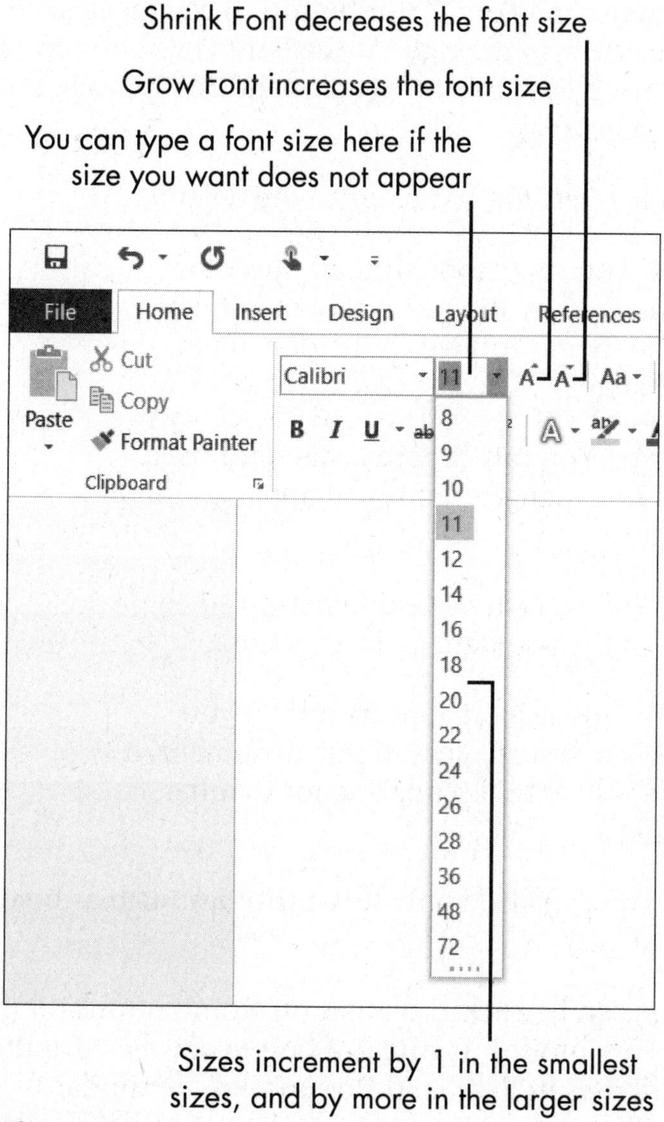

Figure 2-5

Apply Text Formatting

You can modify the appearance and pick the color of text.

The default setting for text color is Automatic, which automatically changes the text color so that it contrasts well with the background. On a light background, text is black; on a dark background, text is white.

Select text, and then use the Font Color button to change its color. When you click the arrow to the right of the Font Color button on the Home tab (see **Figure 2-6**), a palette of color choices appears. You can choose any of the following:

- **Automatic:** This resets the text color to the default.
- **Theme Colors:** You can choose one of the color placeholders defined by the current theme. If you later change the theme applied to the document, this color might change.
- **Standard Colors:** You can choose a standard fixed color that will not change even if you apply a different theme later.
- **More Colors:** You can choose a different fixed color than the ones in the Standard Colors section.
- **Recent Colors:** This section appears only if you select a color with More Colors in this document. It provides shortcuts for reselecting a color that has already been used.

Besides text color, you can also apply text attributes, such as bold (like **this**) and italic (like *this*).

Some text attributes can be clicked on and off from buttons on the Home tab (in the Font group). **Figure 2-7** points out the attributes for Word. The text attributes in Excel and PowerPoint are similar.

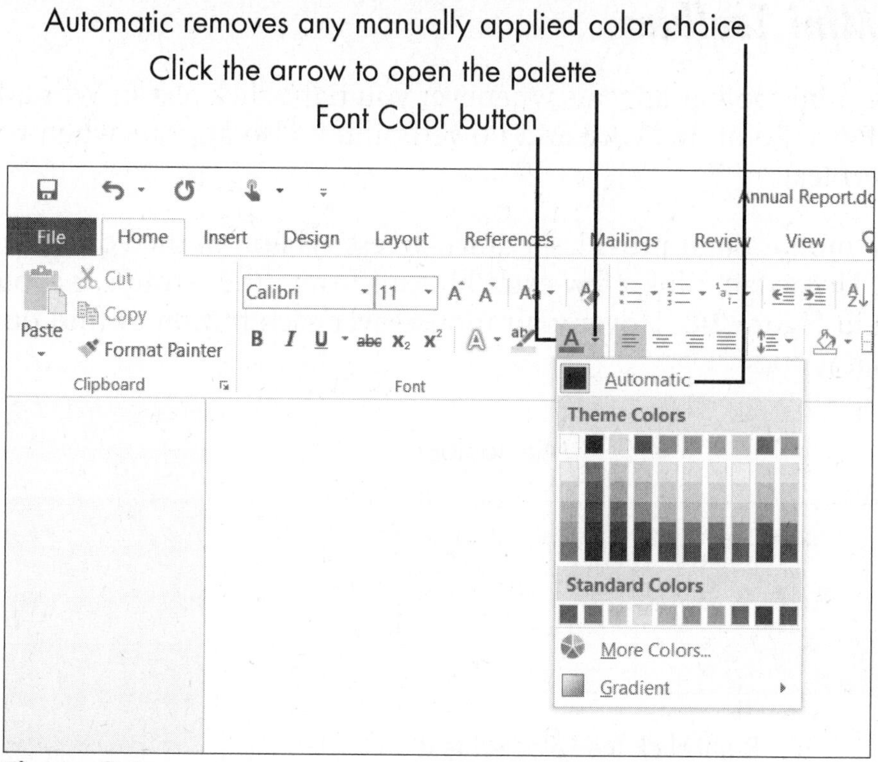

Figure 2-6

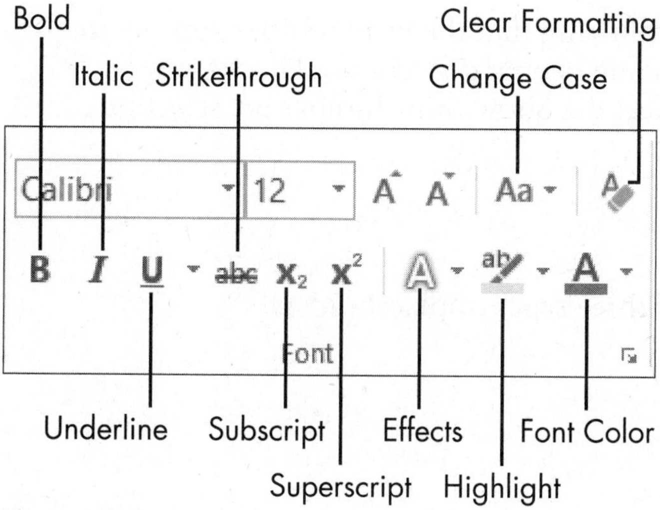

Figure 2-7

Use the Mini Toolbar

The mini toolbar appears whenever you right-click text in Word, Excel, or PowerPoint. In Word and PowerPoint, it also appears when you select text.

The mini toolbar provides a quick-access version of the Font group on the Home tab, plus a few extra buttons from other groups, as you can see in **Figure 2-8**. Hover your mouse over each button to find out what it does.

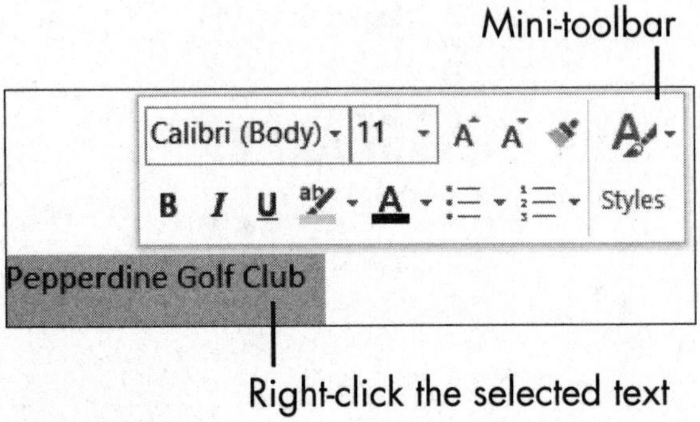

Figure 2-8

If you find it annoying that the mini toolbar appears for selected text (some people do), choose File➪Options and then deselect the Show Mini Toolbar on Selection check box.

Work with Themes

A theme is a set of three types of placeholders:

- Fonts
- Colors
- Graphic effects

Themes are useful when you want to standardize the formatting across multiple documents, or between applications. For example, you might want your résumé and the cover letter that you send with it to be consistent in formatting. Applying the same theme to both would ensure that they use the same fonts and colors.

Or, bigger picture, you can use a theme to apply consistent formatting across lots of documents, and even between applications. For example, you could have a Word document that uses the same theme as your PowerPoint presentation on the same subject, so it looks like they match.

When I use the word "theme" in a general sense in this book, you can assume that I mean a combination of those three types of placeholders: fonts, colors, and effects. However, you can also apply more specific themes that just cover one of those: font themes, color themes, and effect themes. This is great because it lets you combine the parts of different themes to create your own special look. For example, you might use the fonts from one theme and the colors from another.

Instead of choosing a specific font, color, or graphic effect for an item in one of the Office applications, you can instead choose to apply one of the theme placeholders. This formats the item with whatever definition the current theme specifies. Then, if you change to a different theme later, the item changes its appearance. This is a great help in allowing you to quickly change the look of an entire document, spreadsheet, or presentation without having to worry about consistency.

To apply a theme in Word, follow these steps:

1. Choose Design ⇨ Document Formatting ⇨ Themes.
2. Choose a theme from the menu that appears. See **Figure 2-9**.

To apply a theme in Excel, follow these steps:

1. Choose Page Layout ⇨ Themes ⇨ Themes.
2. Choose a theme from the menu that appears.

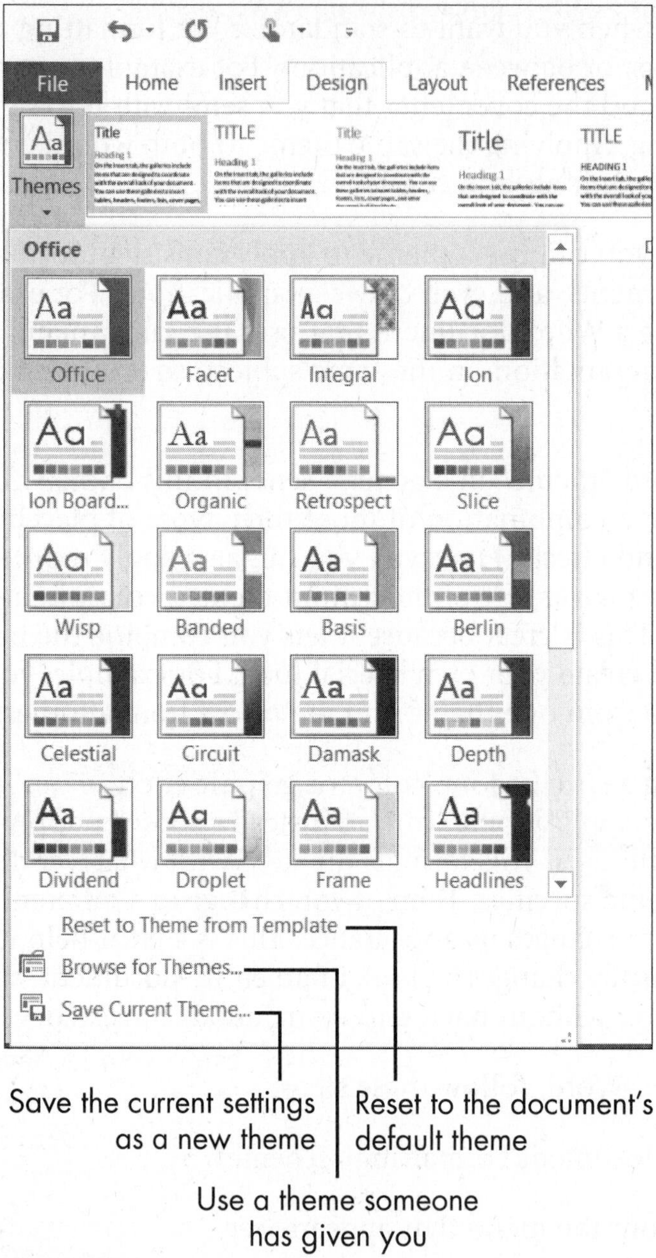
File
Home
Insert
Design
Layout
References
Themes
Office
Office
Facet
Integral
Ion
Ion Board...
Organic
Retrospect
Slice
Wisp
Banded
Basis
Berlin
Celestial
Circuit
Damask
Depth
Dividend
Droplet
Frame
Headlines
Reset to Theme from Template
Browse for Themes...
Save Current Theme...
Save the current settings as a new theme
Reset to the document's default theme
Use a theme someone has given you

Figure 2-9

To apply a theme in PowerPoint, you have two methods:

- On the Design tab, click one of the samples in the Themes group. You can then optionally choose a different color variant from the Variants group. See **Figure 2-10**.
- On the Design tab, click the down arrow in the Themes group and select a theme from the menu that appears.

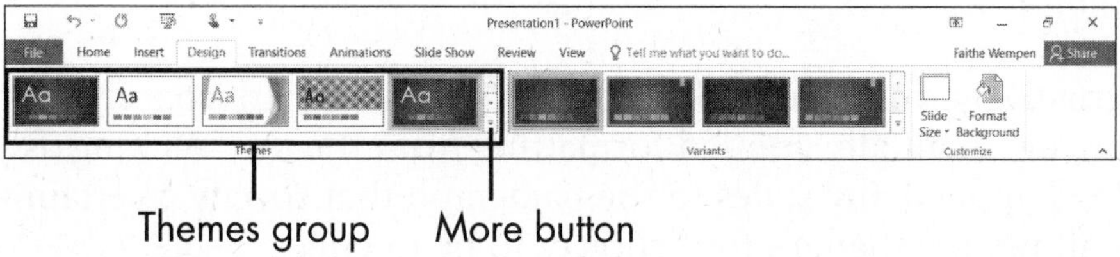

Figure 2-10

Each theme on the menu has a name, but you can't get a very good overall sense of a theme without seeing it in action. Fortunately, there's a quick way to do this. Just hover the mouse pointer over a theme, and the document behind the open menu shows a preview of how the theme will affect it.

Make sure you have some text in the document, in an area that isn't obscured when the menu is open.

If you apply a theme (or preview one) and it doesn't seem to have any effect, you probably have specific fonts and/or colors selected that are overriding the theme choices. Earlier in the chapter, where I show you how to choose a font, I mention the Theme Fonts section at the top of the Font menu. If you choose anything other than what was in the Theme Fonts section, any theme changes you make will not affect that text.

So, say you applied various fonts to a document, but now you decide that you'd rather let a theme handle the font choice. Here are some possible ways to fix that:

1. Reselect the text.

2. On the Home tab, reopen the Font drop-down list and choose the Body font from the Theme Fonts section. Do this for all the body text.

3. Repeat this process by choosing the Heading font for any headings.

   Alternatively, you can reselect the text and press Ctrl+spacebar. This strips any manually applied formatting from the text. As long as you haven't applied any styles to the paragraph that specify a certain font, this allows the theme's font choices to be in effect.

   You can also apply color themes, font themes, and effect themes. Accessing them is somewhat different in each of the three applications:

   - Word: On the Design tab, use the Colors, Fonts, and Effects buttons.
   - Excel: On the Page Layout tab, use the Colors, Fonts, and Effects buttons.
   - PowerPoint: On the Design tab, click the More button in the Variants group to open a submenu, and then click Colors, Fonts, or Effects from that submenu.

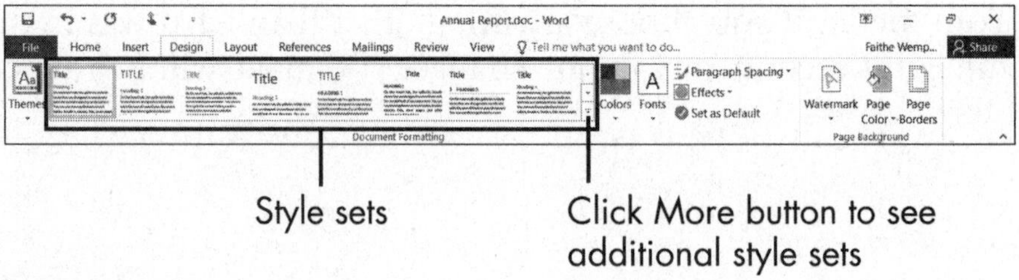

Figure 2-11

You can do a lot more with themes than the little taste I give you here in this chapter. Explore the options at the bottom of the Themes menu (refer to Figure 2-9) on your own, or check out the Help system in each application.

Check Your Spelling and Grammar

All the Office apps share a common spell-check feature that tells you what words don't appear in its dictionary. You can decide what to do with each one.

While you work in an application, your words are compared against the dictionary, and anything that doesn't appear in the dictionary is marked with a red wavy underline. See **Figure 2-12**.

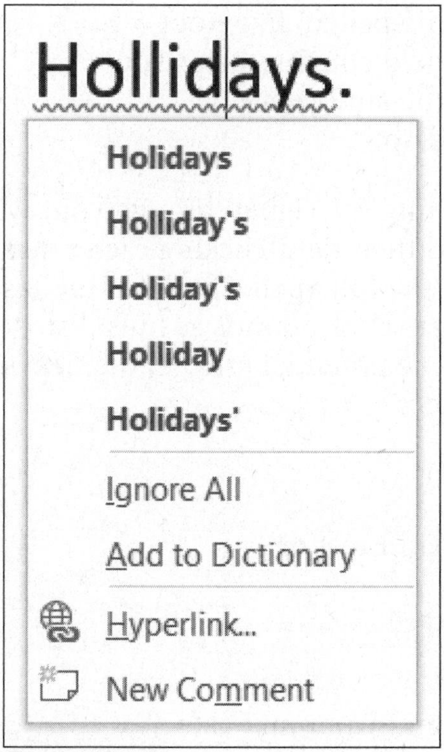

Figure 2-12

Right-click any red-underlined word to see a menu of choices. From this menu, you can

- Click one of the suggestions, and Word immediately changes the red-underlined word to the suggested word.
- Click Ignore All to mark all instances of the word as okay in this document only.
- Click Add to Dictionary to add this word so that it's never marked as misspelled again on your computer, in any document.

Add to Dictionary is useful when you frequently write a word that the dictionary doesn't recognize, like an unusual last name or the name of a company whose name is intentionally misspelled, like Kool Kottage. Adding the word to the dictionary helps you get it right and cuts down on the annoyance of approving it every time it pops up.

If you'd rather not check your spelling by paging through your work, looking for the red underlines, and then right-clicking each one as you find it, I have a better way. Go for the full Spell Check feature instead. It asks you to choose from a similar set of options as I just listed, but it automatically moves you from one potential error to the next so you don't have to hunt for the underlines.

To start a spell check, choose either

- Review ➪ Proofing ➪ Spelling (in Excel or PowerPoint)

  or

- Review ➪ Proofing ➪ Spelling and Grammar (in Word).

The Spell Check task pane in Word, shown in Figure 2-13, contains a few more options than the right-click menu, such as Ignore (which ignores single instances of a word) and Change All (which changes at once all the instances of a misspelled word in the current document).

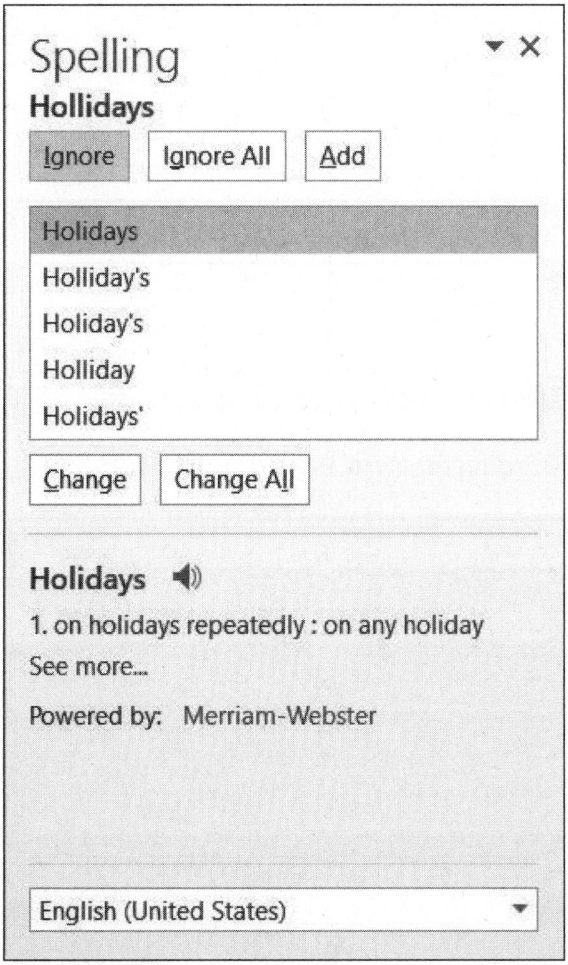

Figure 2-13

Word also has a grammar component. Grammar errors appear with a blue wavy underline, and you can spot-check them just like with spelling. You can also work with them from the Grammar task panel, as shown in **Figure 2-14**. The Ignore Rule button suppresses further checking for the grammar rule that was broken in the notification that appears; the Explain button pops up an explanation of the grammar rule being applied.

Right-click a blue wavy underlined word for a quick grammar correction

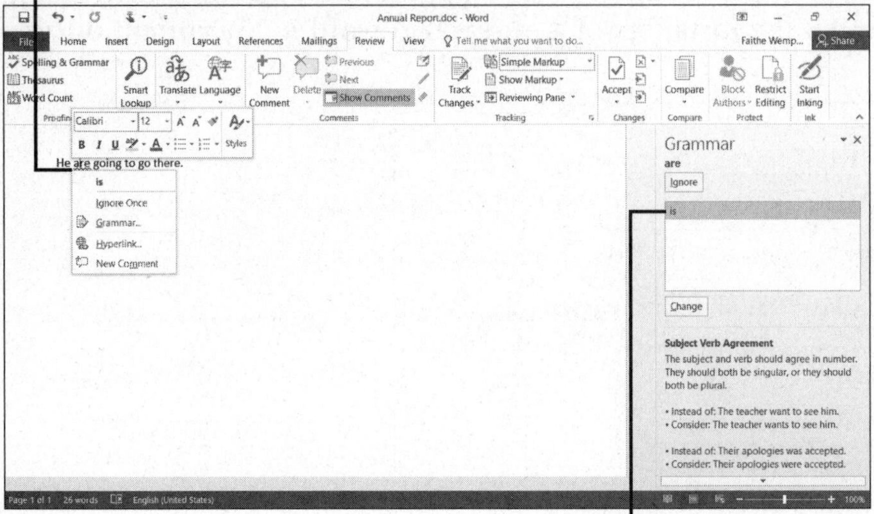

Grammar corrections also appear in the task pane

Figure 2-14

Opening, Saving, and Printing Files

Chapter 3

All Office apps can create, open, save, and print data files. A *data file* stores your work in a particular application. If you don't save your work, whatever you have entered disappears when you close the application or turn off your computer. Not good.

Each Office 2016 application has its own data file format. For example

- **Word:** Document files, `.docx`
- **Excel:** Workbook files, `.xlsx`
- **PowerPoint:** Presentation files, `.pptx`
- **Outlook:** Personal folders files, `.pst`

Word, Excel, and PowerPoint use a separate data file for each project you work on. Every time you use one of these programs, you open and save data files.

Outlook uses just one data file for all your activities. This file is automatically saved and opened for you, so you usually don't have to think about data file management in Outlook.

Get ready to . . .

The steps for saving, opening, and printing data files are almost exactly the same in each application, so mastering it in one program gives you a big head start in the other programs. In this chapter, you'll see the basic skills that will serve you well for working with data files no matter which program you are using.

In this book, the pictures and steps show Office 2016 in the Windows 10 operating system. I provide alternate steps as needed where the process is different in Windows 8.1 and/or Windows 7.

Save Your Work

As you work in an application, the content you create is stored in the computer's memory. This memory is only temporary storage. When you exit the application or shut down the computer, whatever is stored in memory is flushed away forever — unless you save it.

If you want to keep what you're working on, here are some ways to save:

- Click the File tab and click Save.
- Press Ctrl+S.
- Click the Save button on the Quick Access toolbar.

The first time you save a file, the application prompts you to enter a location and name for it. The Save As page appears in Backstage view, as shown in **Figure 3-1.** From there, click one of the save locations, such as OneDrive - Personal or This PC and then click one of the recent folders in that location, or click Browse to start at the default folder.

For example, suppose you want to save the file in the Documents folder on your local hard drive. You would first click This PC. At that point, if Documents appears on the Recent Folders list, you could click it; otherwise you could click Browse to start in the default save location for your local PC (which is, incidentally, the Documents folder). Either way, the Save As dialog box opens, as shown in **Figure 3-2**.

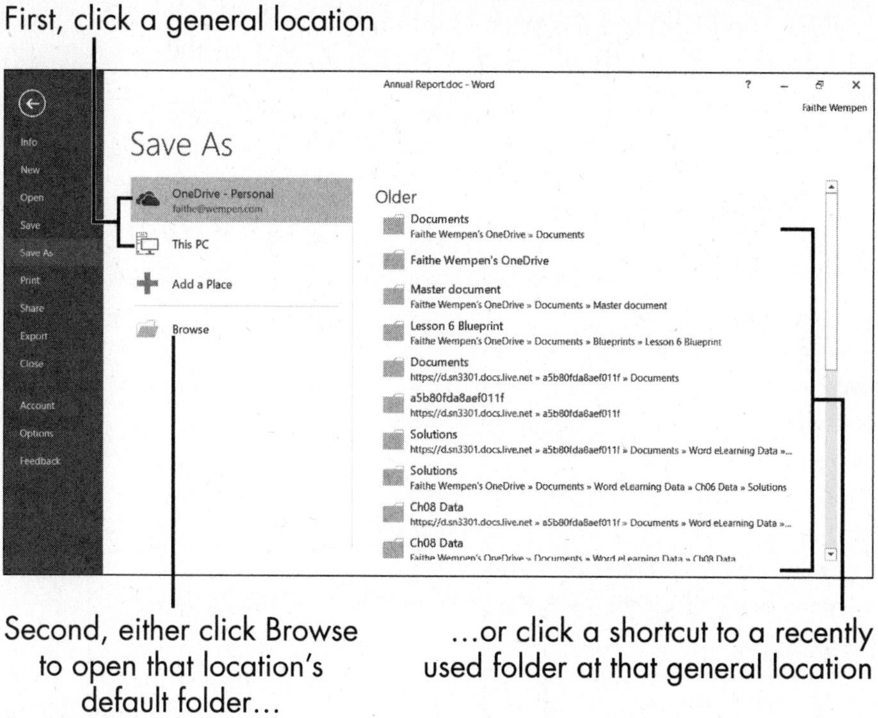

Figure 3-1

When you re-save an already saved file, the Save As screen doesn't reappear; the file saves automatically with the most recent settings. If you want to change the settings (such as the location or file type) or save under a different name, choose File⇨Save As to make the Save As controls appear.

To change the file type, open the Save as Type list in the Save As dialog box (Figure 3-2) and make another selection. In each of the applications, there are three important file types to know about:

- **Default:** The default format in each application supports all features except macros. The file extension ends in the letter X for each one: Word is `.docx`; Excel is `.xlsx`; PowerPoint is `.pptx`.
- **Macro-enabled:** This format supports all features, including macros. The file extension ends in the letter M for each one: `.docm`, `.xlsm`, and `.pptm`.

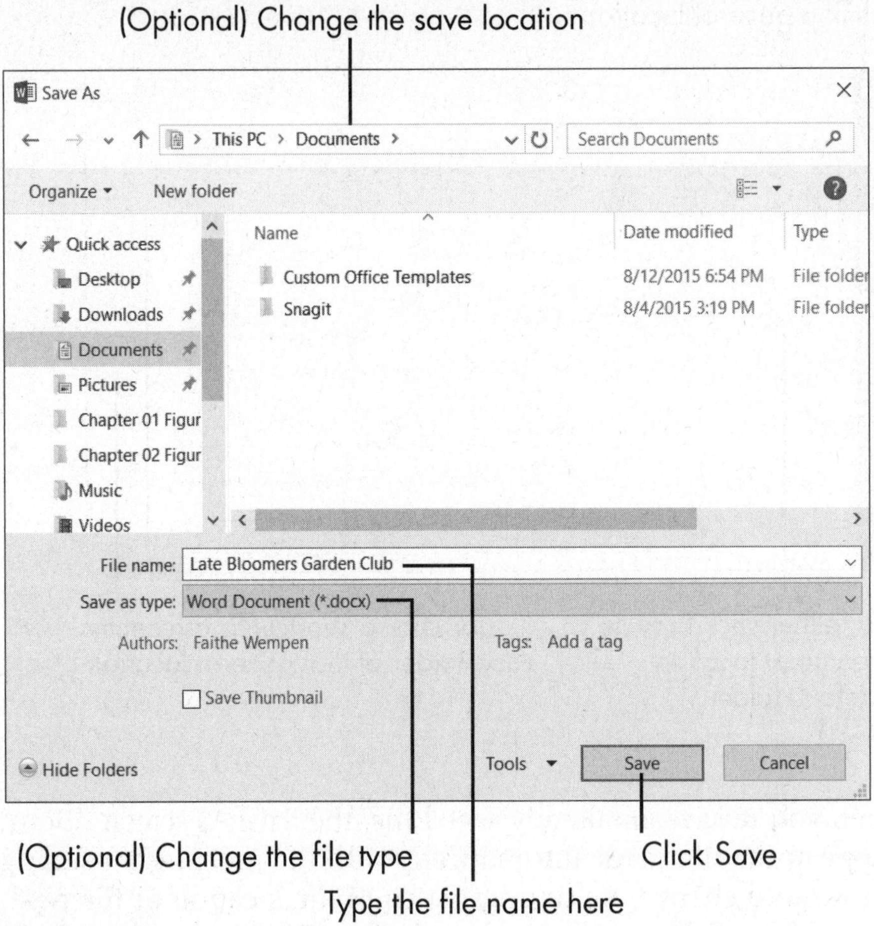

Figure 3-2

Macros are recorded bits of code that can automate certain activities in a program, but they can also carry viruses. The default formats don't support macros for that reason. If you need to create a file that includes macros, you can save in a macro-enabled format.

- **97-2003:** Each application includes a file format for backward compatibility with earlier versions of the application (versions 97 through 2003). Some minor functionality may be lost when saving in this format. The file extensions are `.doc`, `.xls`, and `.ppt`.

In addition to specifying a file name, you must specify a save location. You can stick with the default folder for the location you selected from the Save As screen, or you can browse to a different folder.

To understand how to change save locations, you should first understand the concept of a file path. Files are organized into folders, and you can have folders *inside* folders. For example, you might have

- A folder called *Retirement*
- Within that folder, another folder called *Finances*
- Within that folder, an Excel file called `BankAccounts.xlsx`

The path for such a file would be

```
C:\Retirement\Finances\BankAccounts.xlsx
```

The C at the beginning is the drive letter. The main hard disk on a computer is called C. The backslashes (\) are separators between folder levels.

At the top of the Save As dialog box, the parts of a path are separated by right-pointing triangles rather than by slashes. You can click any of the triangles to open a drop-down list containing all the *subfolders* (that is, the folders within that folder), and then click one of those folders to quickly switch to it. See **Figure 3-3**.

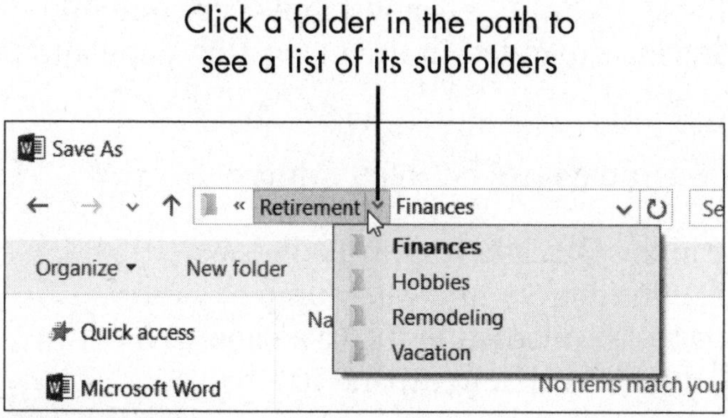

Figure 3-3

Here's a Tricky Thing About Save Locations . . .

Each Windows account has its own separate Documents folder for the local PC; the version of Documents that appears depends on which Windows account is signed in.

Each user also has his or her own OneDrive; the OneDrive that appears depends on which Microsoft account is signed into Office. In Figure 3-1, notice the email address under OneDrive - Personal; this is the email address associated with the user who is currently logged into Word. The signed-in user's name appears in the upper-right corner of the Word window.

In Figures 3-1 and 3-2, the same user is signed into both Windows and Office, but that's not always the case. You can have a different Microsoft account signed into Office than into Windows itself. For example, suppose that Faithe is signed in to Windows and Vick is signed into Office. When browsing the This PC location, the user folders such as Documents are Faithe's, but when browsing OneDrive, the user folders are Vick's. To change the signed-in user in an Office application, click the user name in the upper-right corner of the application window and then click Switch Account.

Paths are also shown as the collapsible/expandable tree, with the drive on the top and all its folders and subfolders beneath. You can double-click a folder to collapse (hide) or expand (show) its contents. Figure 3-4 shows This PC expanded in the navigation pane and the Documents folder selected.

You have several ways to navigate between folders:

- Click a shortcut in the Quick Access list (Windows 10) or Favorites list (Windows 8.1 and 7) to jump to a certain folder. If the list is collapsed in the task pane, as it is in Figure 3-4, double-click it to expand it.

- Click This PC in the Navigation pane (or the Computer pane, if you're using Windows 7) to display a list of all the drives on your PC. From there, double-click to move through the levels of folders to the area you want.

- From the Address bar at the top of the dialog box, click the triangle to open the list for the folder level you want to see the subfolders of, and then click the one you want.
- Click in the Address bar. This changes its display to a traditional path (like `C:\Foldername`); you can manually type in a path and then press Enter.

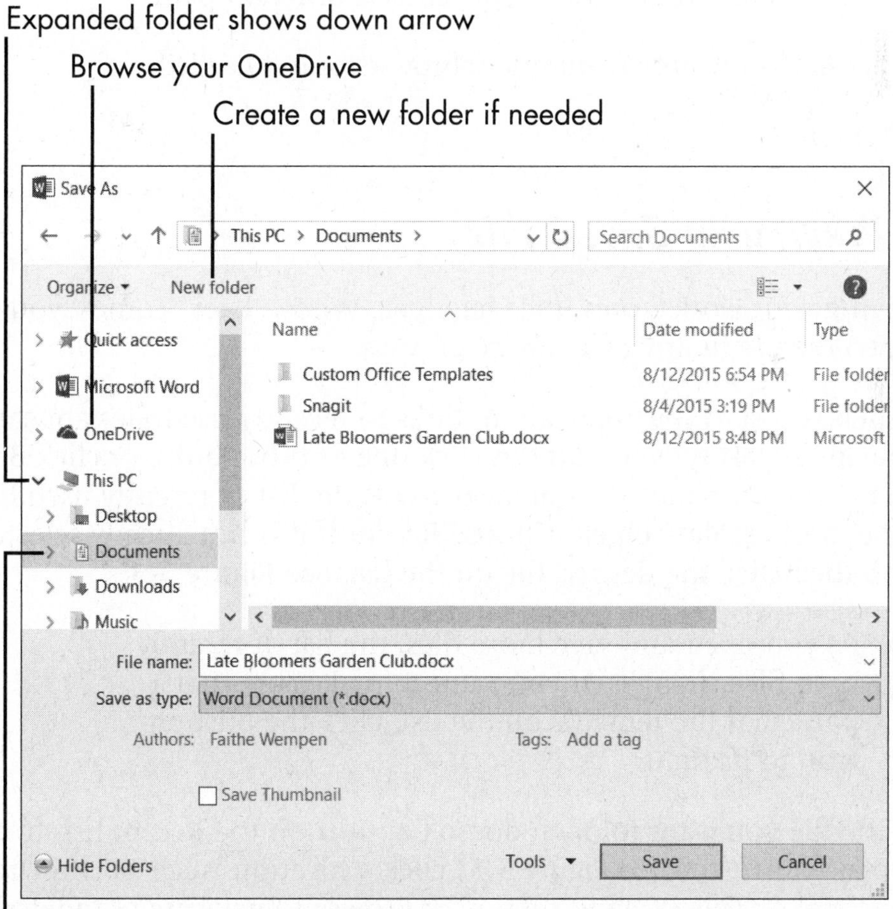

Figure 3-4

You can create a new folder in which to save files. Just click the New Folder button in the Save As dialog box, type a name for the new folder, and then press Enter.

If you find yourself changing the save location frequently, you can set a different location to be the default. Follow these steps in Word, Excel, or PowerPoint:

1. Choose File⇨Options.
2. Click the Save category.
3. In the Default File Location box, enter a different path.

   You can use the Browse button to browse for it if needed.
4. Click OK.

Open a Previously Saved File

Saving your work stores it for later use. When "later" comes, you can open the file in any of a variety of ways.

When you start the application, links to recently used files appear on the app's Start screen. You can click one of those links, or click Browse to browse for a file. You can also access the list of recently used files by choosing File⇨Open. Choose Recent if it is not already selected, and then click the desired file on the list. See **Figure 3-5**.

As you open and save more files, the list of recently used files changes. If you want to make sure that a particular file remains on the list, click the pushpin icon to its right.

If the file you want to open doesn't appear on the Recent list, from the Open screen (refer to Figure 3-5) click a location, such as OneDrive - Personal or This PC, and then click Browse to navigate to the desired file using the Open dialog box (see **Figure 3-6**).

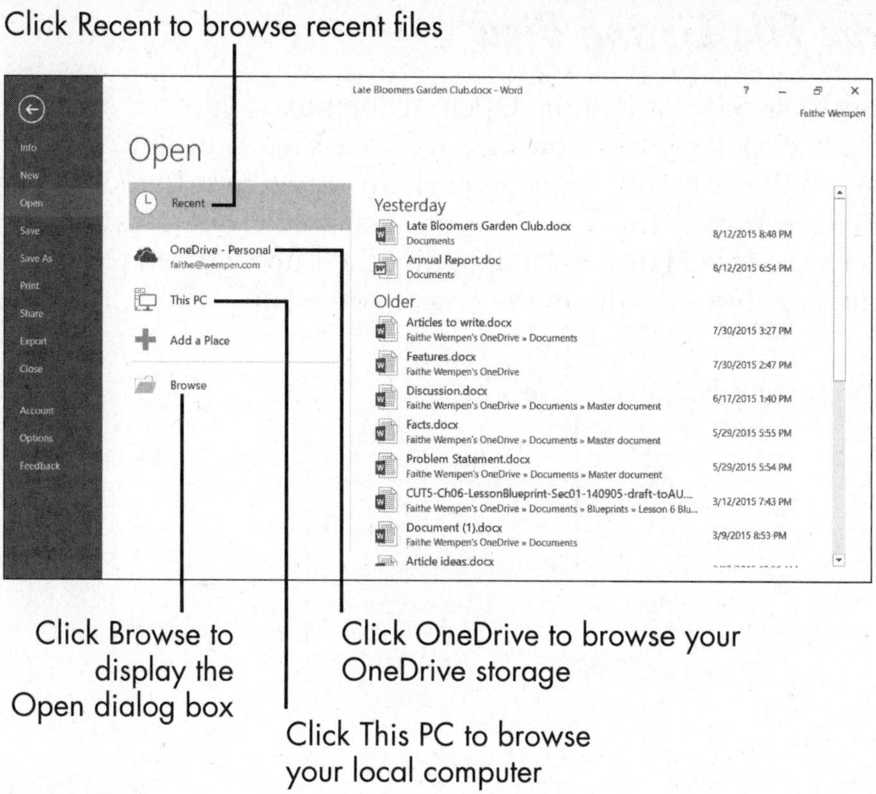

Figure 3-5

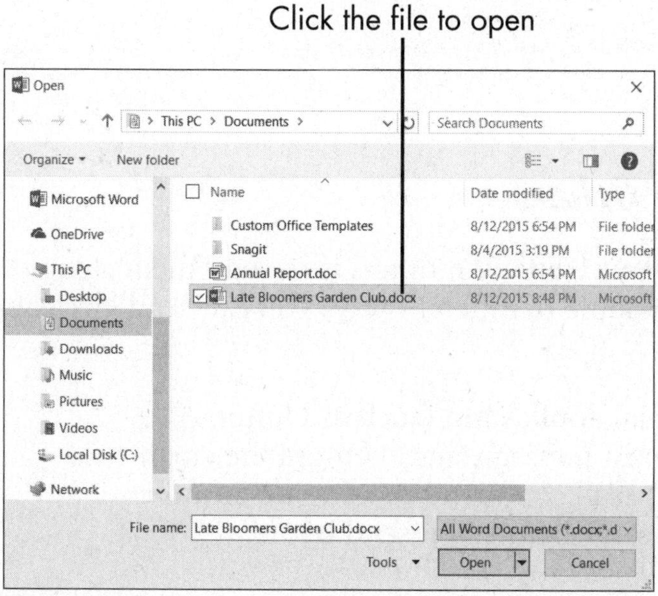

Figure 3-6

Change the File Listing View

In both the Save As and the Open dialog boxes, you can change how files are displayed. Click the Change Your View button to toggle between the available views, or click the arrow next to the Change Your View button to see a list of the available views. This list has a slider on it (see **Figure 3-7**); drag the slider up or down to a different setting, or click directly on the choice you want.

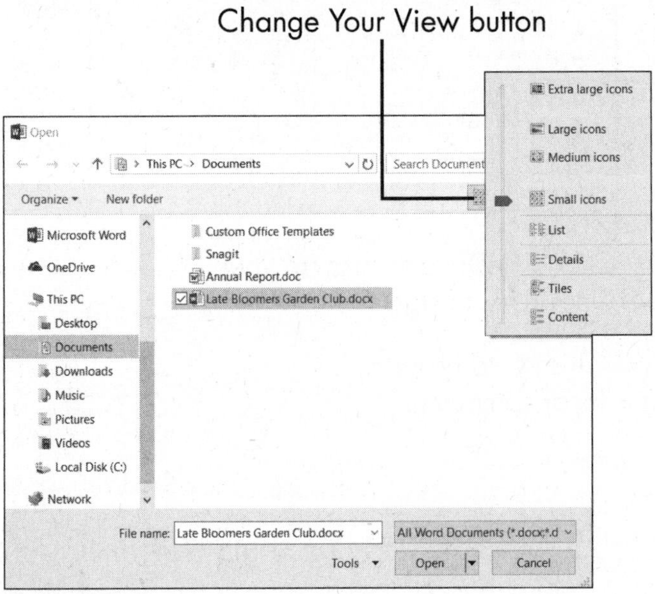

Figure 3-7

Email Your Work to Others

One way to share your work with others is to send them a copy via email. There are a couple of different ways you can send electronic files:

- Open your email application (such as Outlook), start composing a message, and then use the email application's Attach command to add one or more files to the message before you send it.

You can attach any file — not just Office data files. For example, you can send family photos that way, or even video clips. I show you how to do this in Chapter 11, where I cover the basics of Outlook.

- From Word, Excel, or PowerPoint, send the active data file as an email attachment.

Follow these steps to email a file from the application in which you created it:

1. Open the data file that you want to send, in whatever Office app you created it.
2. Choose File⇨Share⇨E-mail⇨Send as Attachment. A new message window appears, with that data file as an attachment.
3. Fill in the email recipient(s) in the To box.
4. The subject line is prefilled with the filename. Change it if you want, as I did in **Figure 3-8**. The file is listed as an attachment in the Attached field.
5. (Optional) If you want to type some explanation of the file, do so in the message body area.
6. Click Send.

You can also copy and paste data from one of the apps directly into the body of an email message that you're composing. This lets you avoid sending an attachment, which might be helpful if you're sending a document or a photo to someone who isn't very experienced with email and might not understand about attachments. Chapter 2 shows how to copy and paste between applications.

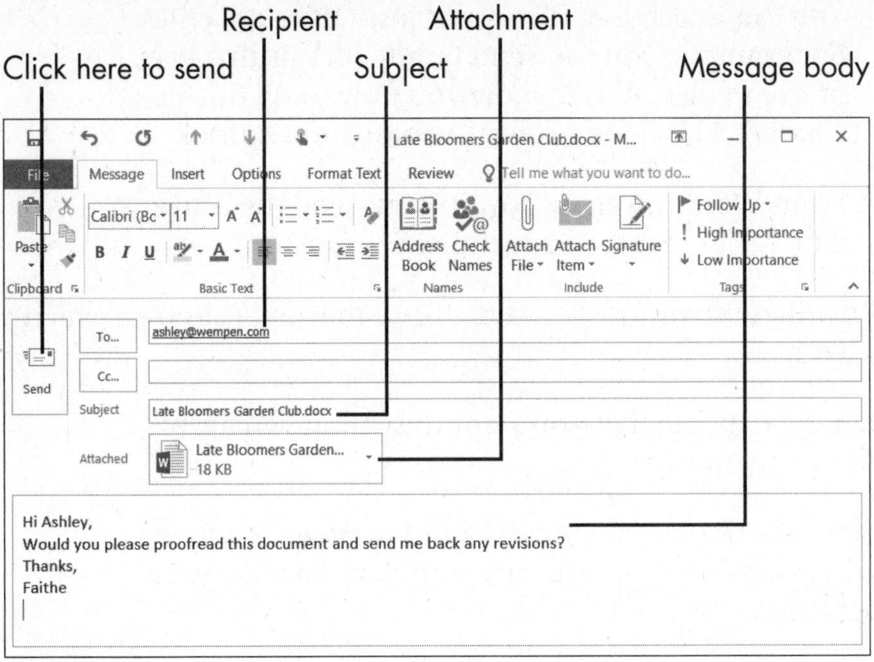

Figure 3-8

Share Your Work in Other Formats

When you're sharing an electronic copy of your work, such as via email attachment, there's a problem if your recipient doesn't have the same application in which to view it. For example, if you send a PowerPoint presentation to a friend who doesn't have PowerPoint, he might not be able to open it.

There are two basic ways around problems of incompatibility: Either the recipient acquires an application that can view the files, or the sender (that's you) can save the file in a format that the recipient can already view.

If you are going to tackle the problem from the recipient side, the easiest way is to have the recipient use the free PowerPoint web-based application, found at `https://office.live.com`. (A Microsoft account is required, which is free.) Web-based versions of Word, Excel, PowerPoint, Outlook, and OneNote are all available. They are not as full-featured as the originals, but they work well for viewing and making simple edits. If you are going about the solution from the sender side, first find out which file formats or applications your recipient uses, and then determine a matching file format that your application will save in. You find the file formats available to your application via the Save As dialog box, from which you can select a different file type.

For text files, Rich Text Format (`.rtf`) is a great choice. It's a near-universal format that almost any word processing program can open, and Word users commonly save in that format when they want to exchange documents with someone who uses a very old or obscure word processing program that doesn't support Word files. **Figure 3-9** shows RTF being selected as the file format in Microsoft Word.

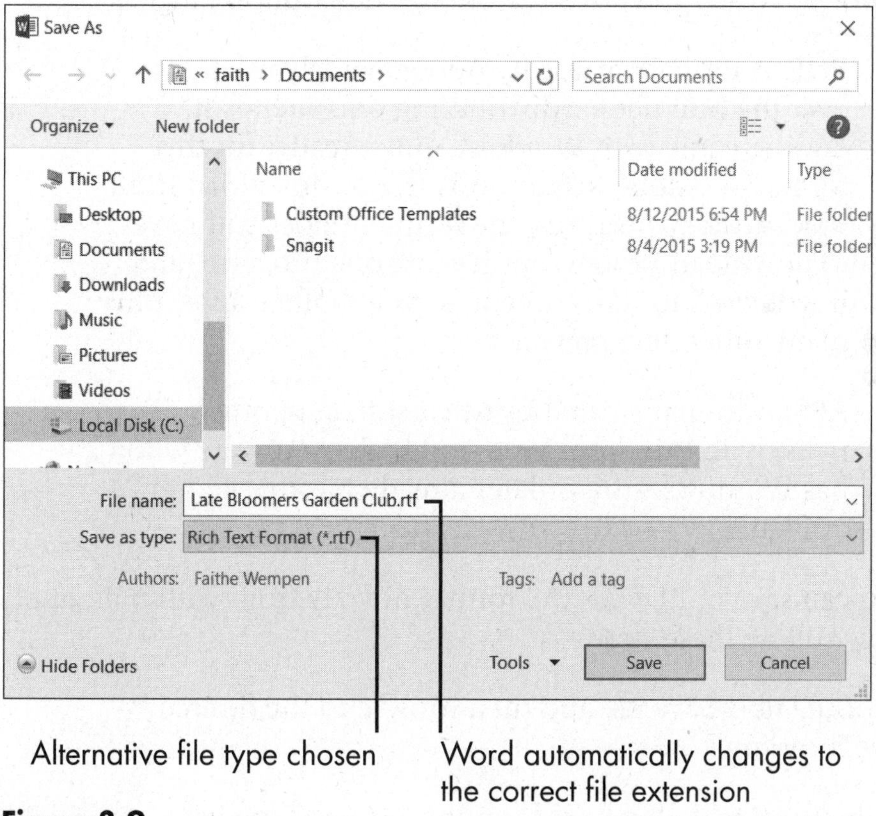

Figure 3-9

Changing to a different file format can result in the loss of some formatting. Some features in Office 2016 applications work only when documents are saved in the application's native format, such as fill-in fields, macros, certain types of editable artwork, and formatting themes. That's why most people don't save in other formats unless it is necessary.

If the recipient will not need to edit the document, your best bet might be to save it in a special format designed for read-only sharing of laid-out pages: a *page description language*. That way, the recipient sees the page exactly as you intended it, without having to find and download a separate viewer for that specific file type.

Office 2016 supports two major page description languages:

- **PDF:** A format created by Adobe, widely used all over the Internet for distributing documents. It doesn't come with Windows, but a reader for this format — Adobe Reader — is free to download from `www.adobe.com`. Yes, the recipient does still have to download Reader, but it's just one program, and it will work for the content from all Office apps, plus many other documents.
- **XPS:** A format created by Microsoft, supported natively in Windows Vista and higher. Anyone who has Windows Vista or later already has this viewer available.

You can save in PDF or XPS format directly from within an application. Follow these steps:

1. Choose File⇨Save As, and then browse to the desired save location.
2. In the Save As dialog box, from the Save as Type list, choose either PDF or XPS Document. The dialog box changes to show some additional controls. See **Figure 3-10**.

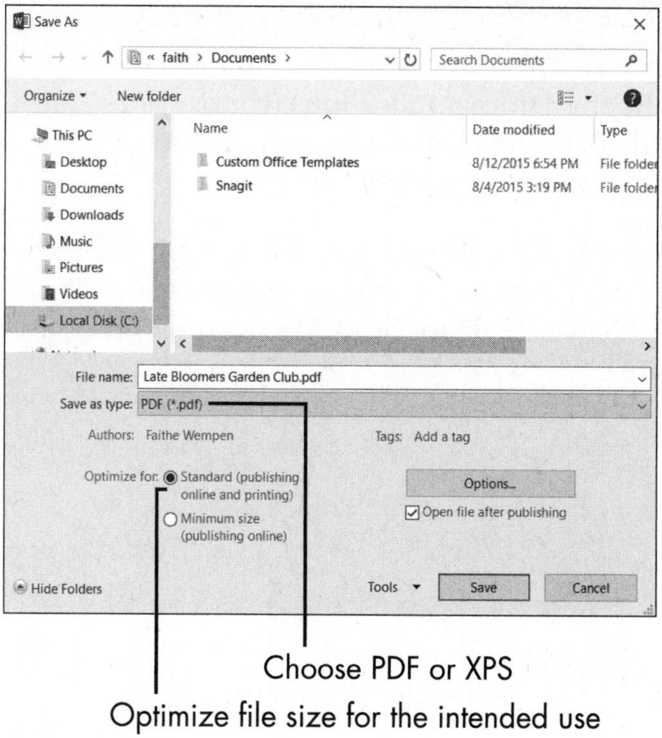

Figure 3-10

Instead of following Steps 1-2, you can choose File ➪ Export ➪ Create PDF/XPS Document ➪ Create PDF/XPS.

3. (Optional) Change the filename if desired. By default, it's the same name as the data file you're working with.

4. Make an Optimize For selection.

   - For documents that might also be printed on paper, choose Standard (the default).

   - For documents that will be shared only online, choose Minimum Size.

5. Click Save. The saved file opens in its native program, which is either Adobe Reader (PDF format) or the XPS Viewer or Internet Explorer (XPS format).

Print Your Work

To print from within any Office applications, choose File➪Print or press Ctrl+P. That displays the Print Settings in Backstage View. Set any print options desired and then click the Print button.

The exact settings found in the Print Settings vary slightly between the applications. **Figure 3-11** shows the settings available for Word. Later chapters of this book cover each application's printing process. The common features are

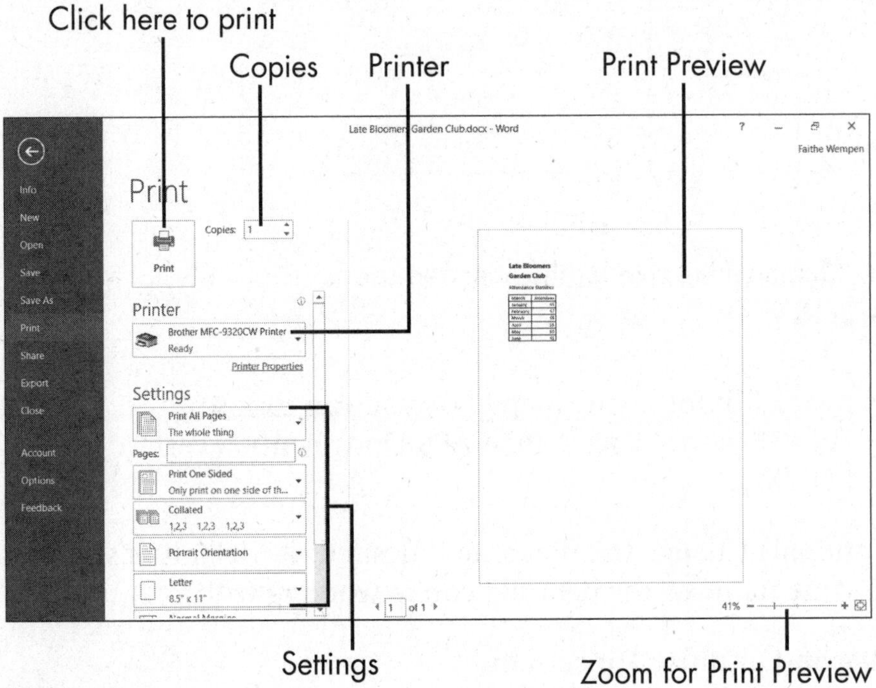

Figure 3-11

- **Copies:** The default is 1; you can choose to print multiple copies instead by specifying some other number.
- **Printer:** Choose from a drop-down list of the printers installed on your system. (If you have only one printer, it's used automatically.)

- **Settings:** Specify which page(s) you want to print, if not the whole thing. You can print all, the current page, a custom page range, or a sheet containing the document's properties. You can also choose collation options, duplexing (one-sided or two sided copies), page size and orientation, and margins.

Sometimes when you print something, it doesn't look exactly how you expected. The view that you work with onscreen isn't the same as the view that will be printed in many cases. (That's especially true in Excel, for example.) *Print Preview* is a special view in which you can see your pages exactly as they will appear when printed. This can help you avoid needlessly printing extra copies and wasting ink and paper. Print Preview appears to the right of the Print Settings in Backstage View, as shown in Figure 3-11.

Recover Lost Work

Computers lock up occasionally, and applications crash in the middle of important projects. When that happens, any work that you haven't saved is gone.

To minimize the pain of those situations, Word, Excel, and PowerPoint all have an AutoRecover feature that silently saves your drafts as you work, once every ten minutes or at some other interval you specify. These drafts are saved in temporary hidden files that are deleted when you close the application successfully (that is, not abruptly due to a lockup, crash, or power outage). If the application crashes, those temporary saved files appear for your perusal when the program starts back up. You can choose to either

- Save them if their versions are newer than the ones you have on your hard drive

  or

- Discard them if they contain nothing you need

To change the interval at which AutoRecover versions are saved, follow these steps:

1. Choose File ➪ Options.

2. Click the Save category.

3. Make sure that the Save AutoRecover Information Every xx Minutes check box is selected. See **Figure 3-12**.

4. If desired, change the value in the Minutes box to another number.

5. Click OK.

Set AutoRecover interval

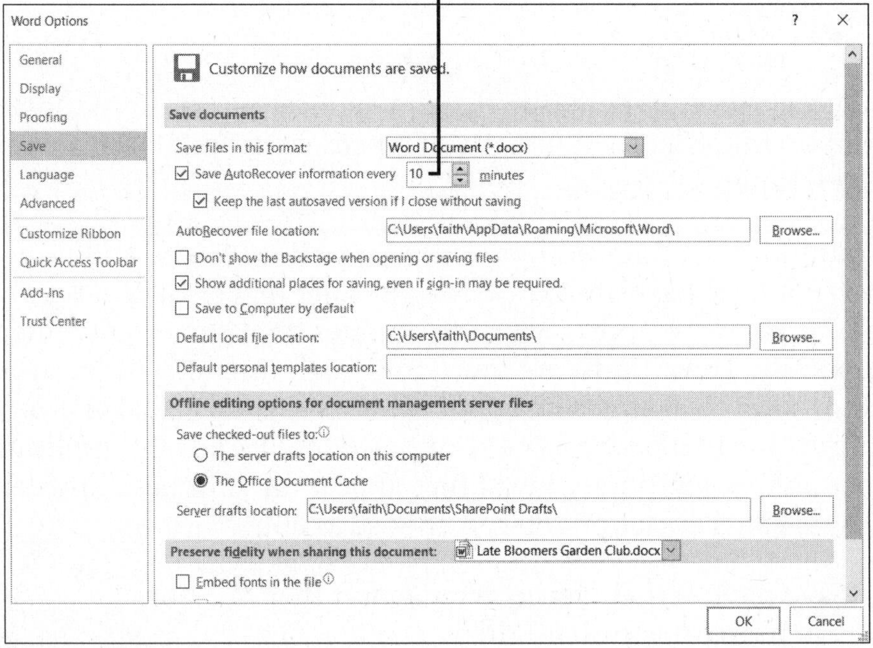

Figure 3-12

Part II
Word

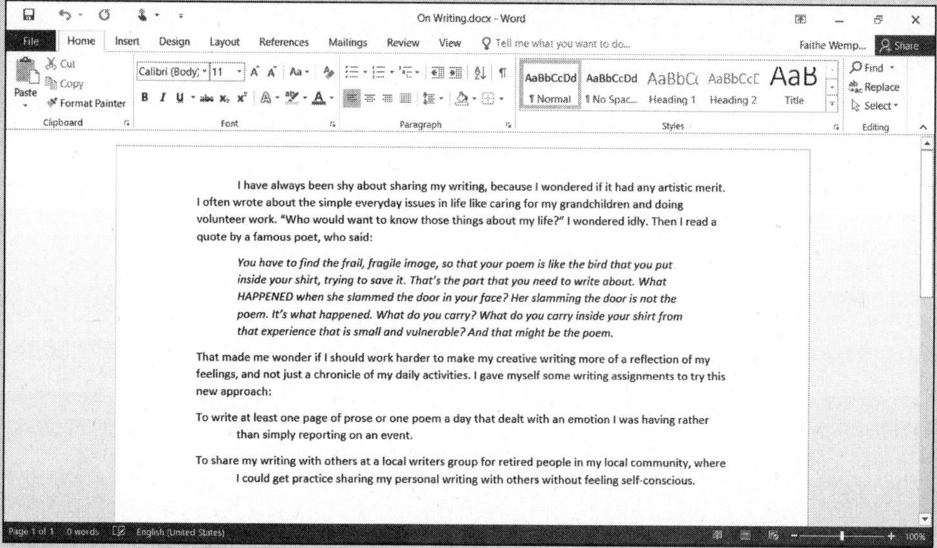

web extras

For a guide on creating your own greeting cards in Word, visit www.dummies.com/extras/office2016forseniors.

Composing Your Thoughts in Word

Chapter 4

If you've read this book to this point, you've seen the common features across the various Office applications, in a general way. In this chapter, it's time to get down to brass tacks with one particular application: Microsoft Word.

Word is a word processing program. That's a fancy way of saying that it specializes in creating and formatting (that is, *processing*) text. Word is ideal for projects that are primarily text-based: in other words, where the text is the main attraction, and the *formatting* (how text looks) plays a supporting role. Suitable projects in Word include correspondence, club newsletters and minutes, flyers and signs, fax cover sheets, mailing labels, brochures, award certificates, and stationery.

That's a pretty broad list of projects!

Because Word is good for so many things, it's usually the first application in the Office suite that a person learns how to use. In this chapter, I show you how to get around in Word; and how to type, edit, and format text.

Get ready to . . .

Examine the Word Interface

Word differs from the other Office applications primarily in the depth of its text-handling tools. Whereas PowerPoint is all about graphics and Excel is all about numbers, Word is all about — well, words! Almost every tab on the Ribbon in Word has a text focus.

Some of Word's strongest unique features include:

- **A complete set of proofreading tools:** You'll find not only a spelling checker, but also a grammar checker, thesaurus, translation utility, and word counter. All these tools are on the Review tab. The spelling and grammar checkers are covered in Chapter 3.

- **Several features for quickly and consistently applying formatting to text:** Word offers convenient themes, styles, and style sets. Styles are on the Home tab, and themes are on the Design tab. Chapter 2 discusses themes in a generic, multi-application sense, and Chapter 5 covers styles and themes specifically in Word.

A *style* applies to an individual paragraph, or a block of selected text. A *theme* applies to the entire document.

- **A full-featured Mail Merge utility:** Use this feature (found on the Mailings tab) to create customized copies of letters, mailing labels, envelopes, and so on. Chapter 6 covers mail merge.

- **Collaboration tools:** Use these tools when working with other people, such as document sharing, change tracking, document comparison, and commenting. All of these are accessed from the Review tab.

Move Around and Select Text

In Chapter 1, I cover how to move around in a document and select blocks of text. In a nutshell, whatever you type in Word appears at the *insertion point,* which is the blinking vertical line on the page. You can move the insertion point by clicking with the mouse where you want it placed, or by using the arrow keys. There are also shortcut keys for moving the insertion point.

Scrolling the document with the scroll bars moves the display (for example, from page 1 to page 2) but does not move the insertion point.

A lot of people are surprised, for example, when they scroll to another page and start typing, but the text appears back on the previous page! That's because the typing appears at the insertion point, which is still back where it was before.

To perform an action upon text — say, make it bold, or move it — you have to select the text first. To select text, drag across it with the mouse, or you can hold down the Shift key and then press the arrow keys to extend the selection. What you selected is highlighted, so that's a good sign. You can also select an entire word by double-clicking it, an entire paragraph by triple-clicking it, or the entire document by pressing Ctrl+A.

You can move around by using keyboard shortcuts. You might find using keyboard shortcuts even more convenient than using the scroll bar. Table 4-1 lists some keyboard shortcuts in Word.

Table 4-2 shows keyboard shortcuts to help you select text. Hold down the Shift key while you press the key in the left column of Table 4-2. The amount of text selected depends on whether you also hold down the Ctrl (Control) key at the same time.

Table 4-1 Movement Shortcuts

Direction key	*Position without Ctrl key*	*Position with Ctrl key*
Up arrow (↑)	One line up	One paragraph up
Down arrow (↓)	One line down	One paragraph down
Right arrow (→)	One character to the right	One word to the right
Left arrow (←)	One character to the left	One word to the left
Home	Beginning of the line	Beginning of the document
End	End of the line	End of the document
Page Down	One screen down (scrolling)	Top of the next page
Page Up	Up one screen (scrolling)	Top of the previous page

Table 4-2 Text Selection Shortcuts

This key plus Shift key	*Selection without Ctrl key*	*Selection with Ctrl key*
Up arrow (↑)	One line up	One paragraph up
Down arrow (↓)	One line down	One paragraph down
Right arrow (→)	One character to the right	One word to the right
Left arrow (←)	One character to the left	One word to the left
Home	Beginning of the line	Beginning of the document
End	End of the line	End of the document
Page Down	One screen down (scrolling)	Top of the next page
Page Up	Up one screen (scrolling)	Top of the previous page

Choose Paper Size and Orientation

The default paper size in Word is 8.5 x 11 inches. That's the standard size (called Letter), which conveniently fits in most printers and copy machines in the United States. (Legal size is the other major size used in the United States: 8.5 x 14 inches.) In other countries, though, standard paper size is different. For example, in Europe, A4 paper is the standard size, at 8.27 x 11.69 inches.

Whenever Word starts a new document, it does so based on a group of settings stored in a template called Normal. A *template* is a configuration file that governs the default settings for the documents that are based on it. These settings include specifications for a paper size of 8.5 x 11 inches. If you want the document to have a different paper size — say, for a brochure — choose Layout➪Page Setup➪Size and then choose a different paper size from the drop-down list. See **Figure 4-1**.

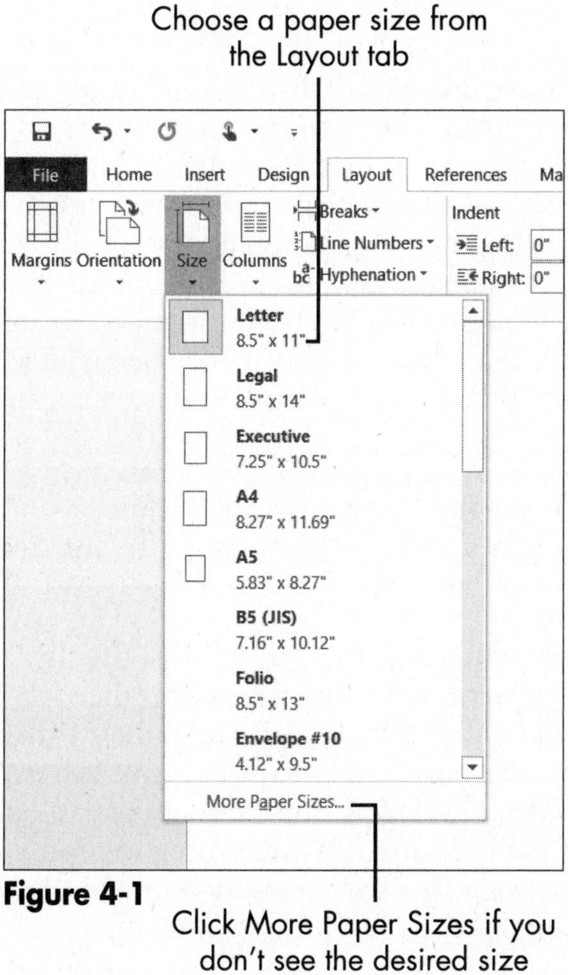

Figure 4-1

Page orientation determines whether the height or the width of the page is greater. If the text is parallel to the narrow edge, that's *Portrait.* If it's parallel to the wide edge, that's *Landscape*.

Portrait (taller than wide) is the more common orientation, used for most correspondence and reports. Landscape orientation (wider than tall) is used for brochures, certificates, and calendars, all of which fit naturally into the wider format.

To change the page orientation, choose Layout ➪ Page Setup ➪ Orientation and then click Portrait or Landscape.

Set Margins

A document's *margin* is the space between the edge of the paper and where the text begins. Ideal margins depend on many factors, including the document type, the need to limit the number of pages (for example, if you're paying by the page to fax or copy a document), and the audience's needs. Adjusting the margins can also control the perception of your document, making it look like it is longer or shorter than it actually is. Many a student who has been assigned a "three-page paper" has tried to get away with writing less by using large margins! (Of course, that generally doesn't work because teachers know that trick.)

Word offers several sets of standard margin settings. Choose Layout ➪ Page Setup ➪ Margins and then choose from the list. See **Figure 4-2**.

Each preset has a value assigned to the four page sides. Usually, a document uses the same margin setting for opposite sides (the same value for top and bottom, and the same value for left and right). This isn't a hard-and-fast rule, though. You might, for example, want extra space at the top of a page when you're printing on stationery with a name and address preprinted at the top. And, if you're going to bind your pages or use a three hole–punch for pages presented in a binder, you might want a larger margin.

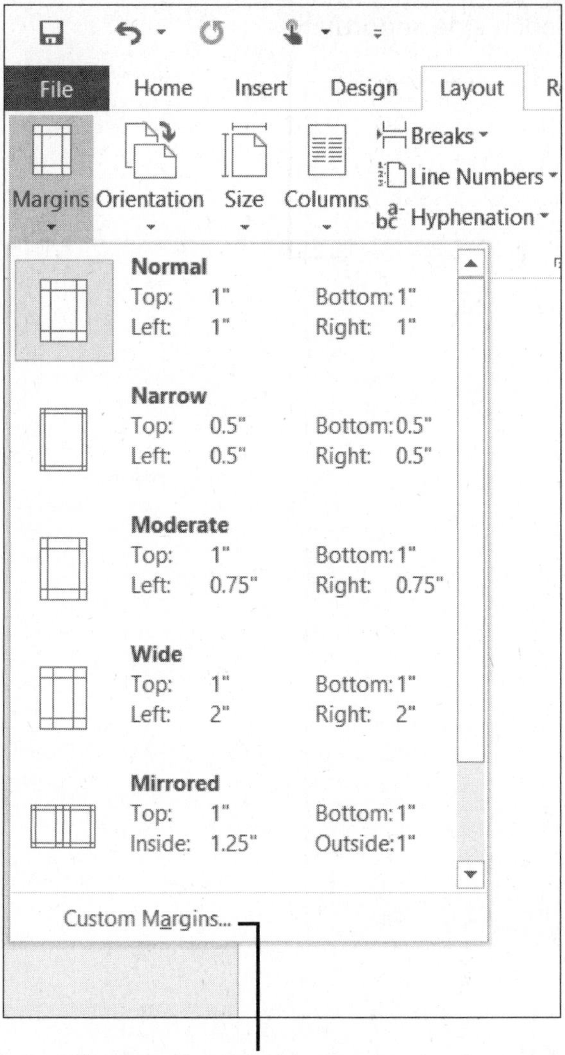

Figure 4-2

If none of the choices on the list match what you want, choose Custom Margins from the bottom of the Margins menu (shown in Figure 4-2) and enter precise values in the Page Setup dialog box that appears, as shown in **Figure 4-3**.

Enter values for each side separately

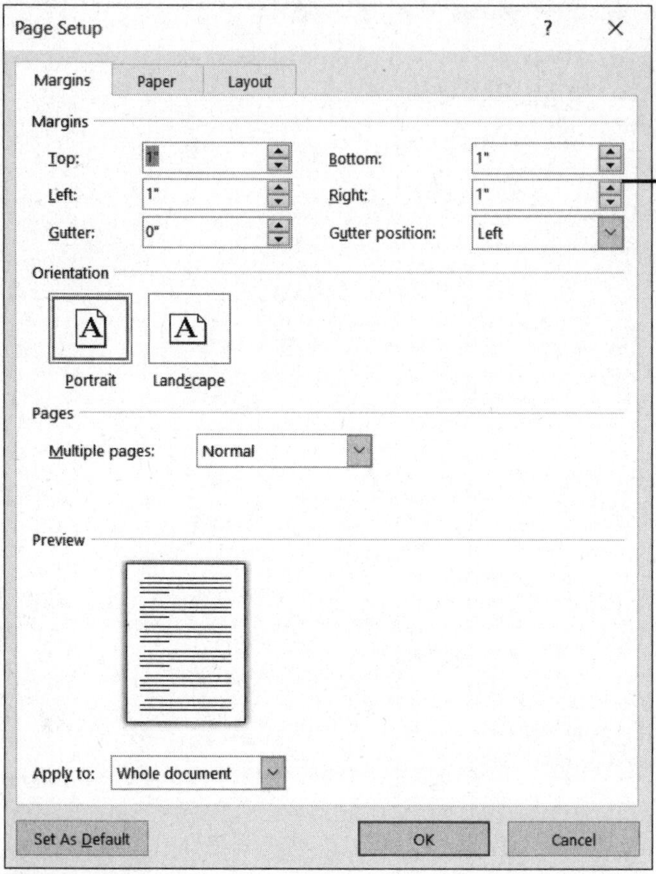

Figure 4-3

Select the Right Screen View

Like with all the Office applications, Word gives you a variety of views to choose from. In Chapter 1, I cover views as a general concept; here, I talk about the specific views in Word.

At different points in the document creation process, you might want to see your document differently. For example, when you're hammering out the text, you might want to see your work in a very plain way, without the distraction of multiple columns and page breaks. Later, when you're fine-tuning the final look, you might want to see the document in a format closer to how it will appear when printed or published on the Web.

As I mention in Chapter 1, the View tab provides access to all the viewing options, and View buttons are also available in the bottom right of the Word window.

The available views in Word are

- **Print Layout:** The default view. You see each page approximately as it will look when printed, including graphics, multicolumn layouts, and breaks. This view is appropriate for most documents and work situations.
- **Read Mode:** A view that simulates an electronic book-reading program, laying out text in an easy-to-read, book-like format. Text can't be edited in this view. This view is good for reviewing someone else's work.
- **Web Layout:** A view of the document approximately as it will look when saved in Web format. Use this view when you are using Word to create content destined from the Web.

Word isn't the most powerful tool for Web page design, but Word does enable you to create and save simple Web content.

- **Outline:** A hierarchical view. Paragraphs are marked as headings (via the Styles feature, covered in Chapter 5) and appear in outline format. You can expand and collapse the outline to show more or fewer outline levels. Outline view is great in the early stage of a project, when you are planning the headings for a long document.

- **Draft:** A plain-text view. You don't see the edges of the page nor any multicolumn layouts. Page and section breaks appear as codes rather than as actual breaks. Some graphics don't appear, and others don't appear in the exact spots they will be in when the document is printed.

In most cases, you will probably be happiest with Page Layout view or Draft view. I use Page Layout view most of the time, and switch to Draft view when I need to edit a multicolumn document. I find it easier to scroll through the text when I don't have to skip from column to column onscreen.

On some less powerful computers, you might notice a difference in Word's performance depending on the view you choose. For example, when you page down or move the insertion point with the arrow keys, you might experience a brief delay, especially in Print Layout view. If you find delays occurring as you edit, switching to Draft view should solve the problem.

Align and Indent Paragraphs

In Chapter 2, I cover text formatting at the individual character level: font, font size, and the like. Now take a look at some formatting that applies to entire paragraphs.

Paragraphs are the building blocks of documents. Every time you press Enter, you create a new paragraph.

You can see the paragraph markers (which don't print) by clicking the Show/Hide (¶) button on the Home tab (in the Paragraph group). This button toggles on/off the display of hidden characters such as spaces, paragraph breaks, line breaks, and tabs. **Figure 4-4** shows a document with the display turned on.

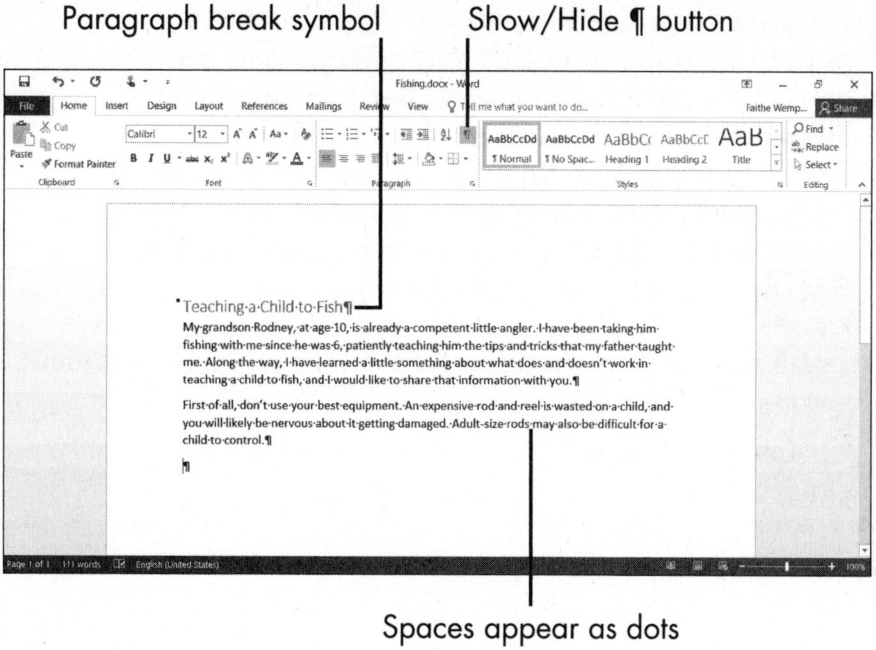

Figure 4-4

Some folks find seeing these characters very distracting. However, showing them can be very helpful when you're trying to make sure you have only one space between words, or when you accidentally press the Tab key and make text skip like this — and then fix it.

Each paragraph has a horizontal *alignment,* which determines how each line aligns between the right and left margins. The default is *left alignment,* where each line begins at the left margin. Left alignment is appropriate for most situations; the text in this book is left-aligned. The alternatives are

- **Right alignment:** Each line ends at the right margin. You might use this to right-align the date in some styles of business letters.
- **Center alignment:** Each line is centered evenly between the margins. You might want to center your name and address on stationery you create.

- **Justified:** Each line has additional space added to it as needed so that it begins at the left margin and ends at the right margin. With justified alignment, all lines of the paragraph except the last one are spaced that way; the final line of the paragraph is left-aligned. If the paragraph consists of only a single line, it is left-aligned. Newsletter text is often justified, making for a tidier-looking page.

Figure 4-5 shows some examples of the four types of alignment.

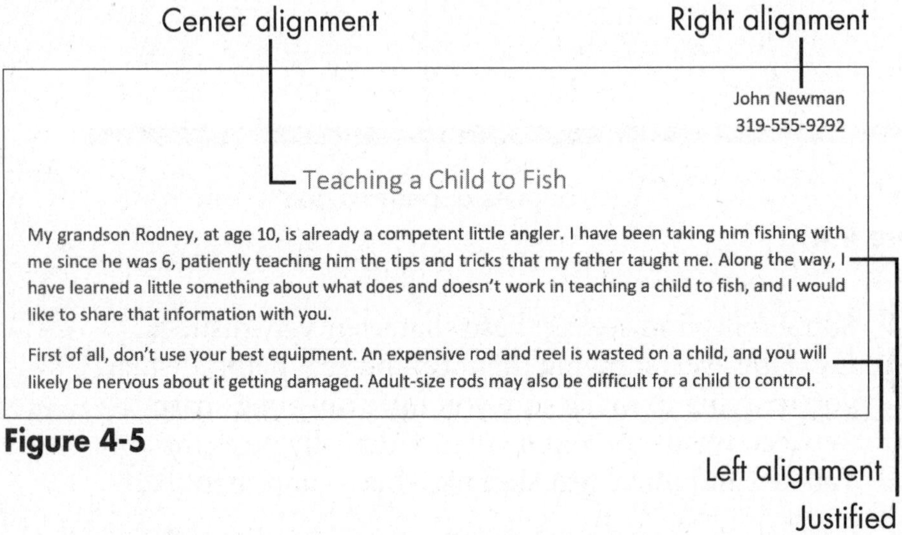

Figure 4-5

To change one paragraph's alignment, move the insertion point into it, or select any (or all) text within it. Then click the paragraph alignment button you want. See **Figure 4-6**.

To apply a different alignment to multiple paragraphs at once, select multiple paragraphs (or any part of them). Then click the paragraph alignment button you want.

By default, each paragraph starts in relation to the right and left margins, depending on what alignment you choose. For example, a left-aligned paragraph starts at the same position as the left margin, like this text. Sometimes you might want to *indent* one or more paragraphs, though: that is, shift their position in relation to the left and/or right margins. For example, in some styles of correspondence, it's customary to indent the first line of each paragraph by one-half inch (or five spaces). Or, when citing a quotation, it's common to indent a paragraph by one-half inch at both the right and the left.

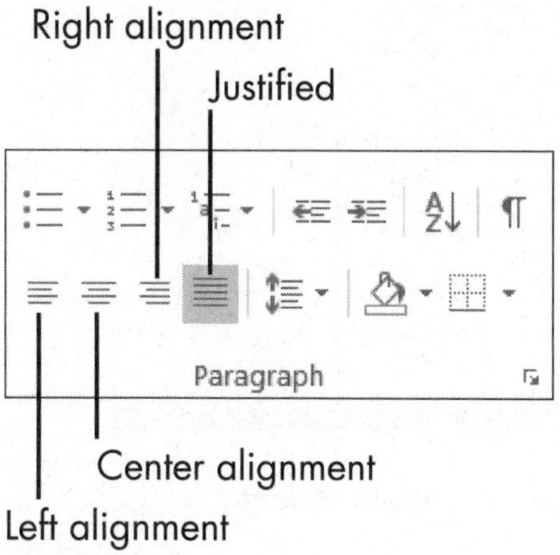

Figure 4-6

Here are the possible types of indents in Word. Each is demonstrated in **Figure 4-7**.

- **First-line indent:** The starting position of the first line of the paragraph is shifted (usually inward) in relation to the left margin.
- **Left indent:** All lines of the paragraph are shifted in relation to the left margin.
- **Right indent:** All lines of the paragraph are shifted in relation to the right margin.

For a simple left indent, use buttons on the Home tab (Paragraph group): Increase Indent and Decrease Indent. See Figure 4-7. Each time you click one of those buttons, it changes the left indent for the selected paragraph(s) by 0.5″.

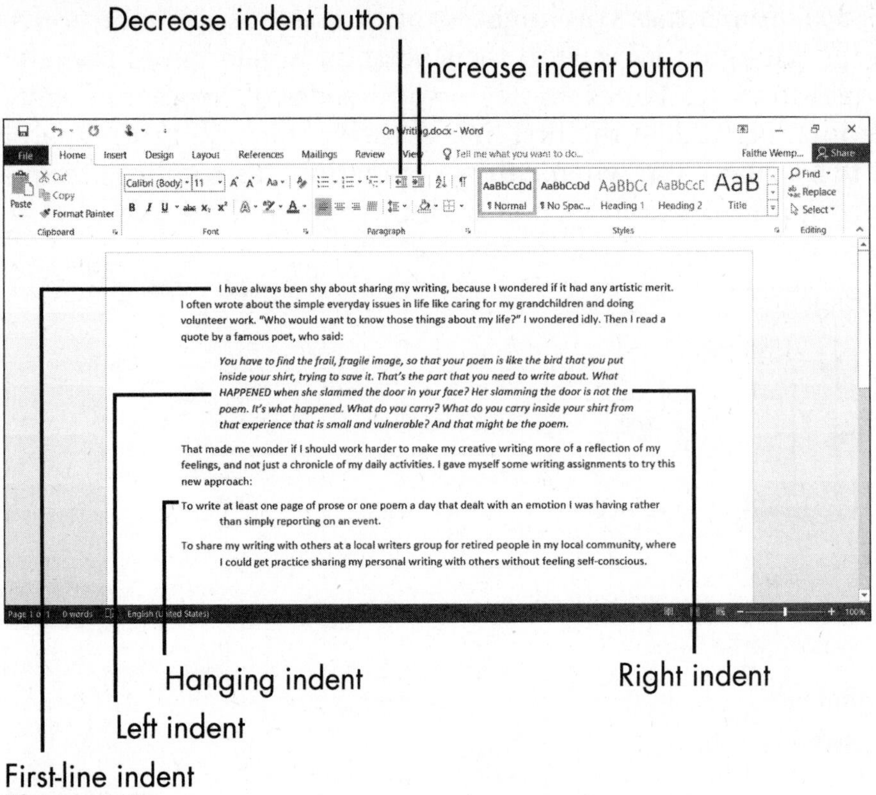

Figure 4-7

If you want to specify the amount of indent or if you want to apply an indent to the right side, use the Indent controls on the Layout tab, as shown in **Figure 4-8**. You can increment the amount of indent up or down in the Left and Right text boxes.

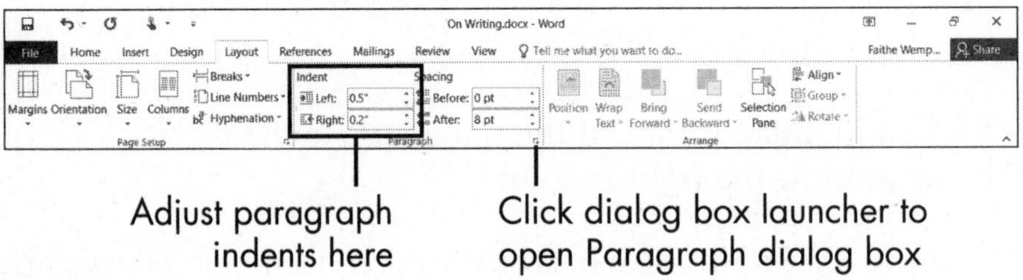

Figure 4-8

If you want a special indent (hanging or first-line), use the Paragraph dialog box. To do so, follow these steps:

1. Select the paragraph(s) to which the setting should apply.
2. On the Home or the Layout tab, click the small icon in the bottom right of the Paragraph group. (It's pointed out in Figure 4-8.)
3. In the Paragraph dialog box that opens, enter values in the Left and/or Right text boxes as desired to create overall indents for the paragraph(s). See **Figure 4-9**.

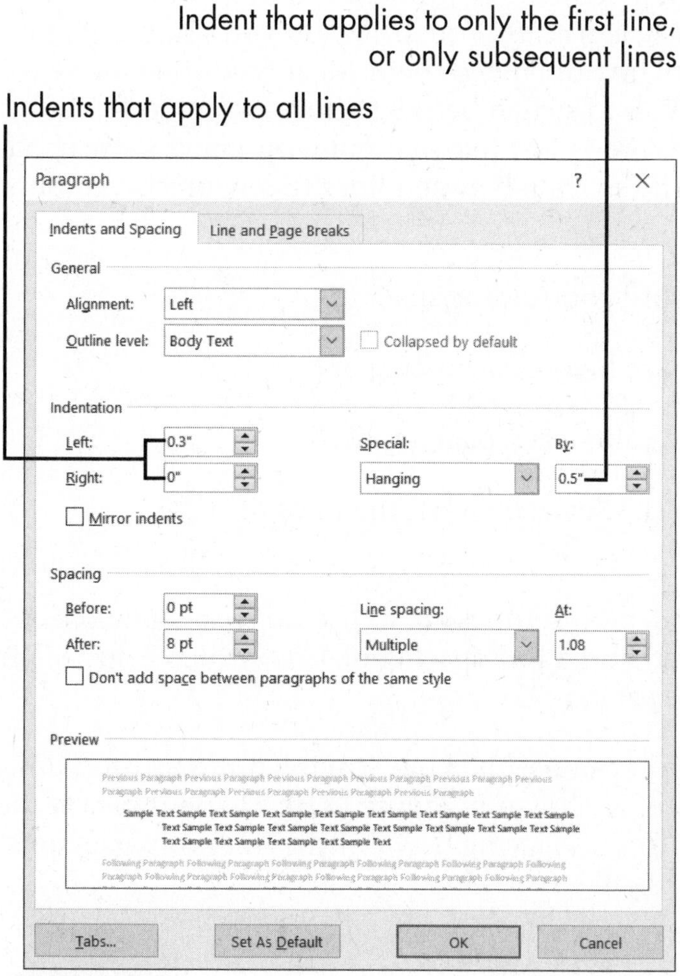

Figure 4-9

4. (Optional) If you want a special type of indent (such as hanging, or first-line), open the Special drop-down list and make your selection. Then enter the amount of the special indent in the text box to the right.

   In Figure 4-9, for example, a hanging indent has been set of 0.9″. That means all lines *except* the first one will be left-indented by 0.9″.

5. Click OK. The indent settings are applied.

Change Line Spacing

If you've used a typewriter, you're probably familiar with the terms *single spacing* and *double spacing*. You know, do you want one line of space between every line of type, or two? Most typewriters have a switch that allows you to switch between those two modes. The Spacing feature in Word is just like that but with many more choices. You can fine-tune the spacing between lines to any precise amount you want.

Three settings in Word control line spacing:

- **Before:** The space before each paragraph
- **After:** The space after each paragraph
- **Line Spacing:** The space between the lines of each paragraph

In Word 2016, the default settings are to use no spacing Before, 8 points of space After, and a line spacing of 1.08, which is just slightly greater than single-spacing.

For basic spacing, you can use the Line Spacing button's drop-down list on the Home tab, as shown in **Figure 4-10**. The numbers at the top of the list refer to line spacing between the lines of paragraphs; the commands at the bottom of the list add or remove spacing before or after the paragraphs. You can also set the Before and After values on the Layout tab, as shown in **Figure 4-11**.

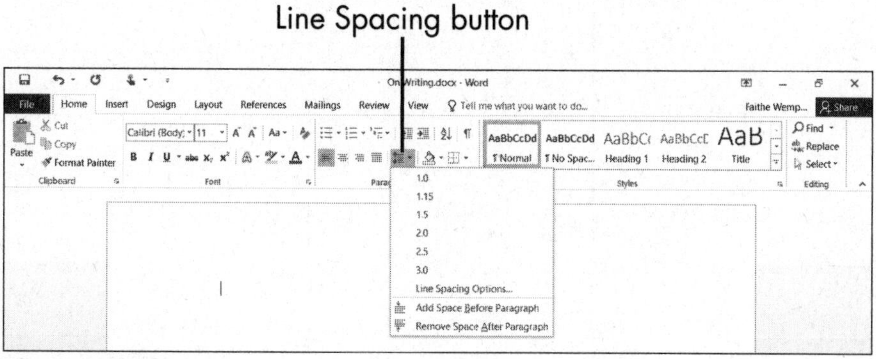

Figure 4-10

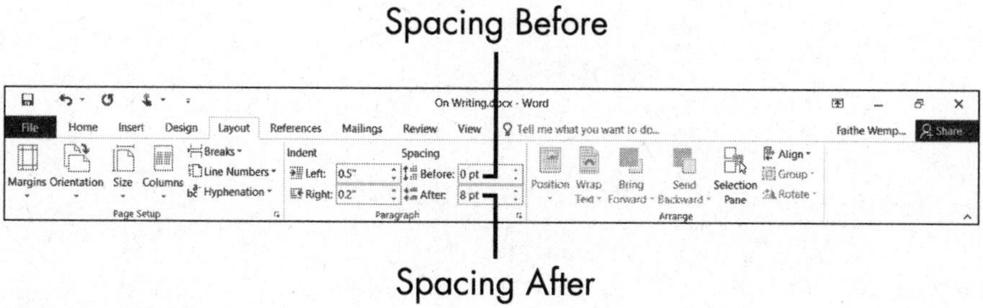

Figure 4-11

If all that still doesn't meet your spacing needs, you can open the Paragraph dialog box (click the little icon in the bottom-right corner of the Paragraph group, on either the Home or the Layout tab) and set specific values for spacing there. As shown in **Figure 4-12**, you can enter Before and After values. In the Line Spacing area, you select a unit of measurement from the drop-down list, and then enter a value.

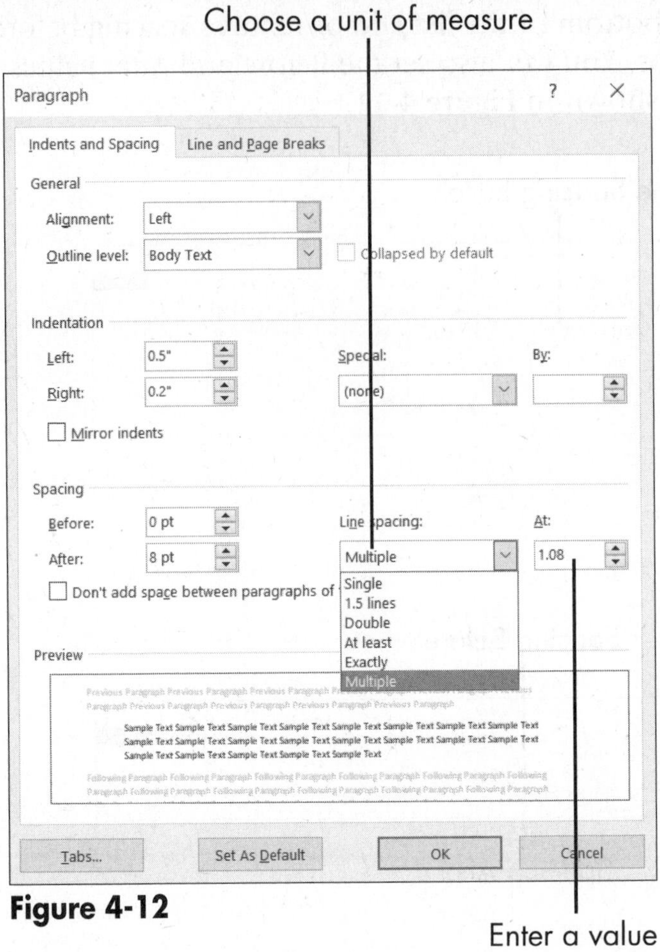

Figure 4-12

Create Bulleted and Numbered Lists

Word makes it easy to create bulleted and numbered lists in your documents. Use a *bulleted list* for lists where the order of items isn't significant, and the same "bullet" character (such as • or ⇨) is used in front of each item. You might use a bulleted list for a packing list for a trip, for example, or a go-forward list. In contrast, use a *numbered list* for lists where the order of items *is* significant, and a sequential step number is used to indicate order. A numbered list might contain the steps for a recipe or a meeting agenda.

You can create a list from existing paragraphs, or you can turn on the list feature and type the list as you go. Either way, you're working with the Bullets button or the Numbering button on the Home tab.

It's just this easy:

- Click the Bullets or the Numbering button to apply a default bullet or number, respectively. The default bullet looks like this (•) and the default numbering treatment uses standard 1., 2., 3., and so on.
- Click the arrow to the right of either button to open a palette of additional choices. **Figure 4-13** shows the Numbering Library and its choices.

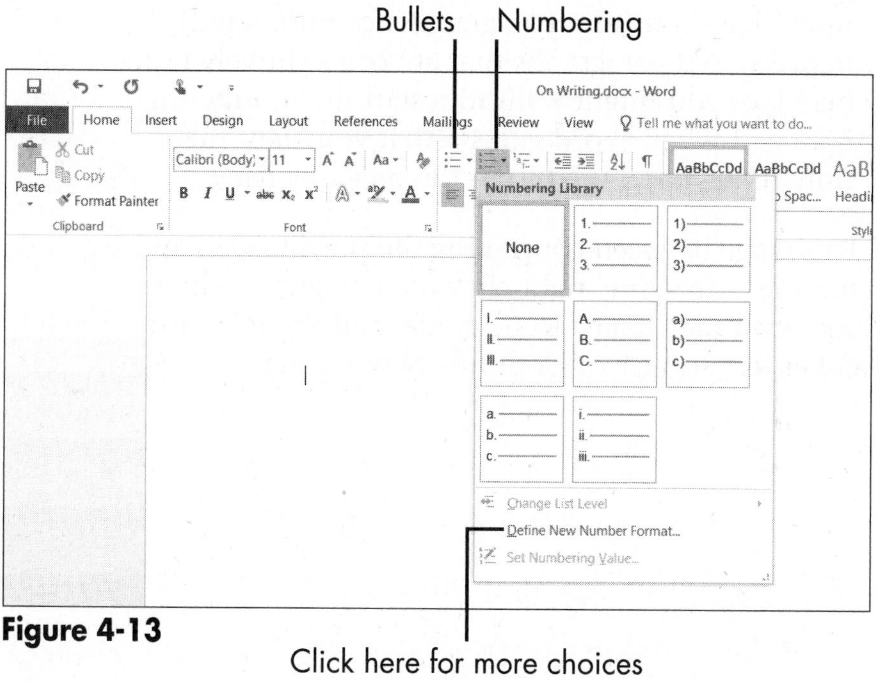

Figure 4-13

If you go the palette route, here's the drill for bullets or numbered lists:

- **Bullets:** Pick one of the bullet characters on the palette. If you don't find what you want, click Define New Bullet to set up a custom bullet.

- **Numbered lists:** Choose from a variety of numeral styles, including Arabic (1, 2, 3) and Roman (I, II, III); or uppercase or lowercase Arabic and Roman letters (A, B, C; i, ii, iii). See Figure 4-13. Clicking the Define New Number Format option opens a dialog box where you can set up your own number formats.

- For each numbered list, Word automatically increments the number. It isn't always perfect at guessing your wishes, though. For example, sometimes you might have a regular paragraph (not numbered) between two paragraphs that are consecutively numbered, or you might want to restart the numbering back at 1 when Word guesses that you want the numbering continued from the previous list.

To change between continuing the previous list and starting a new one, right-click the paragraph where you want the change to be made, and then choose either Restart at 1 or Continue Numbering.

Dressing Up Your Documents

Word makes it easy to create attractive documents with consistent formatting, colorful graphics, and neatly ordered tables. In this chapter, I show you how to take advantage of some of Word 2016's user-friendly features for improving a document's appearance and readability.

In this chapter, I start with the Styles feature, which can save you a lot of time if you like to try different text formatting before deciding on a final look. With styles, you can easily switch between looks without having to worry about maintaining consistency.

Then I show you how to insert photos from your own files and from a web search.

I also explain how to make a page more colorful and attractive by adding a border around the edge of the page, and by coloring its background.

Finally, I walk you through the basics of creating tables that hold multiple columns of information in an orderly way.

Chapter 5

Get ready to . . .

Apply Styles and Style Sets

Using a *style* — a named set of formatting specifications — makes it easy to apply consistent formatting throughout a document. For example, you might apply the style named Heading 1 to all headings in the document and the style named Normal to all the regular body text. Here are the advantages of this approach:

- **Ease:** Applying a style is easier than manually applying formatting. And changing the formatting is a snap. If you want the headings to look different, for example, you can modify the Heading 1 style to change them all at once.

- **Consistency:** You don't have to worry about all the headings being formatted consistently; because they're all using the same style, they're automatically all the same.

Of the several types of styles in Word, the most common type (by far) is a *paragraph style.* A paragraph style can contain formatting specifications, such as font, font size and color, indentation, alignment, and line spacing.

Unless you specify otherwise, each paragraph is assigned a style called Normal. In Word 2016, this default uses a Calibri 11 point (pt) font and left-aligns your text. (Calibri is a font that comes with Office 2016.)

Points (pt) measure how large the text is. Read more about this in Chapter 4.

In the Styles group on the Home tab (see **Figure 5-1**), you can find samples of several different styles. This is the *Styles gallery.* Not all available styles appear in the Styles gallery; each individual style's definition specifies whether or not it appears there.

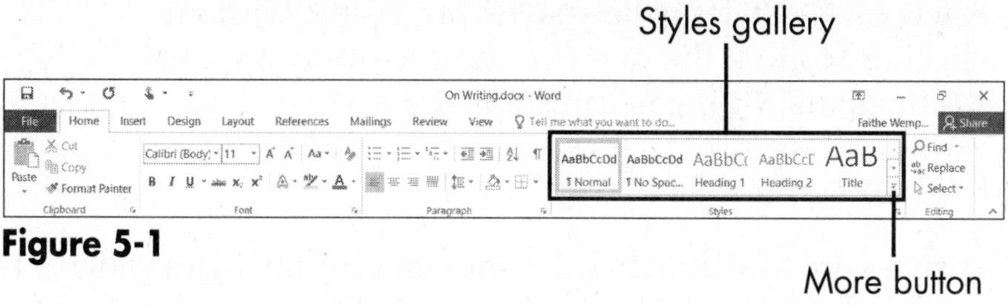

Figure 5-1

To assign a different style to a paragraph, follow these steps:

1. Click your mouse anywhere in the paragraph you want to change.

   If you want to apply the style to multiple paragraphs, select them first. See Chapter 1 for how to select text.

2. Click the Home tab.

3. Click the More arrow (the down arrow with the horizontal line above it) to the right of the Styles gallery, opening the full list of the Styles gallery styles. (See **Figure 5-2**.)

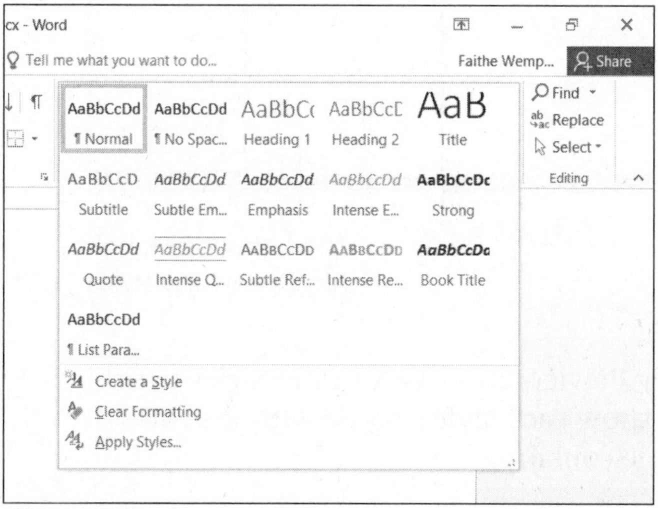

Figure 5-2

A few of the Styles gallery styles are visible without clicking More. If the one you want to apply appears (as in Figure 5-1), you can skip Step 3.

4. Click the style you want.

Other styles are available besides the ones in the Styles gallery. To see them, click the dialog box launcher in the Styles group to open a Styles pane that contains a larger list. See **Figure 5-3**. You can select any style by clicking the style in the Styles pane.

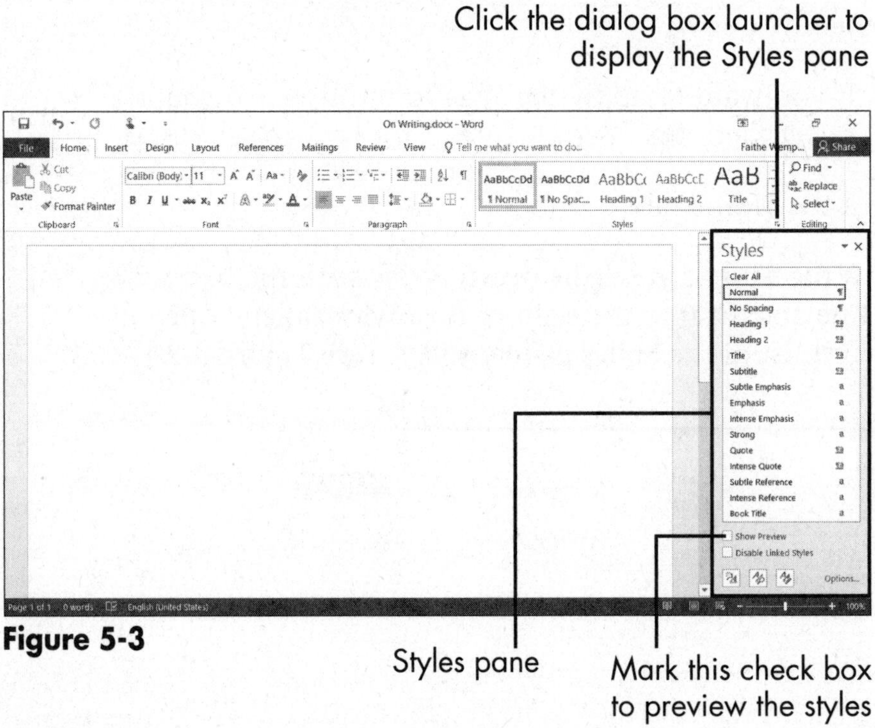

Figure 5-3

Select the Show Preview check box in the Styles pane if you want to show each style's name with the formatting the style contains.

If the Styles pane floats (that is, it's not anchored to the right side of the screen), you can anchor it there by dragging it to the far right until it snaps into place. You can make it float again by dragging it by its title (Styles) back out toward the center of the Word window.

The definitions of the styles are determined by the *style set* in use. Different style sets can quickly change the look of an entire document by redefining each built-in style (fonts, sizes, colors, line spacing, and so on).

To change to a different style set, follow these steps:

1. On the Design tab, point to one of the style sets in the Style Sets gallery in the Document Formatting group. See **Figure 5-4.** The new style set is previewed in your document's existing text.

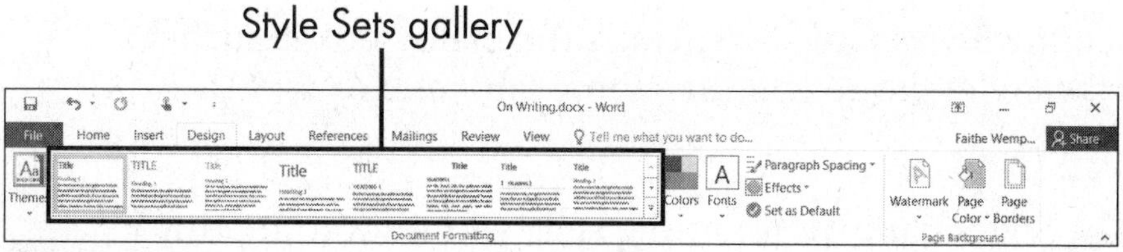

Figure 5-4

2. Click the style set you want.

   If you don't like any of the choices displayed, click the More button for the gallery to open the full gallery of choices, as shown in **Figure 5-5.** Notice that you can reset to the default style set from this gallery menu, or save the current settings as a new style set.

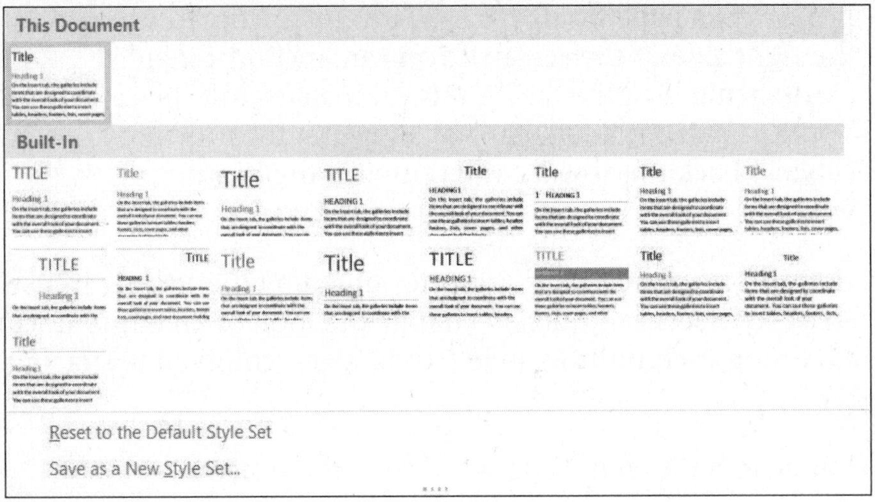

Figure 5-5

You can also manually modify any style's definition. Suppose that you want the body text in a document to be a little larger. To do this, follow these steps:

1. Open the Styles pane by clicking the dialog box launcher for the Styles group (on the Home tab; refer to Figure 5-3).
2. In the Styles pane, point to the style you want to modify so that a down arrow appears to its right.
3. Click the down arrow to open a menu.
4. Click Modify.
5. In the Modify Style dialog box that appears, make any formatting changes as desired. This dialog box contains a variety of text and paragraph formatting settings. See **Figure 5-6**.
6. Click OK.

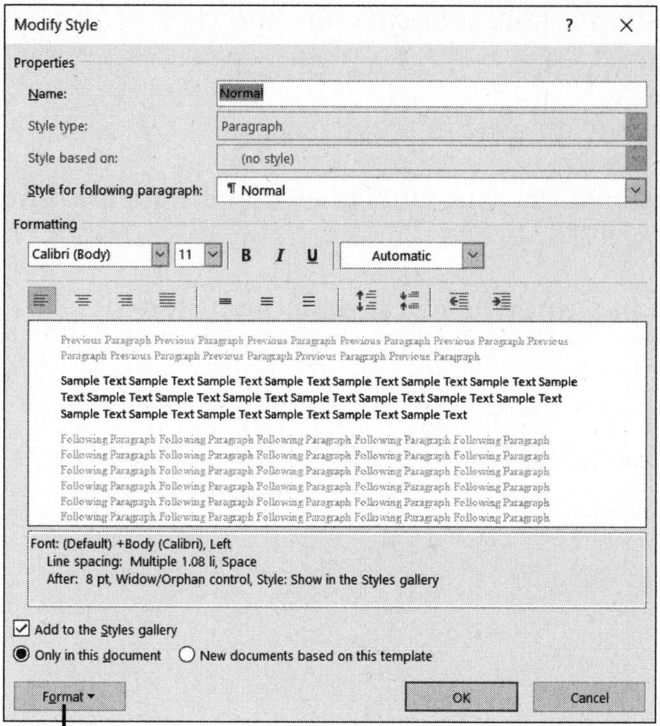

Click here for more formatting settings you can adjust

Figure 5-6

Insert Photos

You can insert pictures into a document from your own picture stash on your local PC, or from online sources such as a Bing image search or your OneDrive.

To insert a locally stored picture, follow these steps:

1. Position the insertion point where you want the picture to appear.
2. Choose Insert ➪ Picture. The Insert Picture dialog box opens.

3. Navigate to the folder containing the picture and click the desired picture.

4. Click Insert. The picture appears in the document.

To insert a picture stored on your OneDrive, the process is slightly different:

1. Position the insertion point where you want the picture to appear.

2. From the Insert tab, click Online Pictures. An Insert Pictures dialog box appears. See **Figure 5-7**.

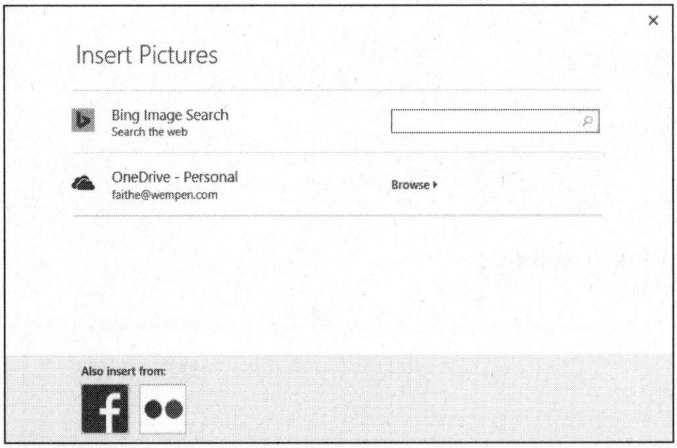

Figure 5-7

3. Click the Browse button next to OneDrive. A list of the folders and files on your OneDrive appear.

4. Click the picture you want.

5. Click Insert.

But what if you don't have the photo you want? Office applications include a means of performing a Bing image search from within the applications themselves, so you can find an image without having to exit out to a web browser. Bing is Microsoft's web search engine.

Follow these steps to find and insert an image with Bing:

1. Position the insertion point where you want the picture to appear.

2. From the Insert tab, click Online Pictures. An Insert Pictures dialog box appears (refer to Figure 5-7).

3. In the search box next to Bing Image Search, type one or more keywords that define what you are looking for, and then press Enter. An assortment of images appear. **Figure 5-8** shows an example.

4. Scroll through the images, select the one you want, and click Insert.

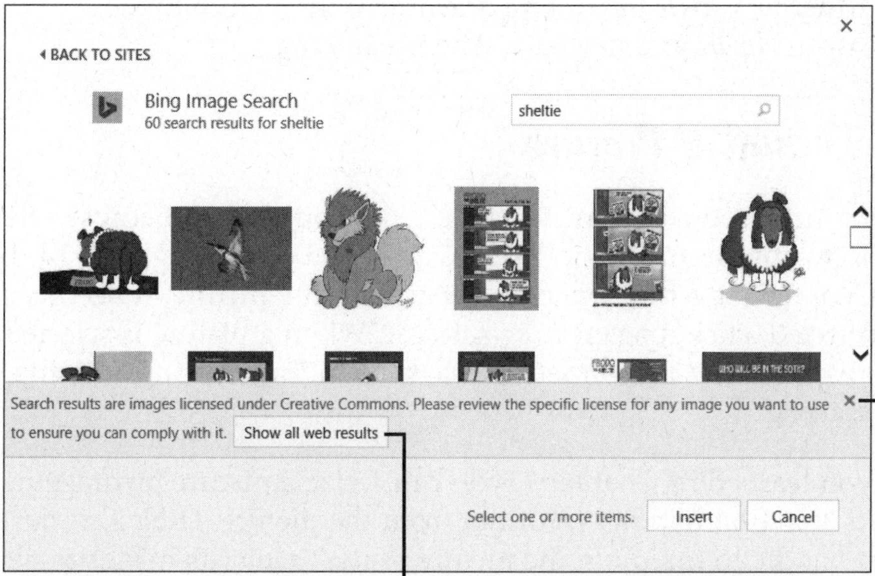

Figure 5-8

As the note overlaid on the search results shows in Figure 5-8, the images that Bing finds within Office are licensed under Creative Commons. This means they are royalty-free images that are okay to use for non-commercial projects. However, don't count on an image being free to use just because it shows up in the Bing search results. If you are creating a publication that will be widely distributed, or sold, you should research the images selected to make sure the owners have not placed any restrictions on their use. When you select an image in the dialog box, a hyperlink appears in the bottom-left corner of the dialog box; you can follow it to the original image source, and from there you can glean information about its usage restrictions, if any.

Microsoft no longer provides clip art for Office users. However, if you are specifically looking for clip art (that is, vector-based line drawings), try including the word *clipart* as a key term when searching.

Size and Format a Picture

After you insert a picture, it is selected. (You can tell because selection handles appear around it, like the ones you saw in Figure 1-14, back in Chapter 1.) When you click away from the picture, it becomes unselected; click it again to re-select it. When a picture is selected, you can work with it in a variety of ways, including moving, resizing, and formatting.

As you learned in Chapter 1, you can resize a picture by dragging one of its selection handles in or out from the picture. Drag a corner selection handle to maintain the picture's *aspect ratio* (its height-to-width ratio) to avoid distorting it.

When a picture is selected, a Format tab appears on the Ribbon (upper right). This tab contains a variety of buttons for working with the picture, such as adding a matte or a border. Tinker with the options there.

If you don't like what you've done, press Ctrl+Z to undo the last action. Or just delete the figure (select it and then press Delete) and start over.

Position a Picture

You can move a picture by dragging it where you want it. (Position the mouse pointer over any portion of the picture except over a selection handle.) Sounds simple, right? There's small snag, though: by default, Word treats pictures as inline images. In other words, it sees a picture as a very large single character of text. As the text floats, the picture floats, too. In this mode, the options are limited as to where you can place the picture because it has to remain associated with a paragraph.

As an alternative, you can change a picture's text wrap setting so that the image can be positioned anywhere on the page. Each of the various text wrap settings has a different way of interacting with any document text that may potentially overlap with the picture. Here are the choices:

- **In Line with Text:** The picture is a part of the paragraph; the text doesn't wrap around it. This is the default setting.
- **Square:** Text wraps around the picture's rectangular outer frame.
- **Tight:** For some images, this is the same as Square. If the image is vector-based line art with no solid background (as with some types of clip art, for example), the text may wrap tightly around the image itself, rather than around its rectangular outer frame.
- **Behind Text:** The text appears as an overlay on top of the picture.
- **In Front of Text:** The image appears over the top of the text, partially obscuring it.

- **Top and Bottom:** The picture interrupts the text, which flows above or below it. The picture is on a line all by itself.
- **Through:** Mostly the same as Tight.

In **Figure 5-9**, the text wrapping is set to Square.

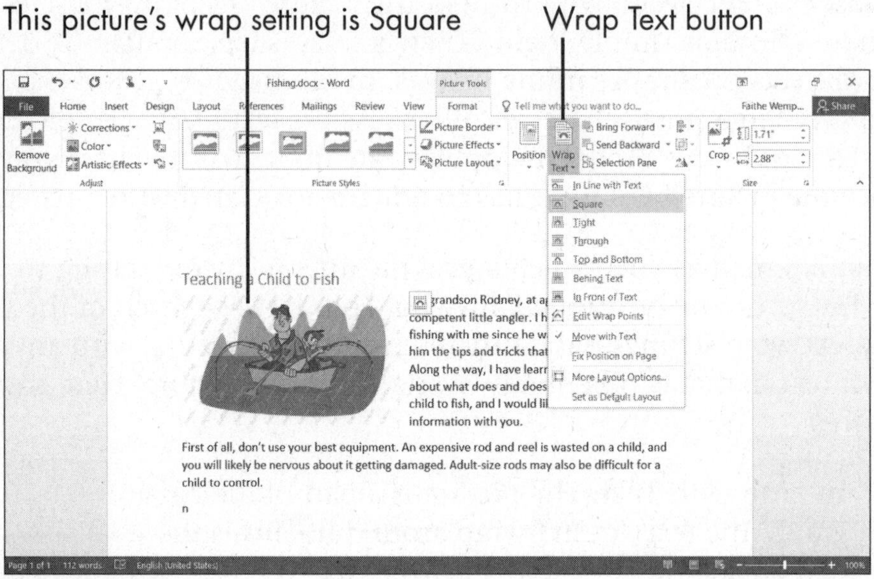

Figure 5-9

Add a Page Border

A *page border* can make a page look more festive and colorful; this feature is great for family newsletters, invitations, and holiday greetings. Page borders can be plain or fancy lines, or can consist of tiny pictures repeated in a pattern (Border Art).

To choose a page border, follow these steps:

1. Choose Design ⇨ Page Background ⇨ Page Borders. The Borders and Shading dialog box opens with the Page Border tab displayed. See **Figure 5-10**.

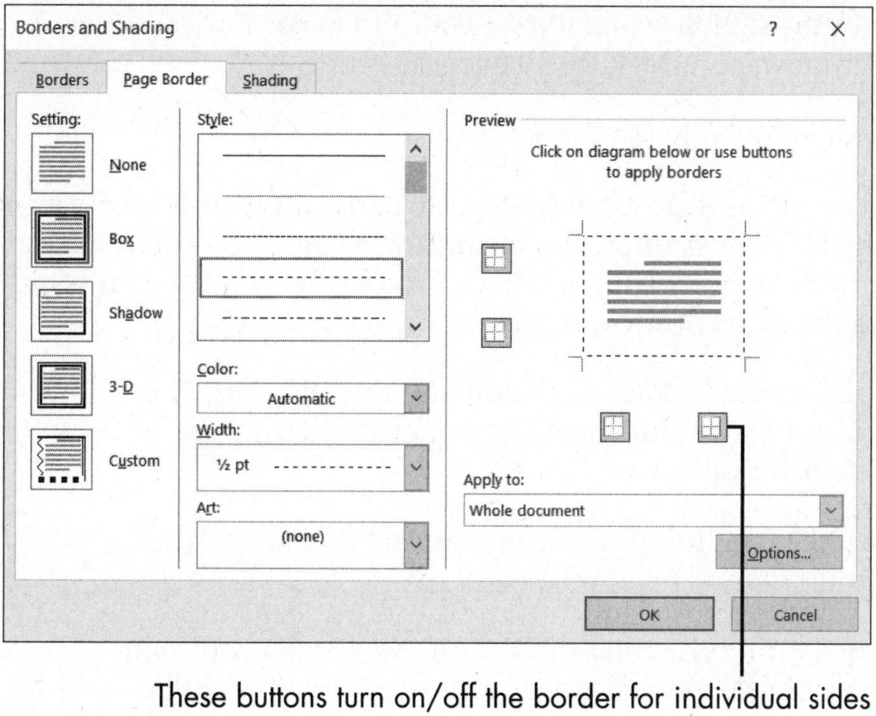

Figure 5-10

2. Choose one of the presets at the left side to describe the type of border you want:

   - *Box:* The border is the same on all sides.
   - *Shadow:* The border is thicker at the left and bottom.
   - *3-D:* A 3-D effect is applied to the border. (The effect is not always obvious, depending on other choices you make.)
   - *Custom:* You can specify different settings for each side of the border individually.

3. Choose a line style from the Style list.
4. Choose a line color from the Color list.
5. Choose a width from the Width list.

6. Check the sample in the Preview area to make sure it's how you want it. Make any changes needed.

7. Click OK to apply the border.

   You can also create a border by using artwork. This is where it gets really fun! For example, for a Christmas letter, you could have a border made of holly leaves or trees; for a birthday party, you could have a border made of slices of cake.

1. Choose Design ➪ Page Background ➪ Page Borders. The Borders and Shading dialog box opens with the Page Border tab displayed.

2. Open the Art drop-down list and select the picture you want to use.

3. In the Width box, enter the size (in points; pt) you want for the border's width. An average size border might be 30pt, for example.

4. Click OK. **Figure 5-11** shows an art-based border.

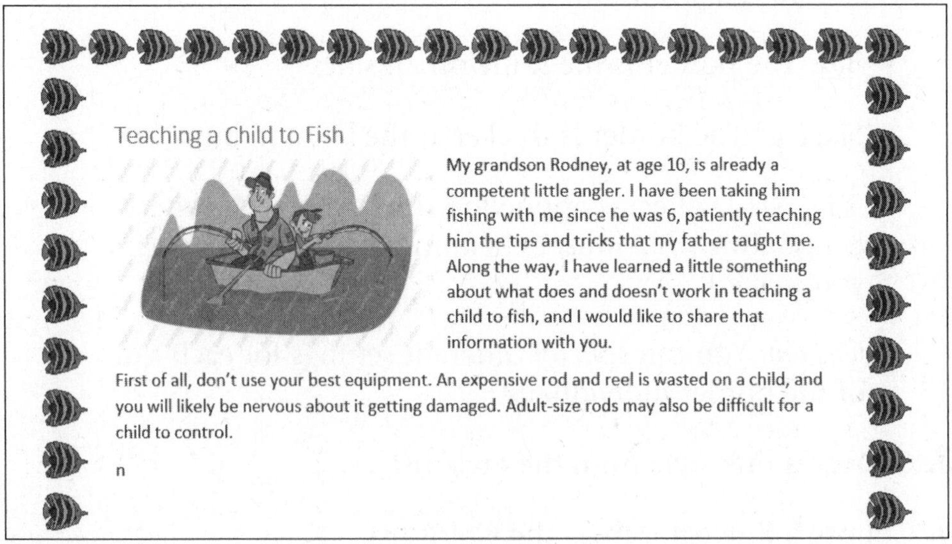

Teaching a Child to Fish

My grandson Rodney, at age 10, is already a competent little angler. I have been taking him fishing with me since he was 6, patiently teaching him the tips and tricks that my father taught me. Along the way, I have learned a little something about what does and doesn't work in teaching a child to fish, and I would like to share that information with you.

First of all, don't use your best equipment. An expensive rod and reel is wasted on a child, and you will likely be nervous about it getting damaged. Adult-size rods may also be difficult for a child to control.

n

Figure 5-11

Apply a Background Color to a Page

Besides page borders, another way to dress up a page is to give it a colored background. Be aware, though, that if you print a page with a colored background, one of two things will happen:

- **Word will print it without the background,** and any special formatting that relies on the background might not look right. For example, if you have a black background and set the text color to yellow, you might end up with a barely readable document with yellow text on a white page.
- **Word will print it with the background,** meaning that you'll use a lot of ink in your printer.

Background colors are most useful in documents that will be distributed online — such as via e-mail — rather than printed.

Background colors do not print by default. If you want to make them print, do this: Choose File⇨Options. Then click the Display tab and mark the Print background colors and images check box.

To set a background color (and "set" can mean to add or remove), follow these steps:

1. Choose Design⇨Page Backgound⇨Page Color. A color palette appears.
2. Make your choice:
   - Click the color you want to use for the page background.
   - Choose No Color to remove any existing background.

Like with many parts of Office, the color palette contains theme colors and fixed colors. As you can read in Chapter 2, *theme colors* are the color placeholders defined by the document's theme; they change if you choose a different theme. Comparatively, *fixed colors* (also called *standard colors*) don't change. See **Figure 5-12**.

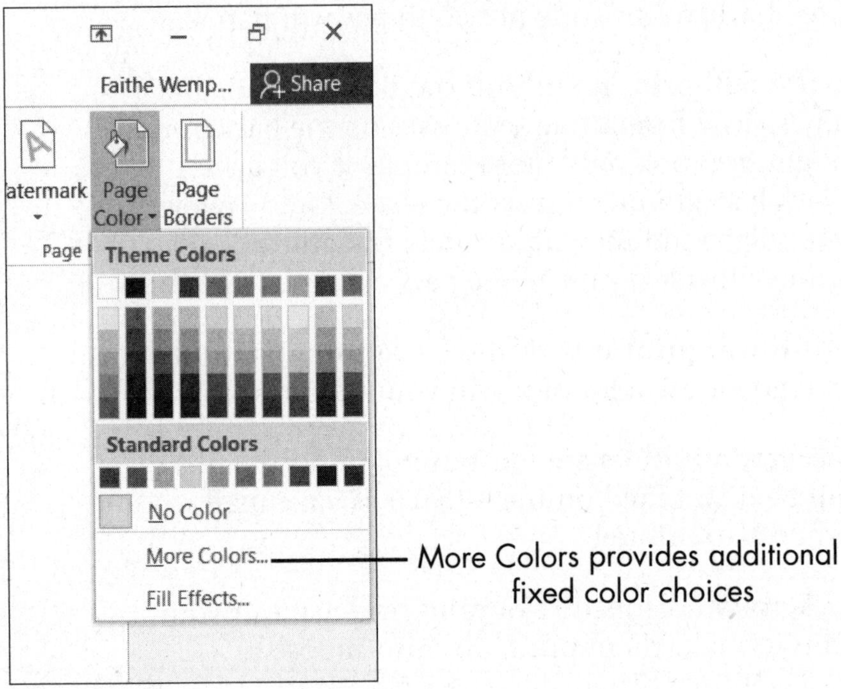

Figure 5-12

You can also choose Fill Effects from the color palette. This opens the Fill Effects dialog box, where you can set up any of four types of fill effects:

- **Gradient:** A gradual blending between one color and another, like with a vibrant sunset
- **Texture:** A repeating graphic that looks like a certain type of surface, such as wood, concrete, or paper
- **Pattern:** A pattern of lines and/or dots in one color, with a contrasting background color

- **Picture:** An image (that you pick from the images stored on your hard drive) that fills the entire background

The details of using each of these fill effects is beyond the scope of this book, but you can experiment with them on your own. And don't forget, you can use the Help system in Word (press F1, click the question mark button, or type your question in the *Tell me what you want to do* box) to get more information about any feature.

Create Tables

A *table* is a grid of rows and columns, somewhat like a spreadsheet in Excel. Tables are useful for displaying information in multicolumn layouts, such as address lists. **Figure 5-13** shows a table in a document.

Budget Committee

The following people have signed up to be on the Budget Committee.

Member	Phone Number	Email	Lifetime Member?
Sally Smith	317-555-8822	sally@microsoft.com	Yes
Henry Ortega	317-555-7183	henry@sycamoreknoll.com	No
Cynthia Slater	219-555-5755	hyacinthia@wempen.com	Yes

Figure 5-13

You can create two kinds of column-based layouts in Word. One kind is a multicolumn table, which I describe here. The other kind is the *newspaper style,* where text flows all the way from the top of the page to the bottom in one column, and then loops up to the next column. I don't cover that feature in this book, but you can play with it on your own by choosing Page Layout⇨Columns.

Here's one way to insert a table:

1. Position the insertion point where you want the table to appear.
2. Choose Insert⇨Tables⇨Table. A menu opens that includes a grid of squares.

3. Drag your mouse across the grid until you highlight how many rows and columns you want. For example, in **Figure 5-14**, I'm selecting three columns and four rows.

4. Release the mouse button. The table appears in the document.

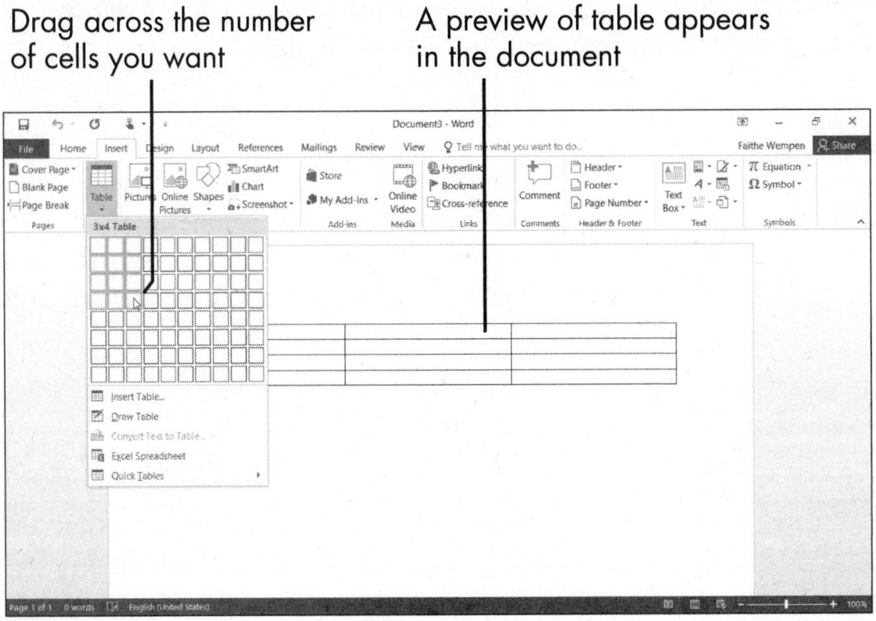

Figure 5-14

If you have trouble selecting the right number of squares on the grid, choose Insert➪Tables➪Table➪Insert Table. In the dialog box that appears, you can type the number of rows and columns you want.

To enter text into the table, just click inside the desired cell and start typing. You can move the insertion point from one cell to the next by pressing the Tab key, or move to the previous cell by pressing Shift+Tab.

When a table is *active* (that is, when the insertion point is anywhere within it), these two extra tabs appear on the Ribbon, under the heading Table Tools:

- **Design:** Contains commands and buttons for formatting the table.
- **Layout:** Contains commands and buttons for changing the structure of the table.

To change the number of rows or columns in the table, use the Layout tab, shown in **Figure 5-15**.

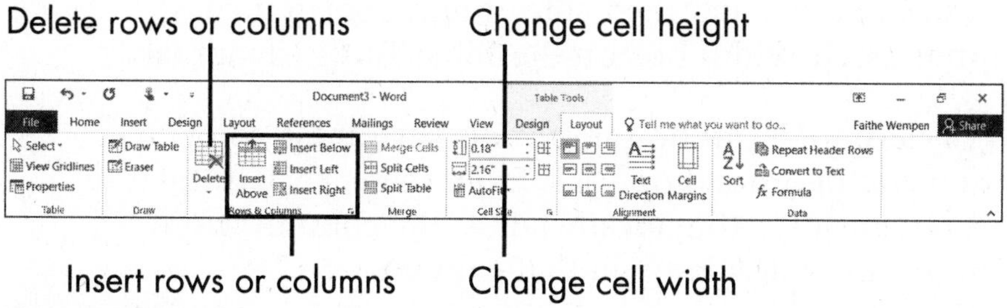

Figure 5-15

- **To delete a row or column:** Select it (drag across its cells) and then choose Table Tools Layout ⇨ Rows & Columns ⇨ Delete.
- **To insert a row or column:** Click in a row or column that is adjacent to where you want the insertion, and then click one of the buttons on the Table Tools Layout tab that describes the insertion you want: Insert Above, Insert Below, Insert Left, or Insert Right.

If you have trouble dragging to select a row or column to work with, try using the Select button on the Table Tools Layout tab. Clicking it opens a menu of things you can select: Cell, Row, Column, or Table.

The height of each cell changes automatically depending on the cell contents. You don't have to change the size unless you want extra vertical blank space in the cell. You can specify a cell height in the Cell Size group on the Table Tools Layout tab. (Refer to Figure 5-15.)

More commonly, you'll need to change a column's width instead of a row's height. Here's how:

- Position the mouse pointer over one of the table's vertical gridlines. The mouse pointer turns into an I-beam with arrows on each side. Then drag to adjust the width.
- Click in a cell and then enter a number (in inches) in the Cell Width box on the Table Tools Layout tab.
- Click AutoFit on the Table Tools Layout tab to open a menu of AutoFit options. From there, click AutoFit Contents to automatically adjust the column width to fit the widest entry in that column.

Format a Table

You can manually format a table and its content in much the same way you format any other text: Use the formatting commands on the Home tab, for example. But the Table Tools Design tab also has special formatting controls that apply specifically to tables.

For example, you can apply table styles to a table to automatically apply border and shading colors and styles, to automatically autofit the content, and to automatically apply different font formatting for the heading rows.

To apply a table style, follow these steps:

1. Click anywhere in the table.

   You don't have to select the whole table.

2. On the Table Tools Design tab, hover the mouse pointer over one of the styles in the Table Styles gallery (shown in **Figure 5-16**). The style is previewed in the table.

3. Click the desired table style. For additional choices, click the More button to open the full gallery of styles, as shown in **Figure 5-17**.

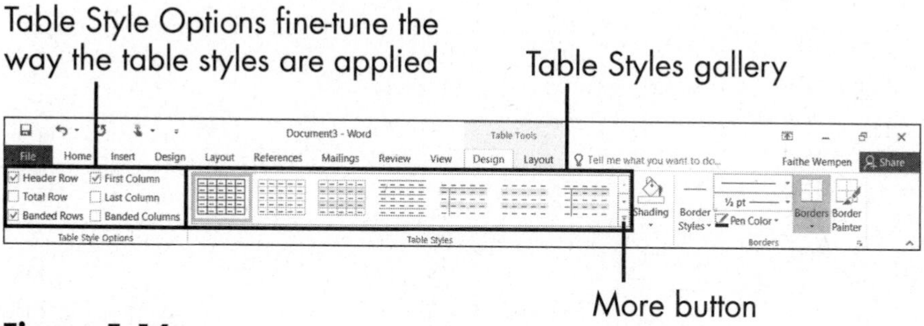

Figure 5-16

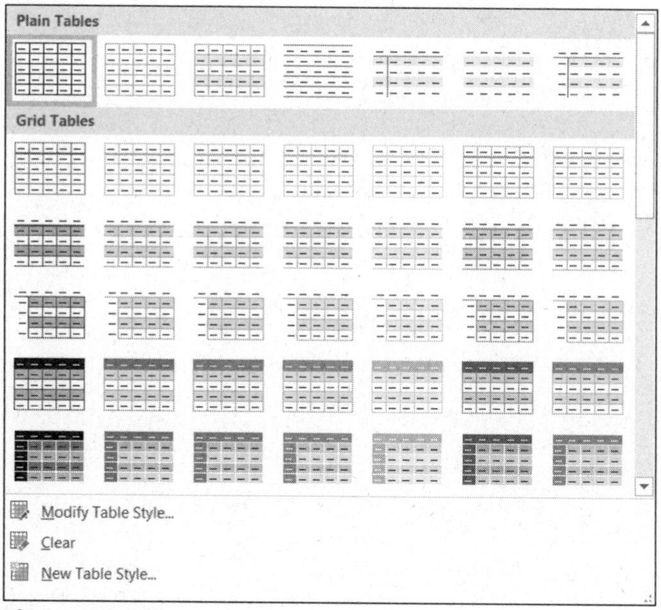

Figure 5-17

The check boxes in the Table Style Options group enable you to specify how the table style will be applied. For example, you can choose whether the header row is formatted differently than the rest of the table. If you choose Banded Rows, every other row will have a different color background, for easier reading.

Taking Word to the Next Level

Chapter

6

Word has so many features and capabilities that most people don't even scratch the surface of what it can do. And that's okay! Word is a good tool partly because it's accessible at a variety of levels. I won't try to transform you into a Word guru, but I do want to show you some fairly simple features that you can use to make a big difference in your documents.

I start this chapter by showing you how to number the pages of a document, and also how to create headers and footers that repeat the same text at the top or bottom of each page. Then I show you how to insert cover pages and other special-purpose elements — *building blocks* — that can add style and beauty to your documents with a minimum of effort.

And when you print a letter, you also often need an envelope, so I show you how to generate envelopes in Word (and how to feed them into your printer).

Finally, I tackle *mail merge:* merging a form letter with a list of addresses. This helpful Word tool really isn't as hard as some people make it out to be.

Get ready to . . .

Number the Pages

Have you ever dropped a stack of papers that needed to stay in a certain order? If the pages were numbered, putting them back together was fairly simple. If not, ugh: what a frustrating, time-consuming task.

Fortunately, Word makes it very easy to number your document pages. And you can choose from a variety of numbering styles and formats.

When you number pages in Word, you don't have to manually type the numbers onto each page. Instead, you place a code in the document that does the numbering for you automatically. Sweet!

Here's how it works. Each document has a header and footer area where you can place information you want repeated on every page. I explain more about headers and footers later in this chapter, but the important thing to know here is that when you use the Page Numbering feature in Word, it automatically inserts the proper code in either the header or the footer so that each page is numbered consecutively. These page numbers are visible only in Print Layout view, Read Mode, Print Preview, and on the printouts themselves. You won't see the page numbers if you are working in Draft view, even though they are there.

For simple page numbering at the bottom of each page (the *footer*), follow these steps:

1. Choose Insert➪Header & Footer➪Page Number.
2. In the menu that appears, point to Bottom of Page. A submenu appears showing various samples of bottom-of-page numbering. See **Figure 6-1**. There are many samples; use the scroll bar on the list to see them.
3. Click a sample to select it. The code for the page numbering is placed in the document footer, in the format you choose.

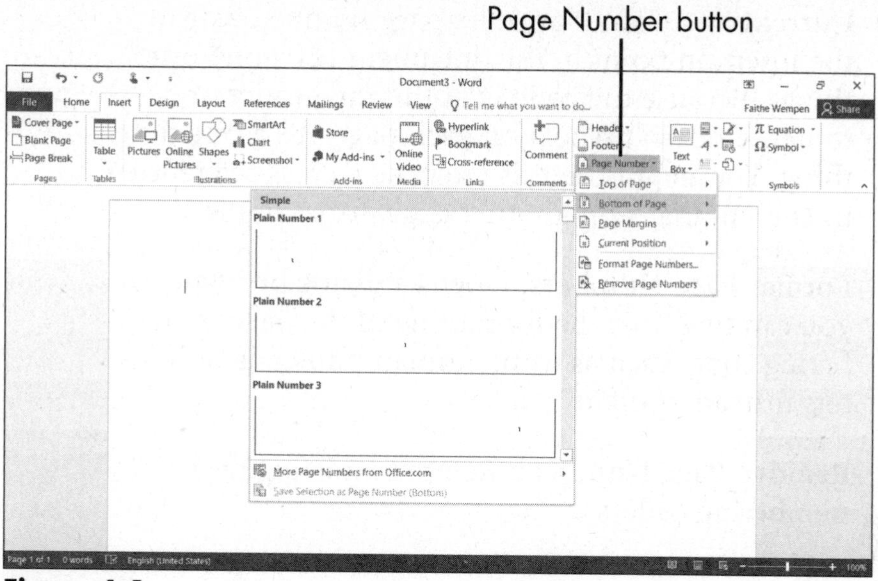

Figure 6-1

For a plain page number, select one of the first three samples: Plain Number 1, Plain Number 2, or Plain Number 3. They are all identical except for the positioning of the number (at the left, center, or right, respectively).

4. To return to editing the main document (leaving the footer), double-click anywhere within the body of your document.

Notice in Figure 6-1 the other page number position options besides Bottom of Page:

- **Top of Page:** Places the page number code in the *header* (top of the page). The page numbers appear on every page.
- **Page Margins:** Places the page number code on the side of the page. The page numbers appear on every page.

- **Current Position:** Places the page number code at the insertion point in the document (as a one-time thing). Because the code is not in the header or footer, it doesn't repeat on each page. It's a one-time thing. You might use this to create a cross-reference to content that's on another page, for example.

- **Format Page Numbers:** Opens a dialog box where you can fine-tune the formatting of the page numbering code, such as using Roman numerals or letters instead of digits.

- **Remove Page Numbers:** Removes existing page numbering code(s).

Use Headers and Footers

In addition to a page number, you can put other content in the header and footer areas of your document. For example, if you're typing the minutes of a club meeting, you might want to put the club's name in the header so that it appears across the top of each page.

Every document has a header and footer area, which are both empty by default. The header and footer appear in Print Layout view, Full Page Reading view, and Web Layout view, and also on the printed page. (If you are in Draft view, you might want to switch to Print Layout view to follow along in this section more easily.)

Here are two ways of putting content into them:

- **Manually:** In Print Layout view, double-click in the header or footer of the page. (Choose View⇨Views⇨Print Layout to enter Print Layout view if needed; see Chapter 1.) This puts you in the Header and Footer editing mode, where you can type text directly into those areas. See **Figure 6-2**.

Double-click the top of the page to edit the Header area

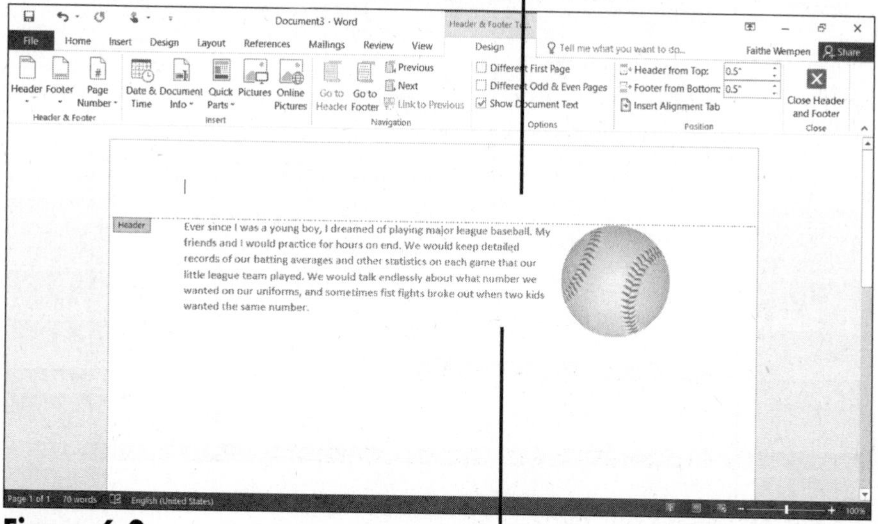

Figure 6-2

When the Header area is active, the main document is read-only

The body of the document cannot be edited while you are in this mode. To resume working within the main part of the document, double-click the main document (anywhere below the header or above the footer).

- **Let Word help:** Choose Insert➪Header & Footer➪Header or Insert➪Header & Footer➪Footer and then select a preformatted header or footer placeholder. This also places you in Header and Footer editing mode automatically, and you can edit the text in the placeholders that were inserted. Depending on the sample you pick, there might be not only a text placeholder but also a page-numbering code. This saves you the step of inserting the page-numbering code separately. **Figure 6-3** shows the Footer menu and an inserted footer.

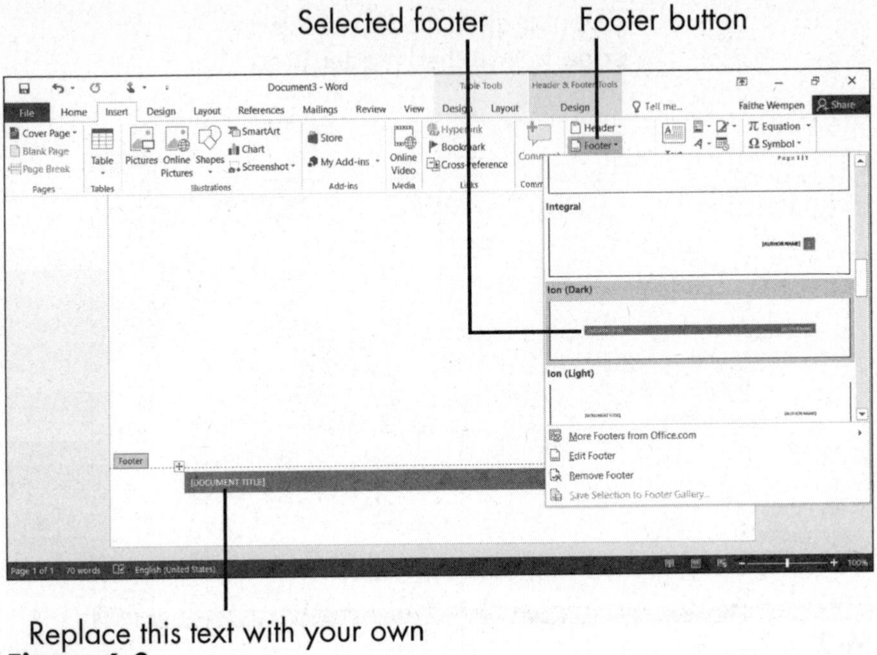

Figure 6-3

You can manually insert a page-numbering code into a header or footer as well as codes for the current date, time, and other information. When the insertion point is in the header or footer area, the Header & Footer Tools Design tab appears on the Ribbon. On that tab are buttons for inserting various types of codes like that. See **Figure 6-4**.

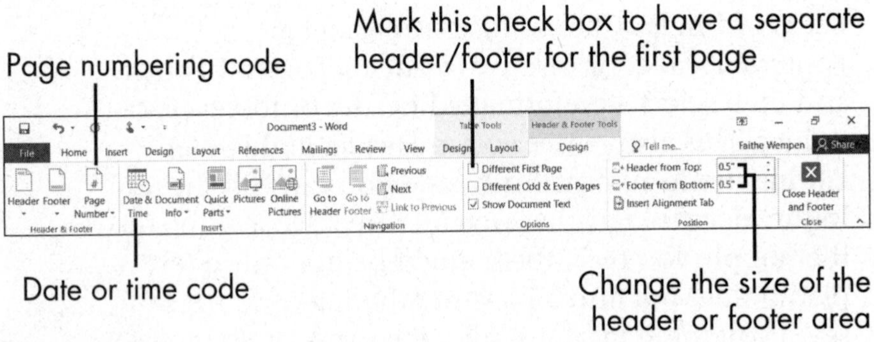

Figure 6-4

Also in Figure 6-4, notice the check boxes in the Options group. Here, you can specify that you want a different header and footer for the first page (for example, so you can have a cover page without header and footer text), or that you want separate headers and footers for odd and even pages (for example, for a double-sided booklet where the page numbers should always be on the outside edge).

Finally, notice in Figure 6-4 that in the Position group, you can control the amount of space allotted to the header and footer. By default, each is one-half inch tall. You can change these values in the Header from Top and Footer from Bottom list boxes.

When you're done working with the header and footer, double-click the main body of the document, or click the Close Header and Footer button on the Design tab.

Insert Cover Pages and Other Building Blocks

Many different document types can benefit from a good-looking cover page: a committee report, a proposal for a home business, or a family album. Word 2016 offers a large gallery of sample cover pages that you can insert in your document and then customize.

Cover pages are automatically placed at the beginning of the document, before the current first page. You don't have to position the insertion point at the beginning of the document before you insert them.

To insert a cover page, follow these steps:

1. Choose Insert⇨Pages⇨Cover Page. A palette of cover page samples appears. See **Figure 6-5**.
2. Click the cover page you want to insert. It is placed at the beginning of the document.
3. Fill in the placeholders on the cover page as desired.

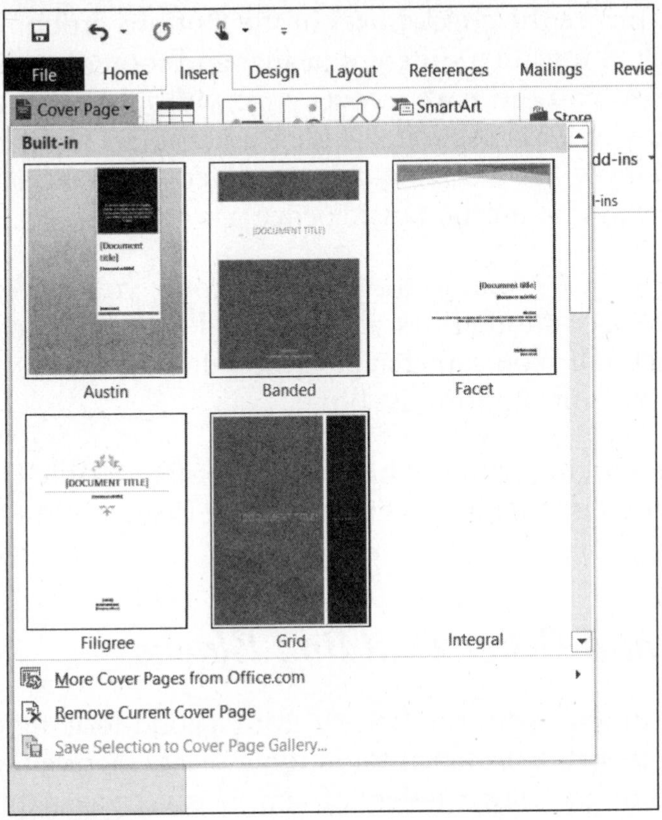

Figure 6-5

To delete a cover page, choose Insert➪Pages➪Cover Page➪Remove Current Cover Page.

Cover pages are just one of several types of preformatted sample content that Word collectively calls *building blocks*. The page numbering samples I show you earlier in this chapter are building blocks, as are preformatted headers and footers.

To see all the building blocks that Word offers in one convenient place, choose Insert➪Text➪Explore Quick Parts➪Building Blocks Organizer. This opens the Building Blocks Organizer dialog box, shown in **Figure 6-6**. From here, you can browse the various types of content and insert anything you find that looks interesting. Some of the content types include equations, tables, text boxes, and watermarks.

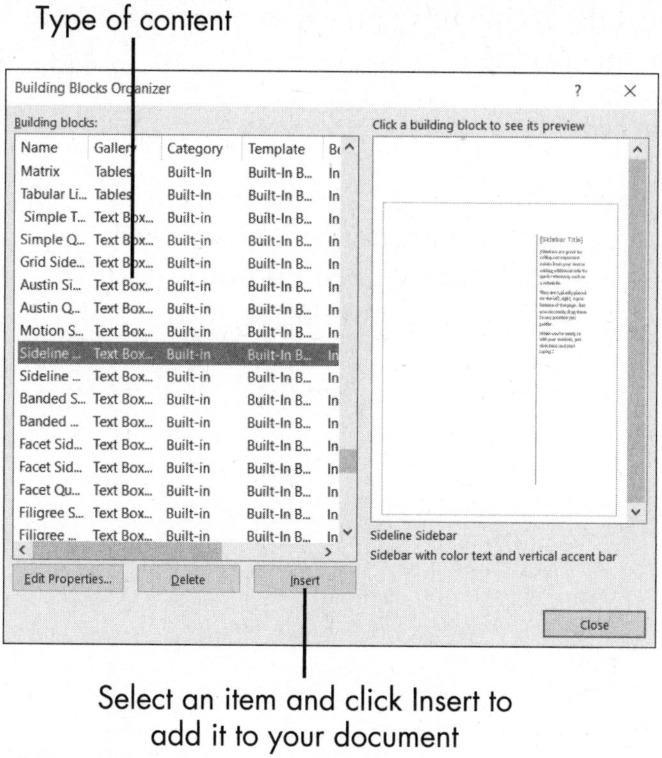

Figure 6-6

Print an Envelope

Envelopes are the natural companions of business and personal letters. Most of the time, when you print a letter, you also want an envelope for it. You can address the envelope by hand, of course, but printing an envelope is quick and easy in Word.

One nice thing about the Envelopes feature in Word is that it can automatically extract the mailing address from the letter, so you don't have to retype it. It also stores your return address and recalls it for you each time you print an envelope.

If your letter contains the recipient's name and mailing address, follow these steps to create an envelope for it:

1. Open the letter in Word.

2. Choose Mailings ➪ Create ➪ Envelopes. The Envelopes and Labels dialog box opens. If the letter contains a valid address, that address is automatically filled into the Delivery Address field, as shown in **Figure 6-7**.

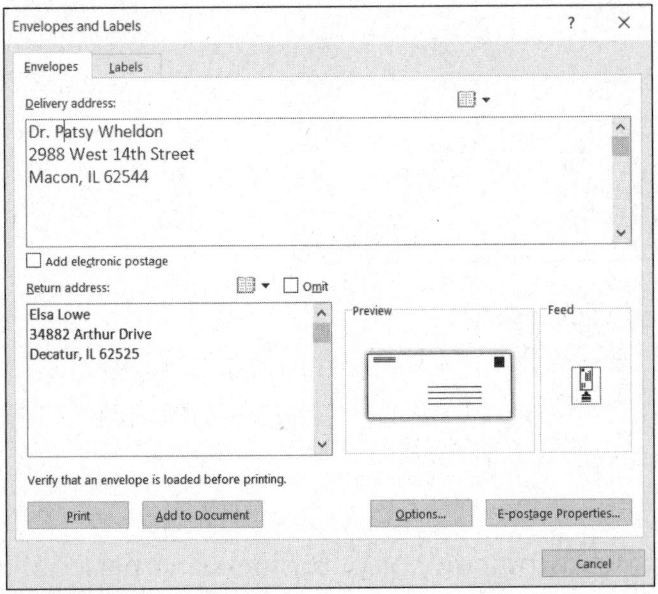

Figure 6-7

3. (Optional) Type your return address in the Return Address field if it doesn't already appear there.

If the return address appears but you don't want to use it (this time only), select the Omit check box. (This keeps the return address on file for later use.) You wouldn't want to use a return address if you're using envelopes with the return address preprinted, or if you're going to use stick-on return address labels.

4. Feed an envelope into your printer.

5. Click Print. The envelope prints.

   If the envelope printing doesn't go as you expected — say, it prints on the wrong side, or it's not lined up correctly — you might need to try again and change the orientation at which you feed it into the printer. For example, you might need to feed it in sideways, rotated 180 degrees, or upside-down.

To avoid wasting an envelope, do a test print using plain paper. Draw an arrow on a piece of paper, and put it into your printer's paper tray, face up, arrow facing in. Then print an envelope on that paper. The relationship between the printout and the arrow can tell you how to orient the envelopes you feed in. For example, if the arrow is on the reverse side from the printing, you know that envelopes need to be fed into the printer flap-up.

Perform a Mail Merge

A *mail merge* combines a list of names and addresses (that is, mailing information) with a form letter, a label, or an envelope template to produce customized copies of the letter for each person. Big companies use mail merge to mail customized advertisements, but it's not just for businesses. Home users can take advantage of mail merge for Christmas card mailing labels, party invitations, club newsletters, and more.

The three steps to a mail merge are

1. Create (or identify) the data source.

2. Create the main document and then insert the merge codes in it.

3. Perform the merge operation between the data source and the main document.

Start with the options for data sources. The data source must be a *delimited* file. In other words, there has to be some consistent way that it distinguishes between one column or row of data and the next.

- **Excel, Word table:** If the data source is an Excel spreadsheet, as in **Figure 6-8**, each type of information is in a separate column. The same goes if the data source is a Word table.

	A	B	C
1	**Name**	**Address 1**	**Address 2**
2	Jan Smith	2987 Rowan Way	Noblesville, IN 46060
3	Karen Clark	118 Main Street	Moweaqua, IL 62550
4	Sylvia Sharp	9444 Stetson Avenue	Indianapolis, IN 46240
5	George Colvin	10785 Riverview Drive	Anderson, IN 46122
6			

Figure 6-8

- **Plain text:** If the data source is a plain text file, each column is delimited by a specific character, such as tab or a comma. In **Figure 6-9**, I used a comma. (When a delimited text file uses commas, it's called a Comma Separated Values, or CSV, file.)

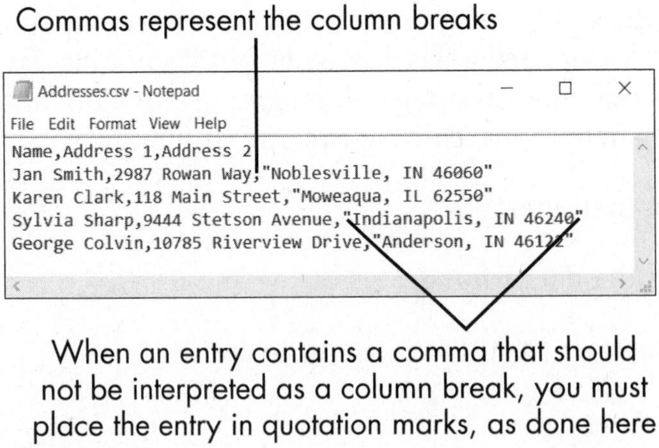

Figure 6-9

- **Outlook:** If the data source is an Outlook Contacts list, each type of information is in a separate field. Outlook Contacts are covered in Chapter 16.
- **Word list:** If you don't have a data source already, you can use the Type a New List feature in Word to create one. Choose Mailings ⇨ Start Mail Merge ⇨ Select Recipients ⇨ Type a New List. See the upcoming **Figure 6-10**.

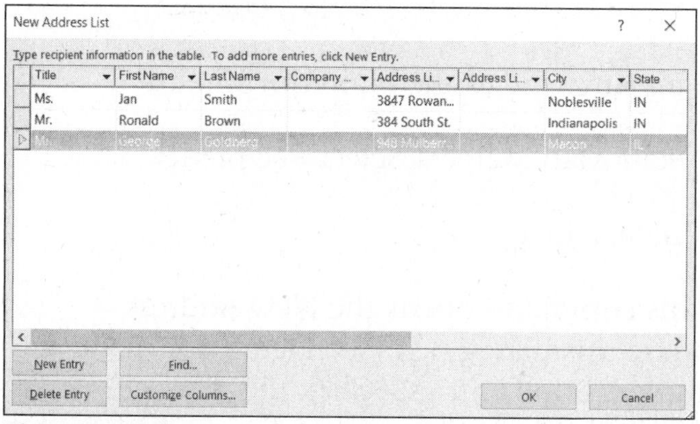

Figure 6-10

A data file shouldn't contain anything except the data (and perhaps a single row of field labels, as in Figure 6-9 with Name, Address1, and Address2). There shouldn't be any blank rows or titles at the top of the page because that confuses the Mail Merge utility. Check your data file to remove extraneous rows before using the file as your mail merge source.

After preparing the data file, you set up the main document. You can either create the main document from scratch, or you can start with an existing document and convert it to be a mail merge main document.

Of the different kinds of main documents you can have, letters, envelopes, and labels are the most common. In this chapter, I show you how to do a letter.

Follow these steps to set up your main document:

1. Start a new document, or open an existing one that you want to use.

2. Choose Mailings ⇨ Start Mail Merge ⇨ Start Mail Merge ⇨ Letters.

Next, attach the data source file to the main document.

1. Choose Mailings ⇨ Start Mail Merge ⇨ Select Recipients.

2. Choose the type of data source:

   - *Type New List:* This command opens the New Address List dialog box. Use this dialog box (see Figure 6-10) to create new address book entries. (Click the New Entry button after each one.) When you're finished, click OK. Then in the Save Address List dialog box that opens, assign a name to the new address list. You can reuse it for other mail merges.

   - *Use Existing List:* This command opens the Select Data Source dialog box. Use this dialog box to select the Excel, Word, Notepad, or other file where you saved your data source. Then click Open to confirm your selection. If you choose a data source file that has multiple sheets or tables, a dialog box might prompt you to pick which one you want.

   - *Select from Outlook Contacts:* This command opens the Select Contacts dialog box. (The first time you do this, you may be prompted to choose a profile. Go with the default one, Outlook.) Click the contact folder you want to use (there might be only one listed) and then click OK. Then in the Mail Merge Recipients dialog box that opens (see **Figure 6-11**), clear the check box for each record that you do *not* want to include in the merge, and then click OK.

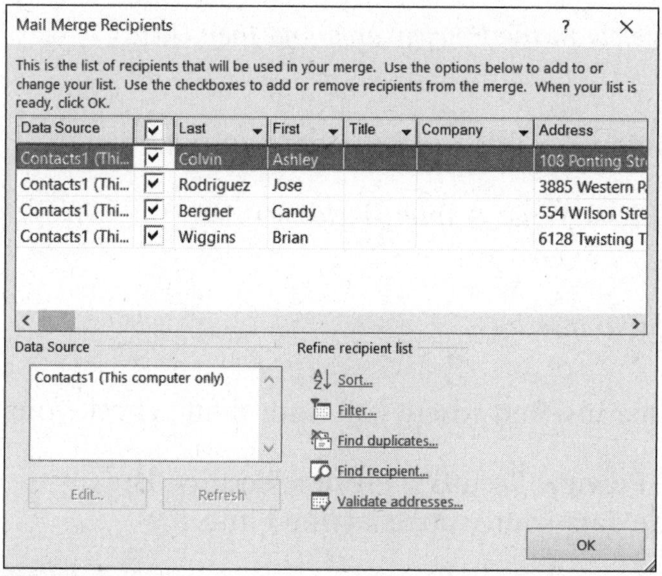

Figure 6-11

Next, insert the field codes into the main document where you want the text to be pulled in from the data source. There are several ways to do this, depending on what you want. Place the insertion point where the field should appear, and then:

- **If you want the recipient's name and address to appear**

  a. Choose Mailings ⇨ Write & Insert Fields ⇨ Address Block.

  b. In the Insert Address Block dialog box that appears, check the preview in the Preview area and then click OK.

➡ **If you want to insert a greeting line (such as Dear Mr. Jones)**

a. Choose Mailings ➪ Write & Insert Fields ➪ Greeting Line.

b. Check the preview in the Preview area and then click OK.

➡ **To insert individual fields from the data source**

a. Choose Mailings ➪ Write & Insert Fields ➪ Insert Merge Field.

b. Select the field to insert.

After all the codes are inserted where you want them, check your work.

1. Choose Mailings ➪ Preview Results ➪ Preview Results. The first record from the data source appears filled into the main document.
2. In the Preview Results group on the Mailings tab, click the right arrow button to move to the next record. Repeat that until you have checked all the records (or at least enough to be confident that you did things right).

When you preview the results, if you have used the Address Block option, you may find that there is more vertical space between the lines of the address than you might like. To fix this, preview the results, and then select all the lines in the address block for the first preview. On the Home tab, click the Line and Paragraph Spacing button in the Paragraph group and choose Remove Space After Paragraph. All the results are corrected.

Finally, time to print the letters.

1. Make sure you have the right kind of paper and enough paper in your printer, and that the printer is powered on and ready.
2. Choose Mailings⇨Finish⇨Finish & Merge⇨Print Documents.
3. In the Merge to Printer dialog box, click OK.
4. In the Print dialog box that opens, check the print settings (such as printer name), and change any if needed. See **Figure 6-12**.
5. Click OK.

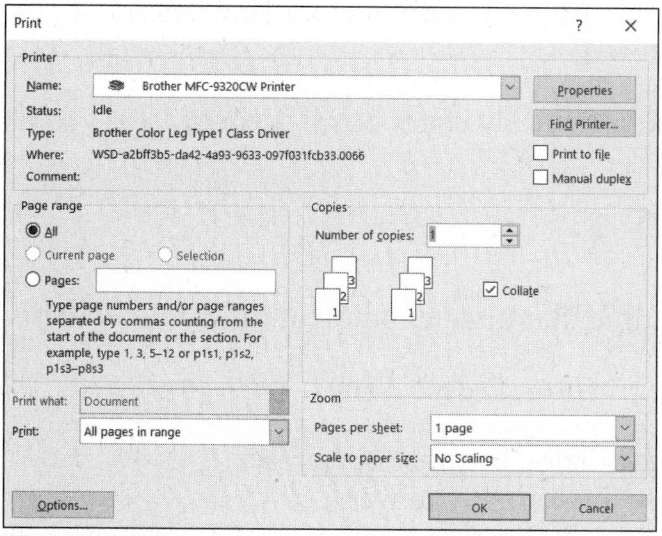

Figure 6-12

Insert the Date and Time

Because you can just type the current date and time into a document, such as when you are writing a letter, you don't need a special feature for that. However, Word offers a feature that inserts the current date and/or time in your choice of many standard formats so that you don't have to worry about whether you've got the punctuation in the right place.

The best part, though, is that you have the option of making the date/time a *field code,* which is a fancy way of saying that the document knows to update the date/time information. So, for example, say you start a letter one day and don't finish it until a week later. If you make the date/time into a field code, the date on the letter will reflect the date when you save or print it, without you having to manually change it. This is a handy feature when you always want the document to display today's date, no matter what day you open it.

To insert a *static* (doesn't change) date or time, follow these steps:

1. Choose Insert⇨Text⇨Insert Date & Time.
2. In the Date and Time dialog box that opens, (see **Figure 6-13**), choose the format you want. The actual date or time will come from the system clock (the date/time clock in Windows).
3. Clear the Update automatically check box if it is not already cleared.
4. Click OK.

To insert a date or time that updates automatically, follow these steps:

1. Choose Insert⇨Text⇨Insert Date & Time.
2. In the Date and Time dialog box that opens (see Figure 6-13), choose the format you want.
3. Mark the Update Automatically check box if it is not already marked.
4. Click OK to complete the insertion.

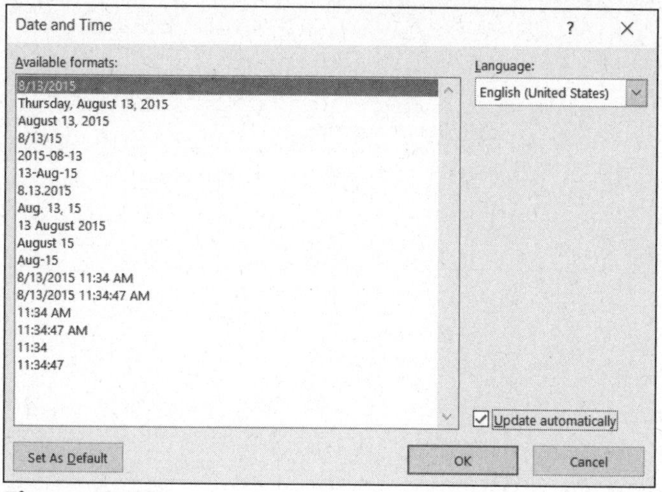

Figure 6-13

If you choose to insert the date/time as a code, it updates automatically whenever you open, save, or print the file. If you want to update it any time other than that, click the date/time so that a pop-up appears with an Update button in it. Click the Update button to update the code. You can also press F9, which updates all field codes in the document.

Part III
Excel

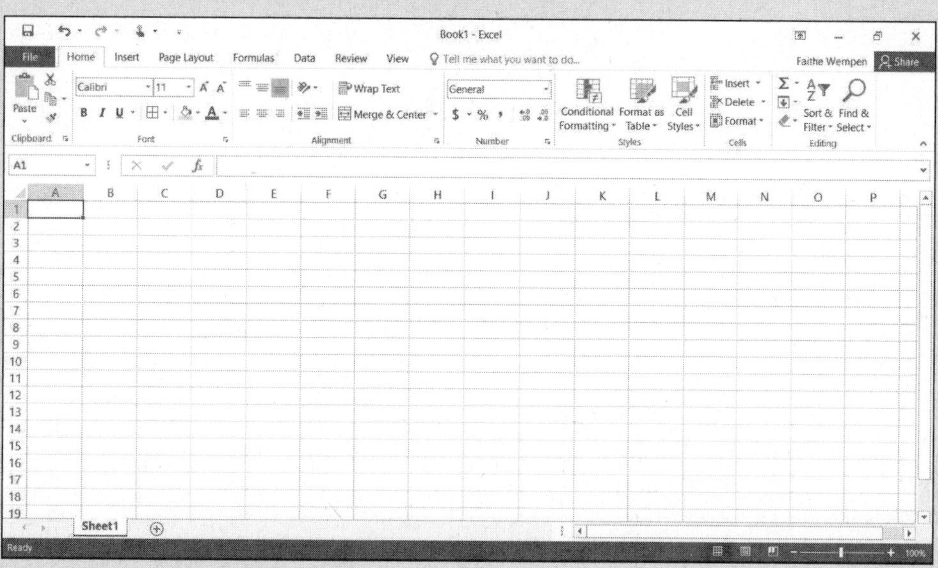

For an explanation of Excel's IF function, visit www.dummies.com/extras/office2016forseniors.

Creating Basic Spreadsheets in Excel

Chapter 7

Get ready to . . .

Microsoft Word works great for typing text, but sometimes you want something a little more structured for data. When you have more complex needs for column-based organizing than what Word's tables can provide, Excel is a great step up to the next level. Excel is much more than just a column organizer, though; it enables you to write formulas that perform calculations on your data. This makes Excel an ideal tool for storing financial information, such as checkbook register and investment portfolio data.

In this chapter, I introduce you to the Excel interface and show you some of the concepts you need to know to work with a spreadsheet. Some of the projects that Excel works great for include

- ➡ Tracking a stock portfolio
- ➡ Recording checkbook transactions
- ➡ Storing an address book list
- ➡ Charting progress toward a goal

Using the skills this chapter covers, you can build all these types of spreadsheets and more.

Understand Excel's Unique Features

Excel shares many elements with the Microsoft Office interface. **Figure 7-1** and the following list, however, show you the features that are unique to the Excel program. (If you need a refresher on the Microsoft Office interface in general, including features such as the Ribbon, Quick Access toolbar, and File tab, take a few minutes to review Chapter 1.)

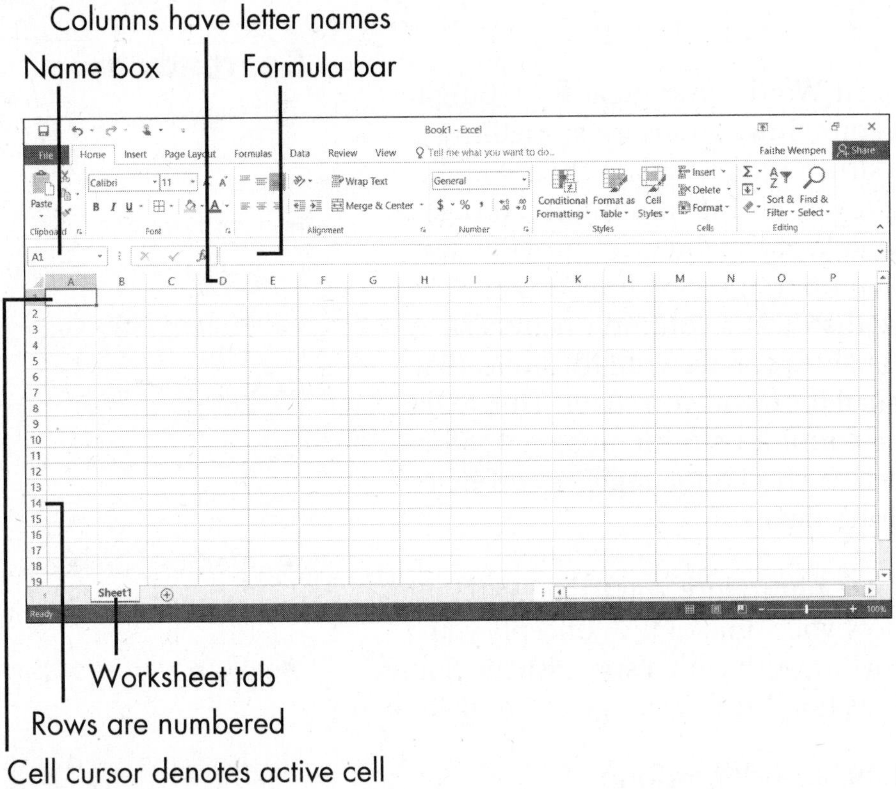

Figure 7-1

As you examine Figure 7-1, you'll see

- **Row numbers:** Each *row* has a unique number. To select an entire row, click its number.

- **Column letters:** Each *column* has a unique letter. To select an entire column, select its letter.

- **Cells:** At the intersection of each row and column is a *cell*. You enter content into a cell by clicking the cell and then typing.

- **Active cell indicator (a.k.a. the cell cursor):** This thick outline indicates which cell is the *active cell* — where your cursor is located at the moment. Whatever you type next appears in the active cell, and whatever commands you issue apply to that cell.

- **Name box:** The active cell's name appears here. For example, if the selected cell is at the intersection of column A and row 1, A1 appears in the Name box.

- **Formula bar:** The contents of the selected cell appears here. If the content is text, that text shows here as in the cell itself. If the content is a formula, the formula appears here, and the result of the formula appears in the cell. For example, if the cell contains the formula `=2+1`, the formula bar shows `=2+1` and the cell itself shows 3.

A *formula* is a math expression, beginning with an equals sign, such as `=2+1`. Formulas can also contain cell references. For example, `=A2+B2` adds the amount found in cell A2 to the amount found in B2.

- **Worksheet tabs:** By default, each workbook file has three *sheets*. They're like pages in a notebook. Each sheet is shown as a tab; click a tab to switch to that sheet.

Sheets are also called *worksheets*. A *workbook* is the entire data file, containing one or more worksheets.

Get Familiar with Spreadsheet Structure

Each cell has a unique *cell address* consisting of its column letter and row number. In Figure 7-1, for example, the active cell is at the intersection of column A and row 1. So, its cell address is A1. See the Name box in Figure 7-1. Each cell must have its own unique address so that you can refer to it when you create a formula. For example, suppose you want to sum (add) the values in cells B3 and B4. You can write a formula like this: `=B3+B4`.

When you copy a formula that refers to cells by their addresses, the references to those cells automatically adjust to take into account the new position. For example, suppose you have the formula `=A1+1` in cell A2. If you copy that formula into cell B2, the copy of the formula reads `=B1+1`. That's called a *relative reference*. In Chapter 8 in the section "Move and Copy Cell Content," you will learn about *absolute references,* which don't change when copied.

A *range* is a group of one or more cells. You refer to a range by the address of the upper leftmost cell in the range, followed by a colon, and then followed by the lower rightmost cell in the range. For example, the range consisting of cells A1, A2, B1, and B2 is written as A1:B2.

Technically, a single cell can be a range, but usually it isn't called a range.

Move the Cell Cursor

As I show you in Figure 7-1 earlier in the chapter, the cell cursor (also called the active cell indicator) is the dark outline around the active cell. To change which cell is active, you can do either of the following:

- **With your mouse:** Click the cell you want to be active.
- **From the keyboard:** Press one of the arrow keys on the keyboard to move the cell cursor one cell at a time in the direction the arrow is pointing until you reach the cell you want to be active.

Table 7-1 provides more shortcuts for moving the cell cursor within a worksheet.

Table 7-1 Movement Shortcuts

Press This . . .	***To Move . . .***
Arrow keys	One cell in the direction of the arrow
Tab	One cell to the right
Shift+Tab	One cell to the left
Ctrl+any arrow key	To the edge of the current data region in a worksheet (the first or last cell that isn't empty)
End	To the cell in the lower-right corner of the window (This works only when the Scroll Lock key has been pressed on your keyboard to turn on the Scroll Lock function.)
Ctrl+End	To the last cell in the worksheet, in the lowest used row of the rightmost used column
Home	To the beginning of the row containing the active cell
Ctrl+Home	To the beginning of the worksheet (cell A1)
Page Down	One screen down (The cell cursor moves, too.)
Alt+Page Down	One screen to the right
Ctrl+Page Down	To the next sheet in the workbook
Page Up	One screen up (The cell cursor moves, too.)
Alt+Page Up	One screen to the left
Ctrl+Page Up	To the previous sheet in the workbook

Select a Range

You might sometimes want to select a multi-cell range before you issue a command. For example, if you want to make all the text in the cell range A1:F1 bold, select that range and then issue the command for applying Bold (by clicking the B button on the Home tab or by pressing Ctrl+B). You can select a range by using either the keyboard or the mouse.

To select a range by using the mouse, follow these steps:

1. Click the upper leftmost cell in the range.
2. Click and hold down the left mouse button and drag to the lower rightmost cell in the range.

To select a range by using the keyboard, follow these steps:

1. Use the arrow keys to move the cell cursor to the upper leftmost cell in the range.
2. Press and hold down the Shift key while you press the → or ↓ keys to extend the selection until all the cells in the range are selected.
3. Release the Shift key.

You can also select a range in reverse order: that is, starting with the lower rightmost cell and dragging upward and to the left or pressing the ← or ↑ keys.

You can also use a hybrid method involving both keyboard and mouse:

1. Select the first cell in the range using any method: either clicking it with the mouse or using the arrow keys to move the cell selector to it.
2. Hold down the Shift key and click the last cell in the range.
3. Release the Shift key.

Table 7-2 provides some shortcut keys to help you select ranges.

Table 7-2 Range Selection Shortcuts

Press This . . .	*To Extend the Selection To . . .*
Ctrl+Shift+arrow key	The last nonblank cell in the same column or row as the active cell; or if the next cell is blank, to the next nonblank cell
Ctrl+Shift+End	The last used cell on the worksheet (lower-right corner of the range containing data)
Ctrl+Shift+Home	The beginning of the worksheet (A1)
Ctrl+Shift+Page Down	The current and next sheet in the workbook
Ctrl+Shift+Page Up	The current and previous sheet in the workbook
Ctrl+spacebar	The entire column where the active cell is located
Shift+spacebar	The entire row where the active cell is located
Ctrl+Shift+spacebar or Ctrl+A	The entire worksheet

Although less common, you can also select a *noncontiguous range* (cells that don't border each other). For example, suppose you want to apply a certain type of formatting to cells A1, A5, and A9. Select those three cells before issuing your formatting command, so that the formatting is applied to the three discrete cells at once:

1. Select the first cell in the range.
2. Hold down the Ctrl key and click more individual cells to be in the range. Or click and drag across more multi-cell blocks to be in the range. The additional selected cells appear highlighted.
3. Release the Ctrl key.

An entire row or column can also be a range. Here's how to select a row or column (for example, to delete it, or to format it a certain way):

- **To select an entire row:** Click its row number to the left of the row.
- **To select an entire column:** Click its column letter at the top of the column.

- **To select multiple contiguous rows or columns:** Select the first row/column and then click and hold down the left mouse button while you drag to include more rows or columns.

- **To select multiple noncontiguous rows or columns:** Select the first row/column and then hold down Ctrl while you click more individual row numbers or column letters. A pale highlight is applied to each row or column you select.

Sometimes, you might want to apply a particular command to every cell on the entire worksheet. For example, you might want all the text in the entire worksheet to be a certain color or font. To select all cells at once, you can drag to create a range that encompasses the entire sheet; but that's somewhat cumbersome. Here are a couple of easier alternatives:

- Press Ctrl+A.

- Click the Select All button, which you can find in the upper-left corner of the sheet at the intersection of the row numbers and column letters. (It's pointed out in see **Figure 7-2**.)

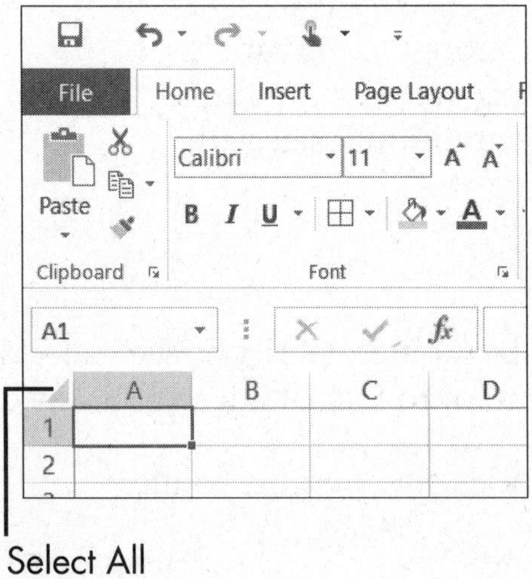

Figure 7-2

Type and Edit Cell Contents

To this point in the chapter, I've introduced you to some spreadsheet basics. Now, it's time to actually do something: enter some text and numbers into cells.

To type in a cell, you simply select the cell and begin typing. Whatever you type appears both in the cell and in the formula bar. (Refer to Figure 7-1 to see where the formula bar is located.) When you finish typing, you can leave the cell in any of these ways:

- Press Enter (moves you to the next cell down).
- Press Tab (moves you to the next cell to the right).
- Press Shift+Tab (moves you to the next cell to the left).
- Press an arrow key (moves you in the direction of the arrow).

If you need to edit what's in the cell, you have these choices:

- Click the cell to select it, and then click the cell again to move the insertion point into it. Edit like you would in Word or any text program.
- Click the cell to select it, and then type a new entry to replace the old one.

If you make a mistake when editing, you can press Esc (top left of your keyboard) to cancel the edit before you leave the cell. If you need to undo an edit after having left the cell, press Ctrl+Z or click the Undo button on the Quick Access toolbar.

Now try typing some text into your spreadsheet. I entered the text shown in **Figure 7-3** to create a simple mortgage calculator. Feel free to enter your own information or type the same text I entered.

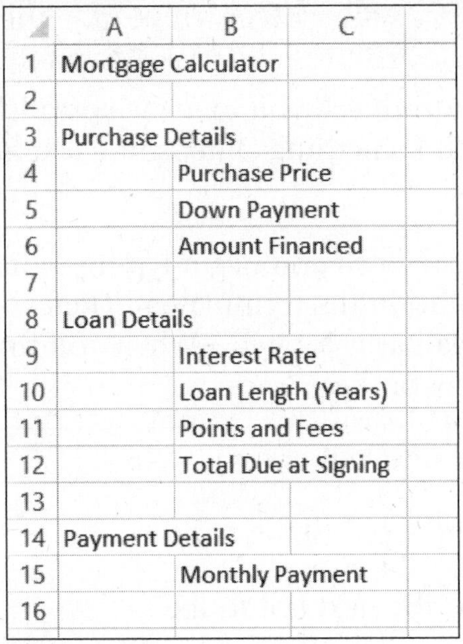

Figure 7-3

If you decide you don't want the text you typed in a particular cell, you can get rid of it in several different ways:

- Select the cell; then right-click the cell and choose Clear Contents from the menu that appears.
- Select the cell; then choose Home⇨Editing⇨Clear⇨Clear Contents.
- Select the cell, press the spacebar, and then press Enter. This technically doesn't clear the cell's content, but it replaces it with a single, invisible character — a space.

Don't confuse Clear with Delete. They are two separate things. There is a Delete command on the Home tab (Home⇨Cells⇨Delete), but using it doesn't *clear* the cell content; instead, it *removes* the entire cell. You find out more about deleting cells in the upcoming section, "Insert and Delete Rows, Columns, and Cells."

And while I'm on the subject, don't confuse Clear with Cut, either. The Cut command works in conjunction with the Clipboard. It moves the content to the Clipboard, from which you can then paste it somewhere else. In Excel, though (unlike in other applications), using the Cut command doesn't immediately remove the content. Instead, it puts a flashing dotted box around the content and waits for you to reposition the cell cursor and issue the Paste command. If you do something else in the interim, the cut-and-paste operation is cancelled, and the content that you cut remains in its original location.

You can also clear only the formatting from a cell by clicking the Clear button on the Home tab and then choosing Clear Formats from its menu. Or, to clear both the content *and* the formatting, choose Clear All.

Try clearing some content from the text you entered in your spreadsheet. Select a cell and use any of the three methods from the preceding bullet list to remove the contents of the cell. From the text I typed earlier, I chose to clear the text from cell A14.

After you type some text in a worksheet, *save your work!* Don't wait until you type a lot of text. Always save early in the process in case something bad happens — like a power outage — that causes your computer to shut down unexpectedly. Refer back to "Save Your Work" in Chapter 3 for details.

Insert and Delete Rows, Columns, and Cells

Even if you're a careful planner, you'll likely decide that you want to change your spreadsheet's layout. Maybe you want data in a different column, or certain rows turn out to be unnecessary. Excel makes it easy to insert and delete rows and columns to deal with these kinds of changes.

Instead of inserting rows and columns, you can move the content between rows or columns. In Chapter 8, read how to move content in a worksheet.

To insert a row or column, follow these steps:

1. Select the row above or the column to the right of where the insertion should occur. Or click in any cell in that row or column.

2. On the Home tab, and click the arrow to the right of the Insert button in the Cells group to open the drop-down list for the Insert button. See **Figure 7-4**.

3. From the menu, choose Insert Sheet Rows or Insert Sheet Columns.

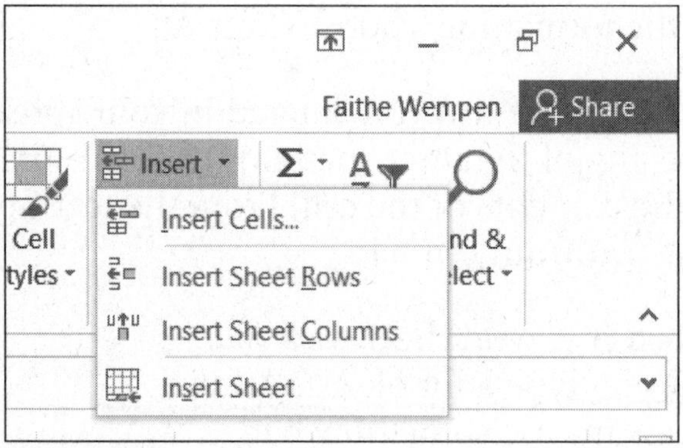

Figure 7-4

Here's another way to insert: from the right-click (contextual) menu:

1. Select a row or column adjacent to where the insertion should occur.

2. Right-click the selection and choose Insert from the menu that appears. Excel inserts either a row or a column, whichever you select in Step 1.

To insert multiple rows or columns at once, select a corresponding number of contiguous rows or columns in Step 1 in the preceding step list. For example, if you select three columns, you get three new blank columns when you choose Insert.

Deleting a row or column works in a similar way:

1. Select the row(s) or column(s) you want to delete.

2. Choose Home➪Cells➪Delete.

   The Delete button has a drop-down list, just like the Insert button does. From it, you can choose what you wanted to delete: cells, rows, or columns. However, in Step 1, you select what you want to delete, so that isn't necessary in this case; you could simply click the button to delete what was selected.

Deleting a cell is different from clearing a cell's content! When you clear only the content, the cell itself remains. When you delete the cell itself, the cells to the right or below shift to the left or up to fill in the gap.

Here's a way to envision what deletion does. Imagine that each cell is a cardboard box, stacked one on top of another in a grid. Each box opens to the front, so you can put things in it and take things out of it. When you delete a cell, you pull the box out of the stack. Gravity dictates that the boxes on top of the space fall down to fill it in. However, in Excel, gravity is backward: The cells fall *up* (or to the right if you specify that).

Excel is smart enough that it tries to guess which direction you want existing content to move when you delete cells. If you have content immediately to the right of a deleted cell, for example, it shifts it left. If you have content immediately below the deleted cell, it shifts it up. You can still override that, though, when needed.

To delete individual cells, follow these steps:

1. Select the cell(s) to delete.

2. Choose Home➪Cells➪Delete. Excel attempts to guess how you want the adjacent cells shifted and then performs that operation.

If Excel didn't shift the other cells in the direction you expected, try again using this slightly longer, but more controllable, alternative procedure:

1. Select the cell(s) to delete.
2. On the Home tab, click the arrow on the Delete button in the Cells group to open its menu.
3. Click Delete Cells. A Delete dialog box opens, as shown in **Figure 7-5**.
4. Select the radio button for the shift you want: Shift Cells Left or Shift Cells Up.
5. Click OK.

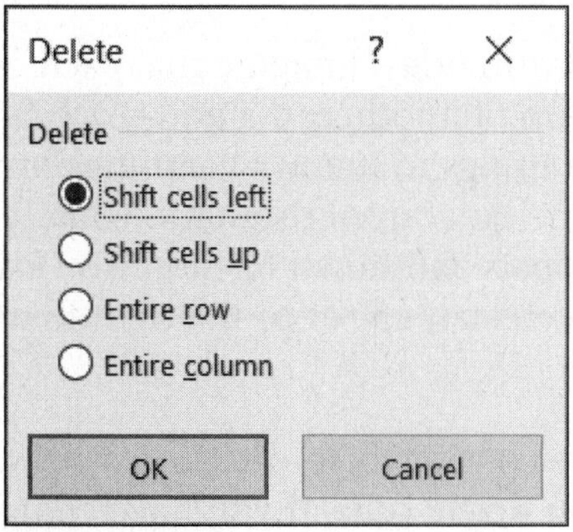

Figure 7-5

Inserting individual cells works in much the same way. You can choose from an easy method that guesses how you want the shift of adjacent content to occur, or a more controllable method where you get to specify how.

Here's the easy method for cell insertion:

1. Select the cell(s) above or to the left of where you want them to appear.
2. On the Home tab, click Insert. Excel attempts to guess how you want the adjacent content shifted and performs that action.

This method gives you direct control:

1. Select the cell(s) above or to the left of where you want them to appear.

2. On the Home tab, click the arrow on the Insert button in the Cells group to open its menu.

3. Click Insert Cells. An Insert dialog box appears.

4. Select the radio button for the shift you want: Shift Cells Right or Shift Cells Down.

5. Click OK.

Here's a shortcut for opening the Insert or the Delete dialog box. Select the cells, right-click the selection, and then choose Insert or Delete from the right-click menu.

Try deleting some individual cells from your spreadsheet. In the Mortgage file I created earlier, I deleted cells A4:A6 and A9:A13. My spreadsheet now looks like **Figure 7-6**.

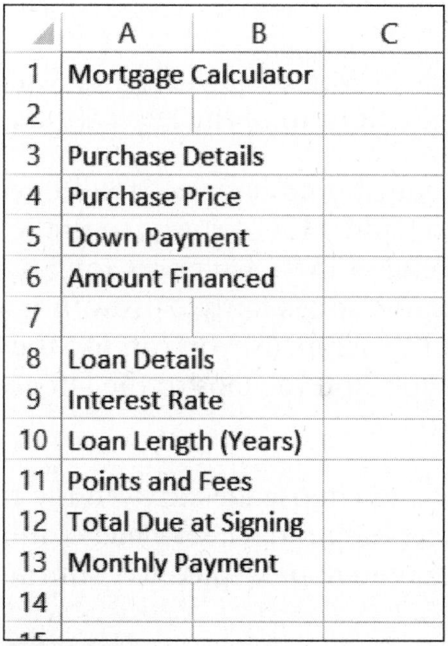

Figure 7-6

Work with Worksheets

Each workbook contains one sheet by default: Sheet1. Sometimes, however, you may want to add more sheets to your workbook. Sheets are like pages. They can come in very handy for creating alternative versions of the same spreadsheet, or for storing different types of information in the same workbook file. For example, you could have separate sheets for your holdings at each investment firm, or separate sheets for the membership rosters of several different clubs.

To create a new sheet, click the Insert Worksheet button shown in **Figure 7-7**, or press Shift+F11. The resulting blank sheet uses the default settings (formatting, column width, and so on).

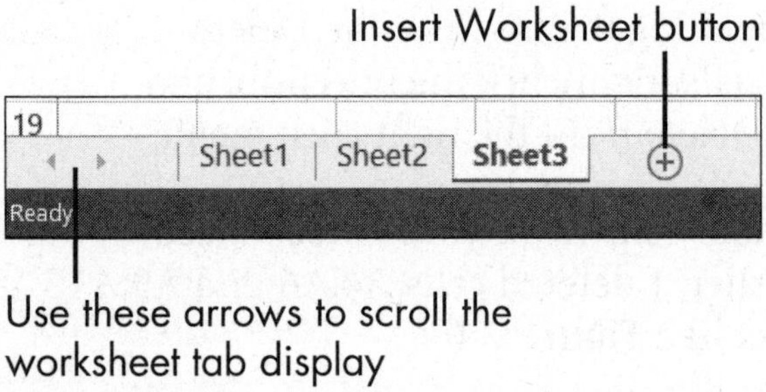

Figure 7-7

When there are multiple sheets present, you can switch from one sheet to another, click the sheet's tab at the bottom of the Excel window.

With a normal Excel window size you should have no trouble seeing several tabs at once. However, if you add a lot of sheets to the workbook or rename the tabs so that some of them have very long names, and/or if you resize your Excel window so it's fairly narrow, not all the tabs may be visible at once. When this happens, you can use the tab scroll arrows to the left of the tabs to scroll the tabs to the left and right.

To delete a sheet, right-click its tab and choose Delete from the right-click menu that appears. If that sheet has no data, it's deleted immediately. If the sheet does contain data, you're prompted to confirm the deletion.

Make sure you really want to delete a sheet because this is an action you cannot undo with the Undo (Ctrl+Z) command.

Give it a whirl. In your spreadsheet, create a couple of new worksheets, and then delete them.

The default names for the sheets aren't particularly helpful in terms of describing what they contain. In a workbook that uses multiple sheets, you will probably want to rename each sheet's tab so that it's meaningful to you.

To rename a sheet, follow these steps:

1. Double-click the sheet's tab. The current name is selected.
2. Type a new name.
3. Press Enter.

If you want, rename the Sheet1 tab in your spreadsheet to something that's easy to remember. For example, I renamed Sheet1 in my Mortgage spreadsheet to *Mortgage*.

You can use up to 255 characters for a sheet name, including most punctuation, but think twice before you use long, fancy names. When creating references to cells on a sheet, you must include the sheet's name in the formula, and long names can be cumbersome to type. In addition, names that include spaces and punctuation can sometimes require special handling to avoid tripping up certain Excel features. Best bet: Stick with single-word sheet names with no punctuation.

Here's a formatting trick to keep your work organized. Each worksheet tab can have a different color, or you can color several tabs all the same to indicate that they're somehow related. The coloring is all up to you!

To assign a color to a sheet tab, follow these steps:

1. Right-click the tab and hover your mouse over Tab Color on the contextual menu.
2. In the Theme Colors palette that appears, click the desired color. (See **Figure 7-8**.)

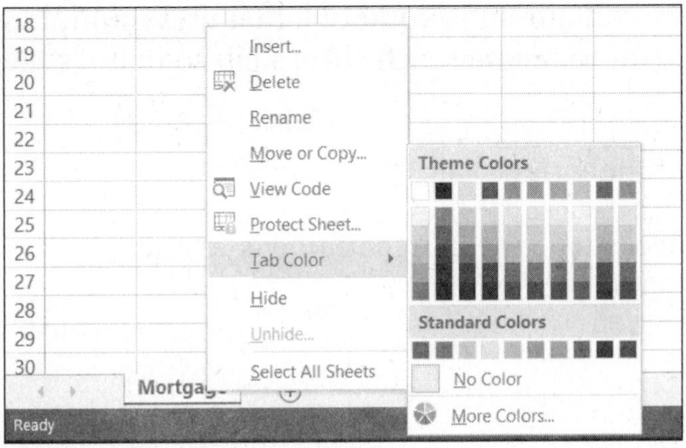

Figure 7-8

When a colored tab is *active* (that is, when that particular sheet is displayed), the color appears slightly washed out in a soft gradient. But when you select a different tab, the inactive tab(s) appear in its full colorful glory. To remove the color, repeat the preceding steps and click No Color in Step 2.

Doing the Math: Formulas and Functions

Chapter 8

The main reason why people choose Excel is that it "excels" at storing and calculating numeric data. With Excel, you can create a grid of numbers, and then insert formulas that perform math calculations on them. That capability makes it possible to build complex worksheets that calculate loan rates and payments, keep track of your bank accounts, and much more.

In this chapter, I show you how to build formulas and functions in Excel, and how to put them to work to do several types of calculation-based jobs.

Get ready to . . .

Learn How Formulas Are Structured

A *formula* is a math calculation, like 2 + 2 or 3(4 + 1). In Excel, formulas are different from regular text in two ways:

- They begin with an equal sign, like this: =2+2
- They don't contain text (except for function names, covered later, and cell references). They contain only symbols that are allowed in math formulas, such as parentheses, commas, and decimal points.

Just like in basic math, formulas are calculated by using an order of precedence. Table 8-1 lists the order.

Table 8-1 Order of Precedence in a Formula

Order	*Item*	*Example*
1	Anything in parentheses	=2*(2+1)
2	Exponentiation	=2^3
3	Multiplication and Division	=1+2*2
4	Addition and subtraction	=10–4

Write Formulas That Reference Cells

One of Excel's best features is its ability to reference cells in formulas. When a cell is referenced in a formula, whatever value it contains is used in the formula. When the value changes, the result of the formula changes, too.

For example, suppose you enter 7 in cell A1 and 8 in cell A2. Then in cell A3, you put the following formula:

```
=A1+A2
```

The result of that formula appears in cell A3 as 15. See **Figure 8-1**. You could have just as easily entered =7+8 in cell A3 and gotten the same result. However, because you reference *the cells* — rather than the *fixed values* — you can modify the result by changing what either A1 or A2 contains. For example, if you change the value in A1 to 4, the result in A3 changes to 12.

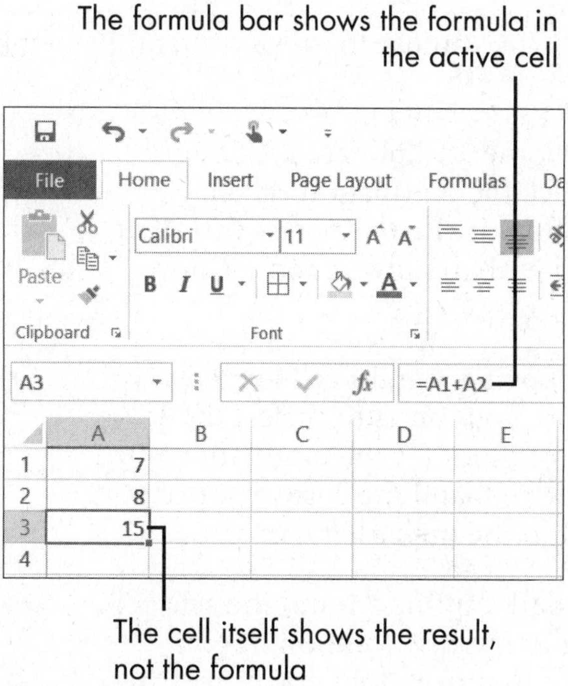

Figure 8-1

You can use a formula to repeat a value between one cell and another. For example, the formula `=A1` repeats whatever value is in cell A1 wherever you put it.

You can combine cell references with fixed numbers in cells, too. Here are some examples:

```
=A1+2
=(A1*A2)/4
=(A1+A2+B1+B2)/4
```

Move and Copy Cell Content

When you're creating a spreadsheet, it's common to not get everything in exactly the right cells to begin with. Fortunately, moving content between cells is easy.

Here are the two methods you can use to move content. Remember to first select the cell(s).

- **Clipboard:** Choose Home⇨Clipboard⇨Cut or press Ctrl+X. Then click the destination cell and choose Home⇨Clipboard⇨Paste or press Ctrl+V. If you want to copy rather than move, choose Copy (Ctrl+C) rather than Cut.

  If you're moving or copying a multi-cell range with the Clipboard method, you can either select the same size and shape of block for the destination. Or you can select a single cell, and the paste will occur with the selected cell in the upper-left corner.

- **Mouse:** Point at the dark outline around the selected range, and then drag to the new location. If you want to copy rather than move, hold down the Ctrl key while you drag. See **Figure 8-2**.

When you move or copy a formula, Excel automatically changes the cell references to work with the new location. For example, suppose you copy the formula in cell A3 (from Figure 8-1) into cell C3. The original formula was `=A1+A2`. When it arrives at C3, it changes to `=C1+C2`. This happens by design, as a convenience to you, because often when you copy formulas, you want them to work relative to their new locations. This is called a *relative reference.*

Sometimes, you might not want the cell references in a formula to change when you move or copy it. In other words, you want it to be an *absolute reference* to that cell. To make a reference absolute, you add dollar signs before the column letter and before the row number. So, for example, an absolute reference to C1 would be `=$C$1`.

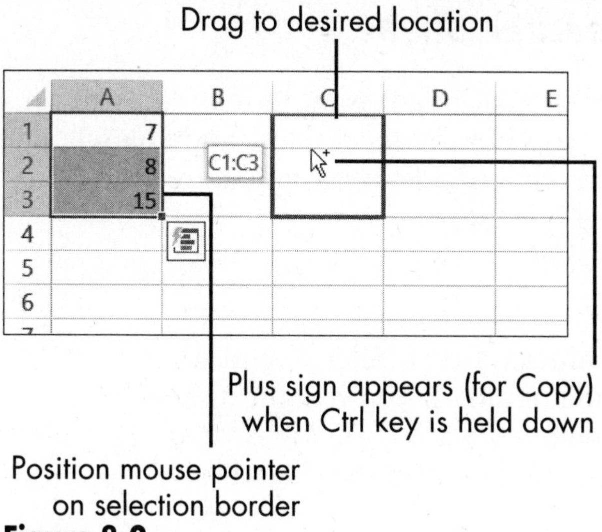

Figure 8-2

You can mix relative and absolute references in the same formula. For example, in **Figure 8-3**, if I copy the formula from D4 to D5, the version in D5 will appear like this:

```
=C5+(C5*$B$1)
```

The C4 reference changed to C5 because it didn't have any dollar signs around it, but the B1 reference stayed the same because it did have the dollar signs.

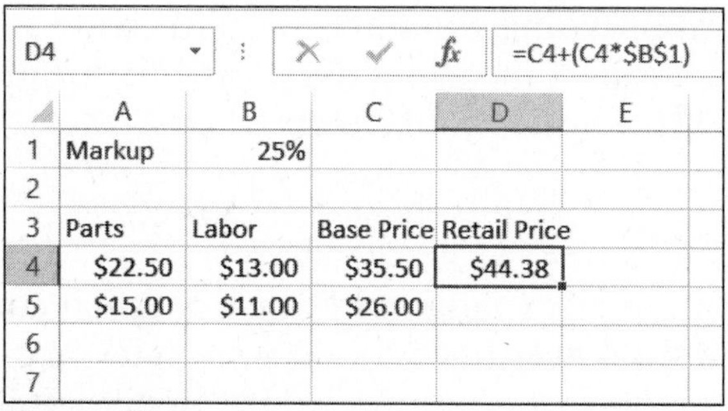

Figure 8-3

Reference a Cell on Another Sheet

In a multi-sheet workbook, you might want to refer to a cell on a different sheet. To do this, you put the sheet name and an exclamation point in front of the cell reference. For example, to refer to cell A1 on Sheet2, you would write it like this:

```
=Sheet2!A1
```

The default sheet names (Sheet1, Sheet2, and so on) have no spaces in the names. If you rename a sheet with a name that includes spaces, you have to put the sheet name in single quotation marks, like this:

```
='Home Budget'!A1
```

Understand Functions

Sometimes, it's awkward or lengthy to write a formula to perform a calculation. For example, suppose you want to sum the values in cells A1 through A10. To express it as a formula, you would have to write out each cell reference individually, like this:

```
=A1+A2+A3+A4+A5+A6+A7+A8+A9+A10
```

In Excel, a *function* refers to a certain math calculation. Functions can greatly shortcut the amount of typing you have to do to create a particular result. For example, instead of the using the preceding formula, you could sum, using the SUM function like this:

```
=SUM(A1:A10)
```

With a function, you can represent a range with the upper-left corner's cell reference, a colon, and the lower-right corner's cell reference. In the case of `A1:A10`, there is only one column, so the upper left is A1 and the lower right is A10.

Each function has one or more arguments. An *argument* is a placeholder for a number, text string, or cell reference. For example, the SUM function requires at least one argument: a range of cells. So in the preceding example, A1:A10 is the argument. The arguments for a function are enclosed in a set of parentheses.

Each function has its own rules as to how many required and optional arguments it has, and what they represent. You don't have to memorize the sequence of arguments (the *syntax*) for each function; Excel asks you for them. It can even suggest a function to use for a certain situation if you aren't sure what you need.

To find a function and get help with its syntax, follow these steps:

1. Click in the cell where you want to insert the function.
2. Choose Formulas ➪ Function Library ➪ Insert Function. The Insert Function dialog box opens.

   If you don't know what function you want, type a few keywords (in the Search for a Function field) that represent what you want to do. For example, if you want to find the minimum value in a range of cells, you might type *Find the minimum value.* Then click Go to see a list of functions that might be what you want. See **Figure 8-4**. Click each function on the list and read the description of it that appears.

3. When you find the function you want, click OK.
4. In the Function Arguments dialog box that opens, fill in the arguments in the field provided. The arguments will be different depending on the function you choose. **Figure 8-5** shows the arguments for the MIN function, for example.

   Here are some ways to fill in the arguments:

   - *Type a number or a cell reference (or range) directly into the box.*

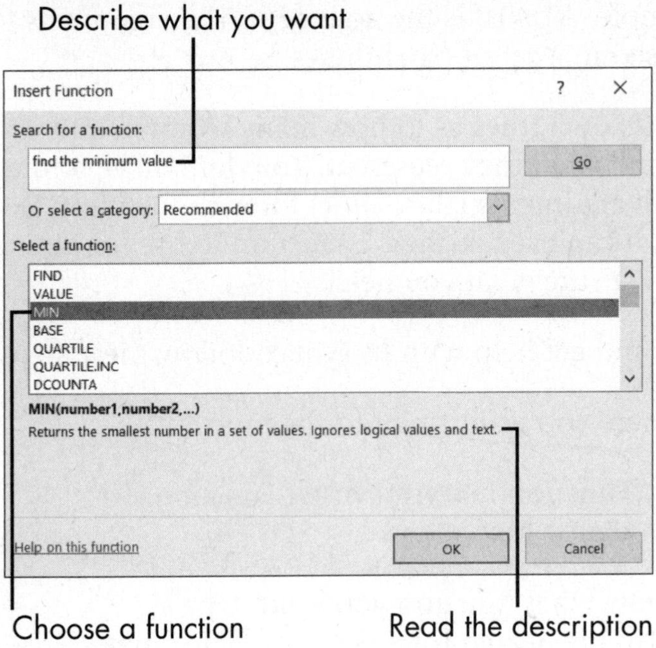

Figure 8-4

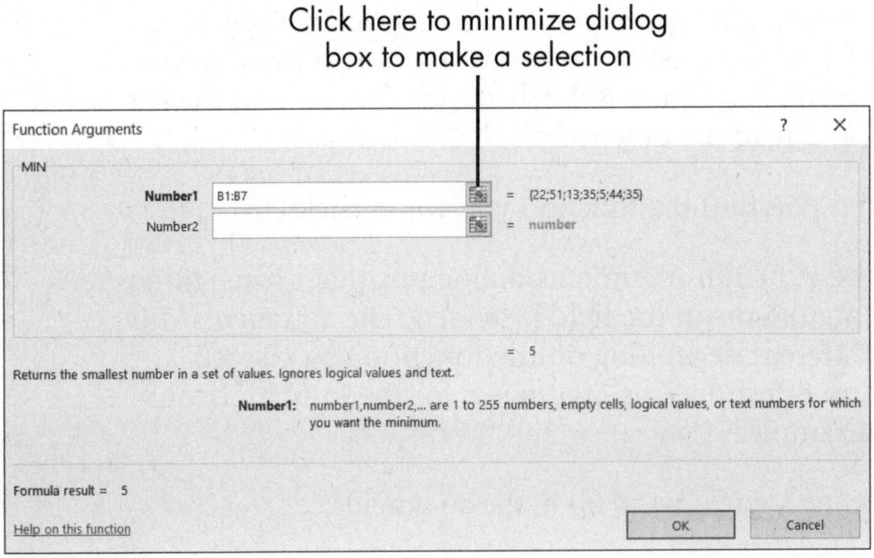

Figure 8-5

Even though the argument is named Number1 in Figure 8-5, you can still enter a range for it. The Number2 argument is optional; you can tell because its name is not bold. This particular function can have an unlimited number of optional arguments; more boxes appear automatically as needed.

- *Click the Selector button to the right of the text box.* This collapses the dialog box temporarily. Select the cell or range in the worksheet, and then press Enter to return to the dialog box.

5. Click OK.

After you get comfortable with a particular function, you might prefer to type it directly into the cell rather than going through the Insert Function dialog box. As you type, Excel helps you by providing prompts for the arguments in a ScreenTip. See **Figure 8-6**.

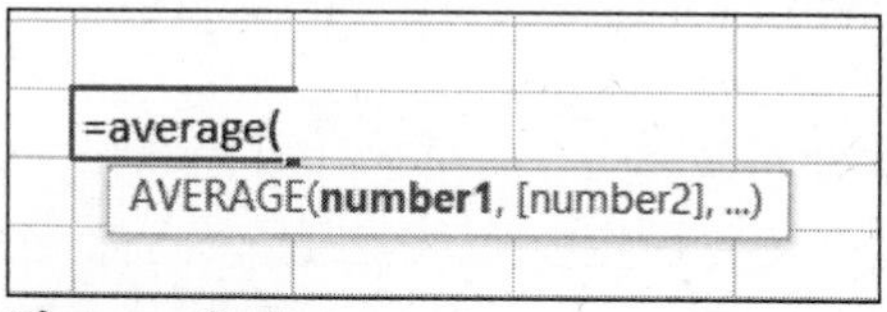

Figure 8-6

Take a Tour of Some Basic Functions

Excel has hundreds of functions, but most of them are very specialized. The basic set that the average user works with is much more manageable.

Start with the simplest functions of them all: those with no arguments. Two prime examples are

- **NOW:** Reports the current date and time.
- **TODAY:** Reports the current date.

Even though neither uses any arguments, you still have to include the parentheses, so they look like this:

```
=NOW( )
=TODAY( )
```

Another basic kind of function performs a single, simple math operation and has a single argument that specifies what cell or range it operates on. Table 8-2 summarizes some important functions that work this way.

Table 8-2 Simple One-Argument Functions

Function	*What It Does*	*Example*
SUM	Sums the values in a range of cells.	=SUM(A1:A10)
AVERAGE	Averages the values in a range of cells.	=AVERAGE(A1:A10)
MIN	Provides the smallest number in a range of cells.	=MIN(A1:A10)
MAX	Provides the largest number in a range of cells.	=MAX(A1:A10)
COUNT	Counts the number of cells in the range that contain numeric values.	=COUNT(A1:A10)
COUNTA	Counts the number of empty cells in the range.	=COUNTA(A1:A10)
COUNTBLANK	Counts the number of non-empty cells in the range.	=COUNTBLANK(A1:A10)

Table 8-3 shows some functions that change how numbers are presented.

Here are some things to note about the items in the preceding table:

- **Absolute value:** This is the positive version of a number. For example, the absolute value of –15 is 15. If the number is already positive, it stays positive.

Table 8-3 Functions That Change Numbers

Function	*What It Does*	*Example*
ABS	Presents the absolute value of the number.	=ABS(B1)
ROUND	Rounds the number up or down by a specified number of decimal points.	=ROUND(B1,0)
EVEN	Rounds a positive number up, or a negative number down, to the next even whole number.	=EVEN(B1)
ODD	Rounds a positive number up, or a negative number down, to the next odd whole number.	=ODD(B1)

- **Multiple arguments:** See the entry for ROUND. There are two arguments: the cell address or number to operate on, and the number of decimal places. A value of 0 for the decimal places results in rounding to the nearest integer.

When a function has more than one argument, the arguments are separated by commas. You can see this in the ROUND example: `ROUND(B1,0)`.

Two other functions, ROUNDUP and ROUNDDOWN, work just like ROUND except they specify which way the rounding will always occur.

Explore Financial Functions

Financial functions are some of the most useful tools for home and small business worksheets because they're all about the money: borrowing it, lending it, and monitoring it. Here's the basic set:

- **PV:** Calculates the present value or principal amount. In a loan, it's the amount you're borrowing; in a savings account, it's the initial deposit.

- **FV:** The future value. This is the principal plus the interest paid or received.

- **PMT:** The payment to be made per period. For example, for a mortgage, it's the monthly payment; in a savings account, it's the amount you save each period. A period can be any time period, but it's usually a month.
- **RATE:** The interest rate to be charged per period (for a loan), or the percentage of amortization or depreciation per period.
- **NPER:** The number of periods. For a loan, it's the total number of payments to be made, or the points in time when interest is earned if you're tracking savings or amortization.

These financial functions are related. Each is an argument in the others; if you're missing one piece of information, you can use all the pieces you *do* know to find the missing one. For example, if you know the loan amount, the rate, and the number of years, you can determine the payment.

Take a look at the PMT function as an example. The syntax for the PMT function is as follows, with the optional parts in italics:

PMT(RATE, NPER, PV, *FV*, *Type*)

The Type argument specifies when the payment is made: 1 for the beginning of the period or 0 at the end of the period. It's not required. (I don't use it in the examples here.)

So, for example, say the rate is 0.833% per month (that's 10% per year), for 60 months, and the amount borrowed is $25,000. The Excel formula looks like this:

```
=PMT(.00833,60,25000)
```

Enter that into a worksheet cell, and you'll find that the monthly payment will be $531.13. You could also enter those values into cells, and then refer to the cells in the function arguments, like this (assuming you entered them into B1, B2, and B3):

```
=PMT(B1,B2,B3)
```

Here is the syntax for each of the above-listed functions. As you can see, they're all intertwined with one another:

```
FV(RATE, NPER, PMT, PV, Type)
PMT(RATE, NPER, PV, FV, Type)
RATE(NPER, PMT, PV, FV, Type)
NPER(RATE, PMT, PV, FV, Type)
```

Here are some common ways to use Excel functions in everyday life:

If I borrow $10,000 for 3 years at 7% yearly interest, what will my monthly payments be?

Use the PMT function. Divide the interest rate by 12 because the rate is yearly, but the payment is monthly. Here is the syntax:

```
=PMT(0.07/12,36,10000)
```

If I borrow $10,000 at 7% interest and I can afford to make payments of $300 per month, how many months will it take to pay off the loan?

Use the NPER function. Again, divide the interest rate by 12 to convert from yearly to monthly. Here's the syntax:

```
=NPER(0.07/12,300,10000)
```

If I deposit $10,000 into a bank account that pays 2% interest per year, compounded weekly, how much money will I have after 5 years?

You want the future value of the account, or FV. The period is weekly, so the interest rate should be divided by 52, and the length of the loan is 260 periods (52 weeks multiplied by 5 years). The PMT amount is 0 because no additional deposits will be made after the initial deposit. The initial deposit is expressed as a negative number because the calculation is from the perspective of the interest earner, not the interest payer. Here is the syntax:

```
=FV(0.02/52,260,0,-10000)
```

As a final example, let's return to that mortgage spreadsheet I started in Chapter 7 and fill in some numbers, as in **Figure 8-7**. I've annotated each field to explain what I put into each one.

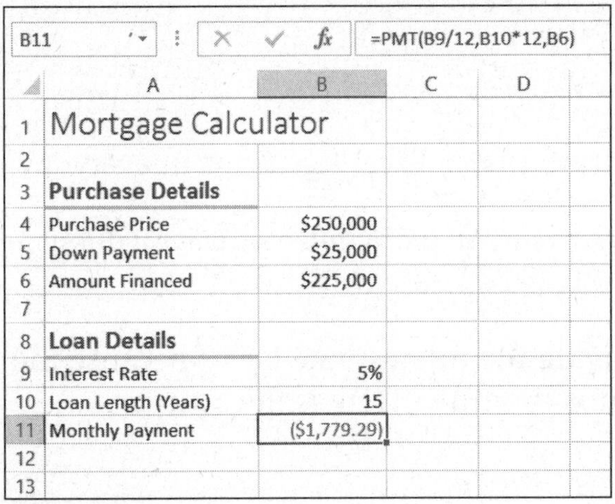

Figure 8-7

It's all pretty self-explanatory, except the PMT function in cell B11:

```
=PMT(B9/12,B10*12,B6)
```

The PMT function requires these three arguments:

- **Rate (RATE):** For the rate, I use B9/12 because I want to calculate a *monthly* payment, and the amount in B9 is per year. The interest rate per month is 1/12 of the interest rate per year.

- **Number of periods (NPER):** The number in B10 is years, and there are 12 periods (months) in each year — so I multiply B10 by 12.

- **Present value (PV):** For the present value, I simply refer to B6, which contains the amount to be financed.

This example is especially useful because it shows how a function can be modified to fit a situation. In this case, I had to convert from years (which is how most people think about loans) to months (which is how Excel calculates loans).

One more thing: did you notice that the payment is negative in cell B11? To make it a positive number, I could have enclosed the function in an absolute value function: ABS. Then it would have looked like this:

```
=ABS(PMT(B9/12,B10*12,B6))
```

When one function is nested inside another, there is only one equal sign, at the very beginning.

Creating Visual Interest with Formatting and Charts

Chapter 9

Get ready to . . .

Large spreadsheets with many rows and columns of numbers can be confusing or boring to look at. What do the numbers really mean? Which number goes with what descriptive text?

You can make a spreadsheet less boring and more informative by applying formatting. You can change font and text size, apply background shading, add borders, and lots more. You can also adjust the row and column sizes to create space between columns or rows of text.

To help users interpret the data, you can also add charts that summarize the data and/or show trends in the data. Excel offers a wide variety of chart types, enabling you to customize virtually every aspect of a chart's formatting.

Adjust Row Height and Column Width

By default, each column is the same width. If you type text that exceeds the column width, one of two things happens:

- **If the cell to the right is blank:** The text overflows into it.
- **If the cell to the right is not blank:** The text appears cut off *(truncated)*. The full text is still stored there, though.

Figure 9-1 illustrates each case.

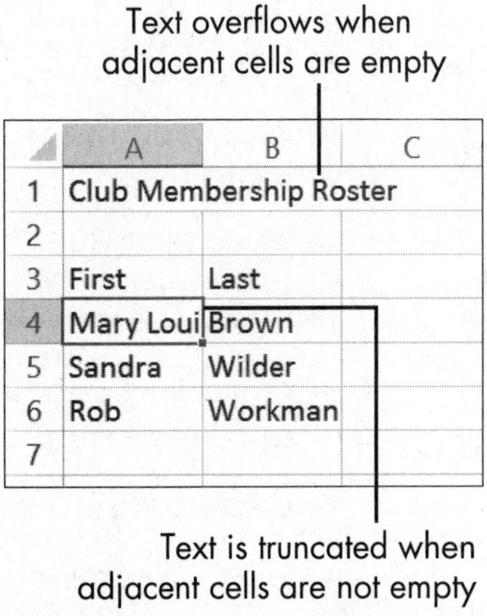

Figure 9-1

To fix such a problem, you must widen the column. Here are some ways how:

- **To widen the column exactly enough to hold the longest entry in it:** Double-click the divider between the column headers, or choose Home⇨Cells⇨Format⇨AutoFit Column Width.

- **To widen the column manually:** Drag the divider between the column headers. See **Figure 9-2**.

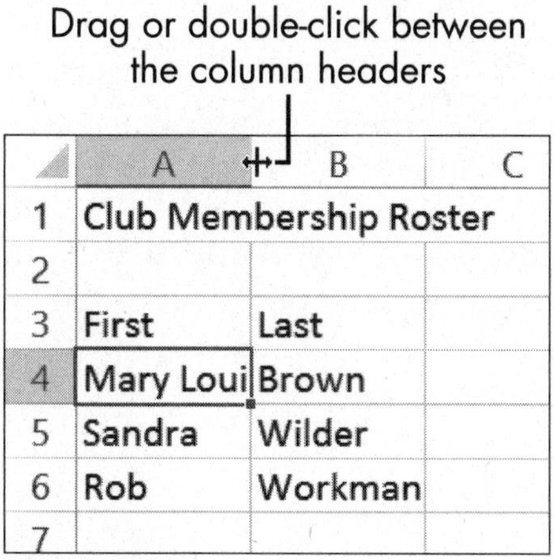

Figure 9-2

You can also make a column narrower; just drag to the left, rather than to the right.

This process also works with row heights. You can drag the divider between two row numbers to change the row height, or double-click the divider to autofit to the content.

Row heights adjust automatically to fit the tallest text in them, so you don't have to worry about text being vertically truncated in rows — usually. If you manually adjust the height of a row and then put some larger text into it, the larger text might become truncated because the row height has been fixed. To make it autofit again, choose Home➪Cells➪Format➪AutoFit Row Height.

Wrap Text in a Cell

Sometimes, rather than making a row wider to make its content fit, you might want the content to wrap to multiple lines within the cell (like a paragraph in a Word document). To do this, select the cell and then choose Home➪Alignment➪Wrap Text. (See **Figure 9-3**.)

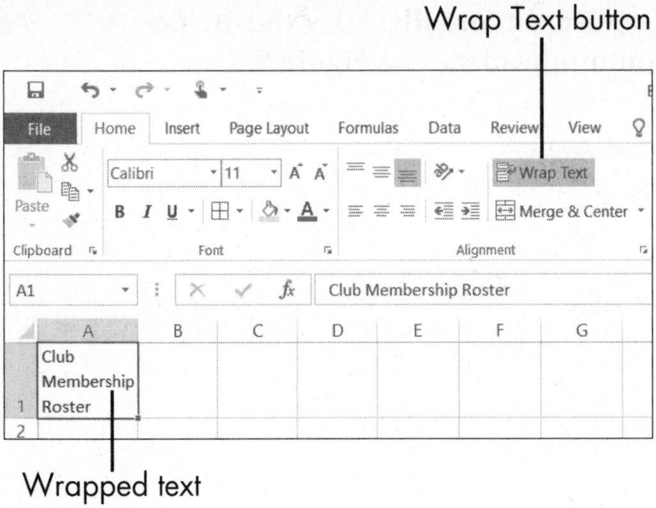

Figure 9-3

Wrapping is handy for column headings and long explanations.

Apply Gridlines or Borders

When you look at your worksheet onscreen, you see faint lines — *gridlines* — that separate the rows and columns.

By default, gridlines appear onscreen but not in print. To control how gridlines appear, display the Page Layout tab and then mark or clear the View and/or Print check boxes in the Sheet Options/Gridlines group. See **Figure 9-4**. (There is also a Gridlines check box on the View tab, but it controls only the onscreen display, not the print setting.)

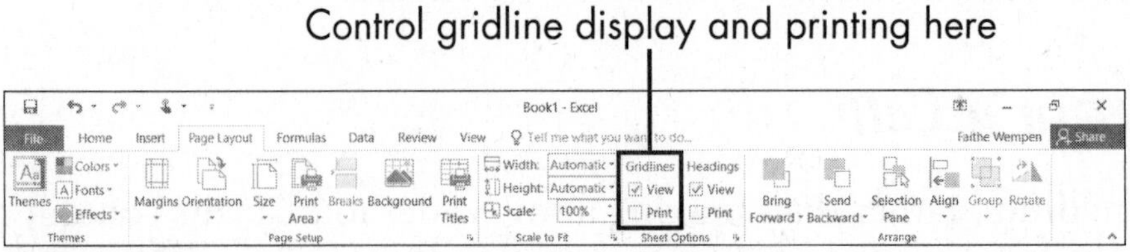

Figure 9-4

You can also apply other lines around one or more sides of each cell: *borders.* These lines can be any color or thickness you want. Borders always display onscreen and always print, regardless of settings. Borders are useful for helping the reader's eyes follow the text across the printed page, and for identifying which parts of a spreadsheet go together logically.

The easiest way to apply and format borders is to use the Borders button's drop-down list on the Home tab. (It's in the Font group, as shown in **Figure 9-5**.) Here's how:

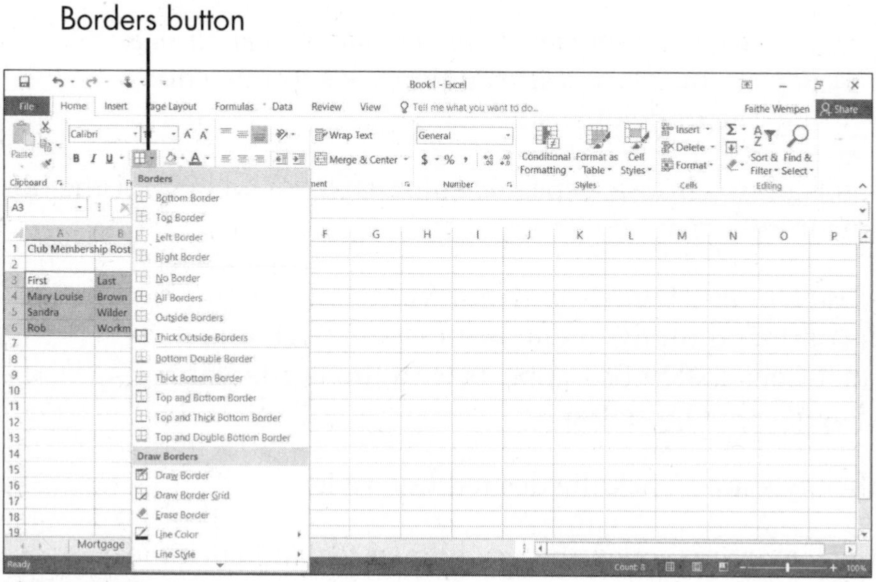

Figure 9-5

1. Select the range of cells to which you want to apply the border.

2. Choose Home ➪ Font ➪ Borders.

3. From the list of borders that appears, choose one that best represents the side(s) to which you want to apply the border.

The border will apply to the outside edges of the range you select. So, for example, choosing Top Border applies a top border only to the cells in the top row of the range, not to the top of every cell in that range.

- *To add a border on all sides of each cell in the range:* Choose All Borders.
- *To remove the border from all sides of all cells in the selected range:* Choose No Border.
- *To add borders on more than one side but not all sides:* Repeat the process several times, each time choosing one individual side.

If you want to choose a specific color, style, or weight for the border, follow these steps:

1. Choose Home➪Font➪Borders➪More Borders (the bottom command on the menu from Figure 9-5). The Format Cells dialog box appears with the Border tab displayed. See **Figure 9-6**.
2. In the Style area, click the desired line style.
3. In the Color area, open the drop-down list and click the desired color.
4. In the Presets area, click the preset for the sides you want to apply the border to: None, Outline, or Inside.

   If you want the border around each side of each cell, click both Outline and Inside.

   or

   In the Border area, click the button(s) for individual sides, or click directly on the sample area in the desired spots, which applies the border to only certain sides.

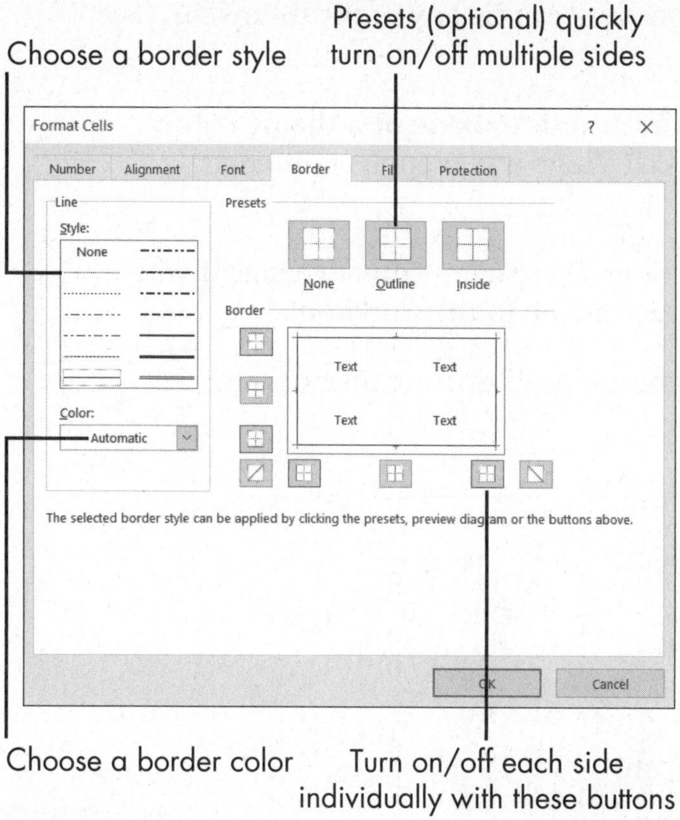

Figure 9-6

Step 4 is necessary. If you choose a border style and color but don't apply it to any sides of the range, that's like selecting nothing at all.

5. Click OK.

Apply Fill Color

Fill color — also called *shading* — is the color or pattern that fills the background of one or more cells.

Shading can help the reader's eyes follow information across a page, and can add color and visual interest to a worksheet. In some types of spreadsheets, such as a checkbook register, it's common to shade every other line, for easier reading.

The fill color you choose can be any of the following. (See Figure 9-7.)

- **A theme color, or a tint/shade of a theme color:** These colors *do* change if you apply a different theme.
- **A standard color:** These colors don't change if you apply a different theme to the workbook.
- **No Fill:** This removes all existing fill from the selected cells.

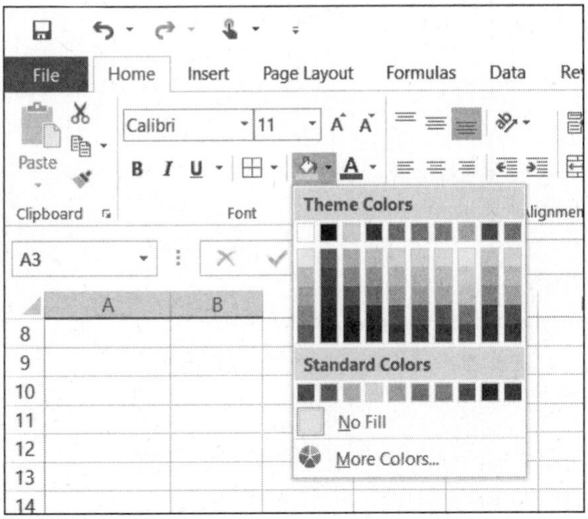

Figure 9-7

To apply fill color, follow these steps:

1. Select the cell(s) to be filled.
2. On the Home tab, click the down arrow to the right of the Fill Color button, opening its menu.

Clicking the Fill Color button applies whatever color is selected (that is, the color that currently appears on the button's face) without opening the menu.

3. Choose your color using one of these methods:

   - *Click one of the color swatches in the Theme Colors palette.*
   - *Click one of the colors in the Standard Colors palette.*
   - *Click More Colors to open a dialog box of additional standard colors.* Choose one and then click OK.

To change the workbook's theme, choose Page Layout⇨Themes. Changing themes changes the fonts and colors used. To change only the colors, choose Page Layout⇨Themes⇨Colors.

Format Text in Cells

Text formatting within a cell works very much like it does in Word and PowerPoint. To change the font, font size, color, or attributes (such as bold or italic) for an Excel spreadsheet cell or range, follow these steps:

1. Select the cell(s).
2. On the Home tab, use the buttons and drop-down lists in the Font group to apply text formatting. **Figure 9-8** points them out.

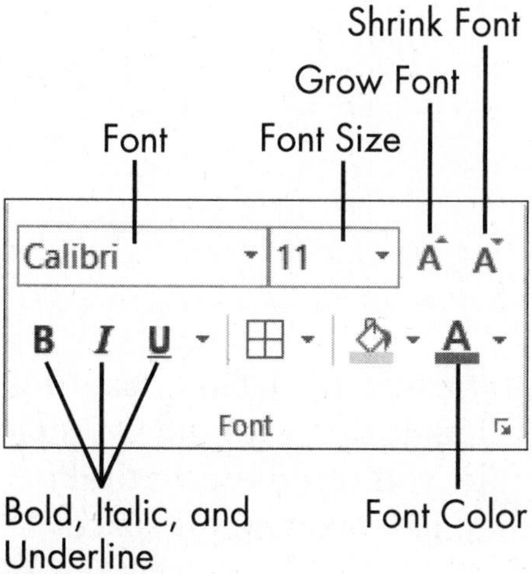

Figure 9-8

Text alignment controls how the text lines up within cells. **Figure 9-9** points out the controls on the Home tab for working with cell alignment, and also shows some examples. *Cell alignment* refers to how the text interacts with the available space in the cell.

- *Horizontal orientation* describes whether the text is left-aligned, right-aligned, or centered when the cell is wider than needed to accommodate the entry.

- *Vertical orientation* describes whether the text aligns with the top or bottom of the cell, or is centered vertically between the top and bottom, when the cell is taller than needed to accommodate the entry.

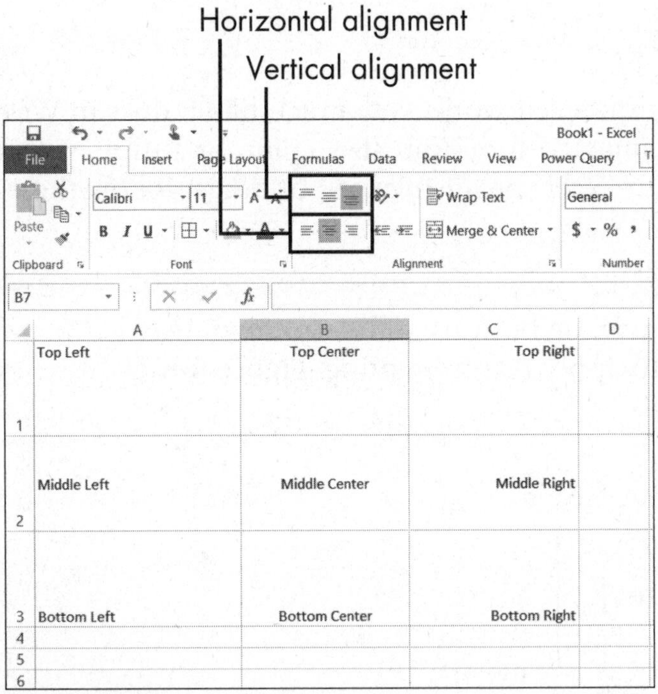

Figure 9-9

Orientation refers to the direction of the text. By default, text runs horizontally from left to right. You can change that with the Orientation button on the Home tab. For example, you could use vertical or slanted text so that labels in a heading row take up less space horizontally.

1. Select the cell(s).
2. Click the Orientation button.
3. Make a selection from its menu.

   Figure 9-10 shows the menu and also some rotated text.

Excel differentiates between angled and rotated text on the Orientation menu (shown in **Figure 9-10**). *Angled text* is diagonal; *rotated text* is straight up-and-down.

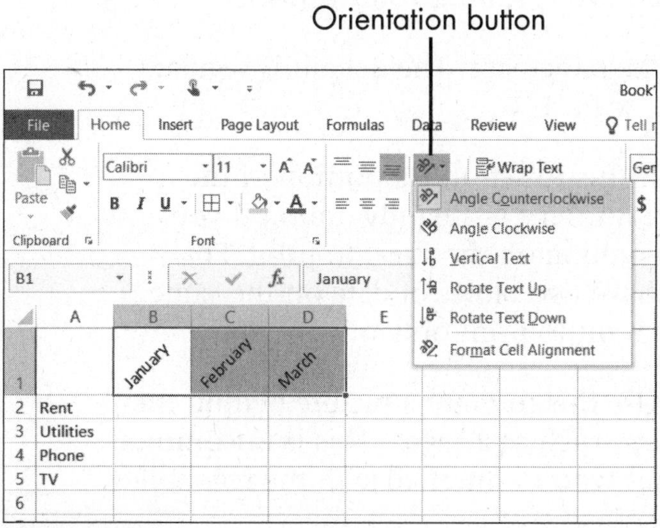

Figure 9-10

Format the Spreadsheet as a Whole

The Page Layout tab contains various formatting controls that affect the entire worksheet.

These controls affect the worksheet when it's printed. (See **Figure 9-11**.)

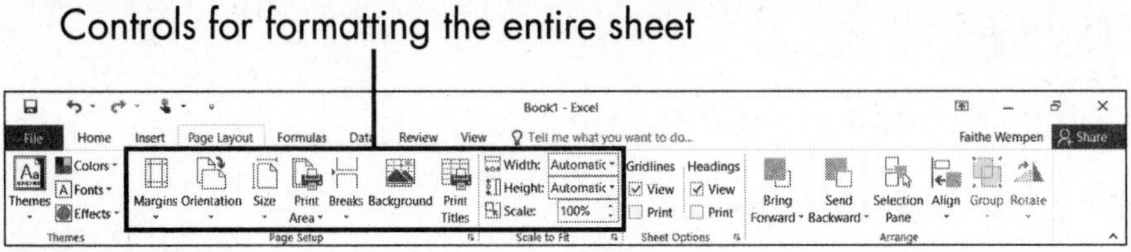

Figure 9-11

- **Margins:** Here, you can set the page margins for printing your worksheet. Choose from among the presets or choose Custom Margins to set your own.
- **Orientation:** Choose from Portrait (tall) or Landscape (wide) for printing your worksheet.
- **Size:** Choose the paper size. The default is regular letter size (8.5″ x 11″).
- **Print Area:** Use this to set only a portion of the worksheet to print. This is a handy option if you don't want everything on the sheet to print. For example, you have two tables of data on the same sheet, but you want to print only one.
- **Background:** Use this to place a picture behind the cells of the sheet, such as a logo. (This is uncommon because pictures tend to interfere with the readability of the data.)
- **Print Titles:** Click this button to open the Page Setup dialog box with the Sheet tab displayed. From there, you can select certain rows and columns to repeat on every page of a multipage printout (such as a row containing column headings, for example).
- **Scale to Fit (group):** Options here enable you to force your printout to fit on a certain number of pages by automatically decreasing the size as needed. You can scale to a certain number of pages (with the Height and Width lists), or you can set an overall scale percentage. Refer to Figure 9-11.

Create a Basic Chart

When you have a lot of numeric data on a sheet, it can be difficult to discern its meaning. Look at **Figure 9-12** to see what I mean. Even though this worksheet is attractively formatted, there are still a lot of numbers. Using a chart might help make more sense out of them.

	A	B	C	D	E	F	G	H	I	J	K	L	M	N
1	My Budget													
2														
3		January	February	March	April	May	June	July	August	September	October	November	December	Total
4	Rent	$ 800	$ 800	$ 800	$ 800	$ 800	$ 800	$ 800	$ 800	$ 800	$ 800	$ 800	$ 800	$ 9,600
5	Electricity	$ 75	$ 75	$ 75	$ 75	$ 75	$ 75	$ 75	$ 75	$ 75	$ 75	$ 75	$ 75	$ 900
6	Gas	$ 100	$ 100	$ 90	$ 50	$ 20	$ 20	$ 20	$ 20	$ 30	$ 40	$ 70	$ 80	$ 640
7	Phone	$ 50	$ 50	$ 50	$ 50	$ 50	$ 50	$ 50	$ 50	$ 50	$ 50	$ 50	$ 50	$ 600
8	Trash	$ 75			$ 75			$ 75			$ 75			$ 300
9	Water		$ 30			$ 30			$ 30			$ 30		$ 120
10	Cable TV	$ 60	$ 60	$ 60	$ 60	$ 60	$ 60	$ 60	$ 60	$ 60	$ 60	$ 60	$ 60	$ 720
11	Internet	$ 40	$ 40	$ 40	$ 40	$ 40	$ 40	$ 40	$ 40	$ 40	$ 40	$ 40	$ 40	$ 480
12	Groceries	$ 150	$ 150	$ 150	$ 150	$ 150	$ 150	$ 150	$ 150	$ 150	$ 150	$ 150	$ 150	$ 1,800
13	Gasoline	$ 50	$ 50	$ 50	$ 50	$ 50	$ 50	$ 50	$ 50	$ 50	$ 50	$ 50	$ 50	$ 600
14	Total	$ 1,400	$ 1,355	$ 1,315	$ 1,350	$ 1,275	$ 1,245	$ 1,320	$ 1,275	$ 1,255	$ 1,340	$ 1,325	$ 1,305	$ 15,760
15														

Figure 9-12

Excel offers various chart types, each suited for a different type of data analysis. For example, **Figure 9-13** shows two different charts created from portions of the data from Figure 9-12.

To create a chart, follow these steps:

1. Select the data to include on the chart. Include any cells that contain text labels that should be in the chart, too.

   You might need to select a range of cells that don't touch each other *(noncontiguous)* for Step 1. If that's the case, hold down the Ctrl key while you select the cells you want.

2. On the Insert tab, click a chart type. (Use the buttons in the Charts group.) A menu opens showing a few common subtypes for that type. For example, in **Figure 9-14**, you can see some column chart subtypes. Choose one of these. A new chart is created and placed on the current sheet as a floating object.

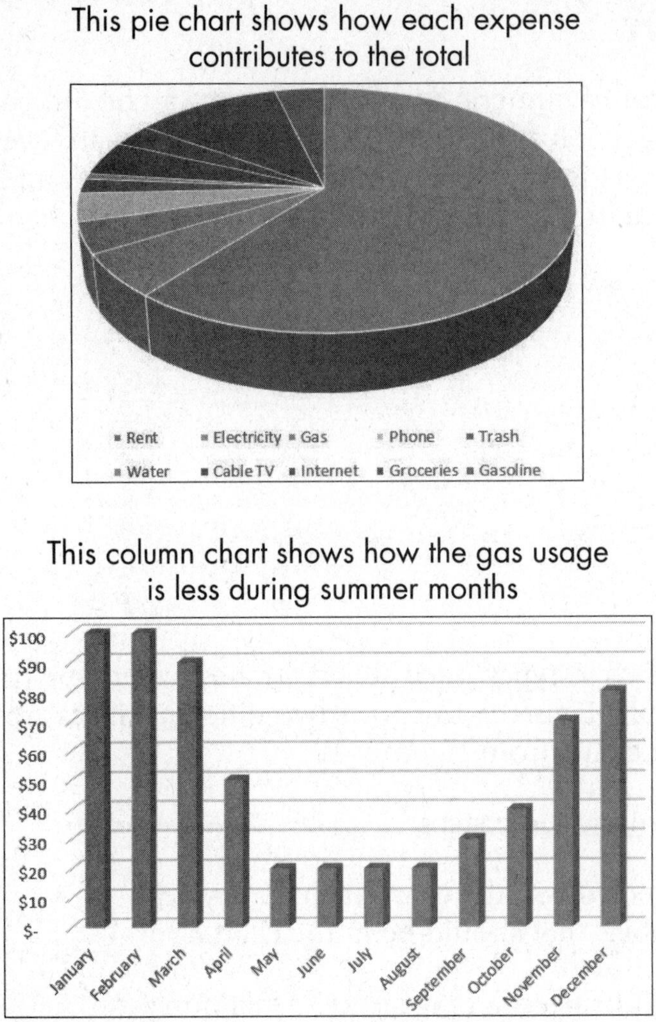

Figure 9-13

For more chart subtypes, click More Charts at the bottom of the menu in **Figure 9-14**. (The exact command name depends on the button; in Figure 9-14 it is More Column Charts.) Then you can choose from the Insert Chart dialog box.

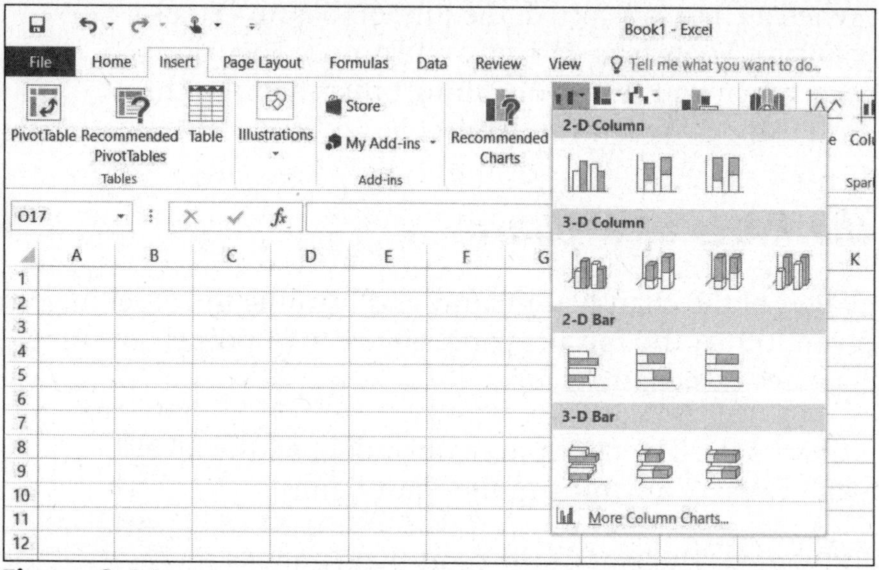

Figure 9-14

After you create the chart, you can

- **Resize it.** Drag one of the corners of its frame, or one of the selection handles on a side (represented by several dots).
- **Move it.** Drag any part of its frame except a corner or a side selection handle.
- **Place it on its own tab.** Choose Chart Tools Design⇨Location⇨Move Chart. Then in the Move Chart dialog box, click New Sheet and then click OK.

If the chart isn't what you expected data-wise, try one of these techniques:

- Delete the chart and try again, selecting different ranges.
- Change how the data is plotted by choosing Chart Tools Design⇨Data⇨Switch Row/Column.
- Choose Chart Tools Design⇨Data⇨Select Data to redefine what cells are used to make the chart.

When a chart is selected, the Ribbon has an extra set of Chart Tools tabs: Design and Format. They disappear when you select something other than the chart, and reappear when you reselect it.

Identify the Parts of a Chart

Every part of the chart has a name, and learning the Excel lingo can help you format the specific parts. **Figure 9-15** points out some of the key features of a chart.

- **Chart area:** The entire chart, including all the labels and extras: everything in the chart frame
- **Plot area:** The part of the chart that contains the data bars/area/pie/points
- **Legend:** The key that shows what each color represents
- **Wall:** The background of the plot area, if any
- **Floor:** On certain types of 3-D charts, the bottom of the plot area
- **Data series:** All the data points in the same data series (represented by a single color or legend key item)
- **Data point:** A single numeric value represented on the chart (for example, a single bar or point)
- **Chart title:** A text label that describes the entire chart
- **Axis:** A line on which data is plotted

A column chart has both a vertical and a horizontal axis.

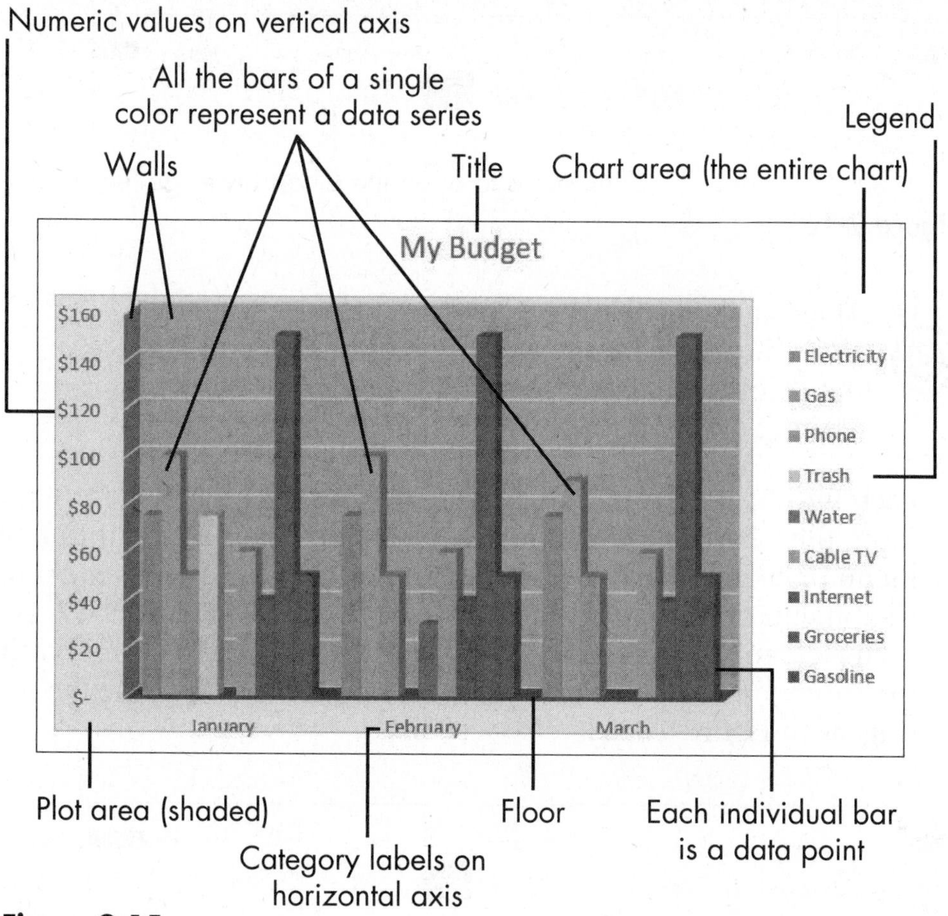

Figure 9-15

Format a Chart

Nearly every aspect of a chart can be formatted differently. You can change the color of every data series, for example, and change the font and size of each text item. You can adjust the rotation of a 3-D chart, move the legend to different positions, add or remove the chart title and various types of labels, and much more.

The easiest way to change the look of a chart is to apply a chart style to it. Chart styles are located on the Design tab. With the chart selected, open the Chart Style gallery and select one of the style presets. See **Figure 9-16**.

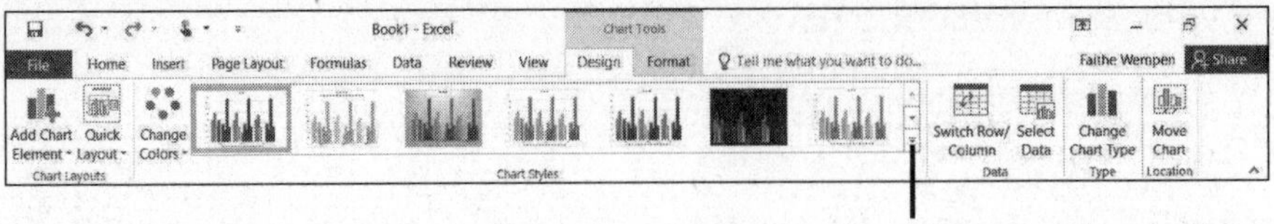

Figure 9-16

The chart style colors come from the color theme that you applied to the workbook. To choose a different color theme, choose either Page Layout ➪ Themes ➪ Themes or Page Layout ➪ Themes ➪ Colors.

Each individual element of a chart can also be separately formatted. From the Chart Tools Design tab, click Add Chart Element to open a menu of chart elements, and then point to the desired element to see a submenu of formatting you can apply to it. See **Figure 9-17**. For each element you can also select the More command at the bottom of the submenu to open a task pane where you can fine-tune the formatting, as in Figure 9-17.

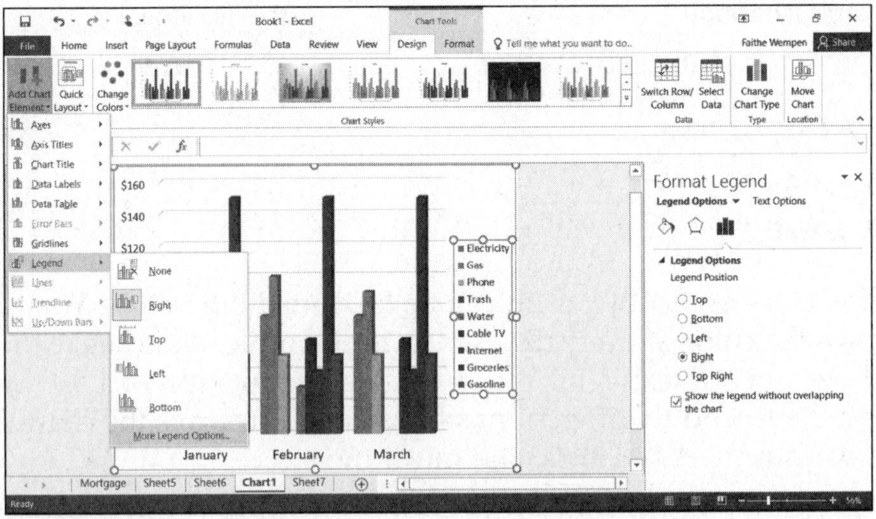

Figure 9-17

Here's an easy way to turn a certain chart element on or off: Click the Chart Elements icon, which is the plus sign near the upper-right corner of the chart when the chart is selected. On the fly-out menu that appears, you can mark or clear the check box for the chart element. There is also a fly-out submenu with the same additional options as on the menu system on the Ribbon. See **Figure 9-18**. By the way, the other two icons nearby are the Chart Styles icon (which provides shortcut access to the various chart styles from the Chart Tools Design tab) and the Chart Filters icon (which enables you to quickly exclude certain data from the chart).

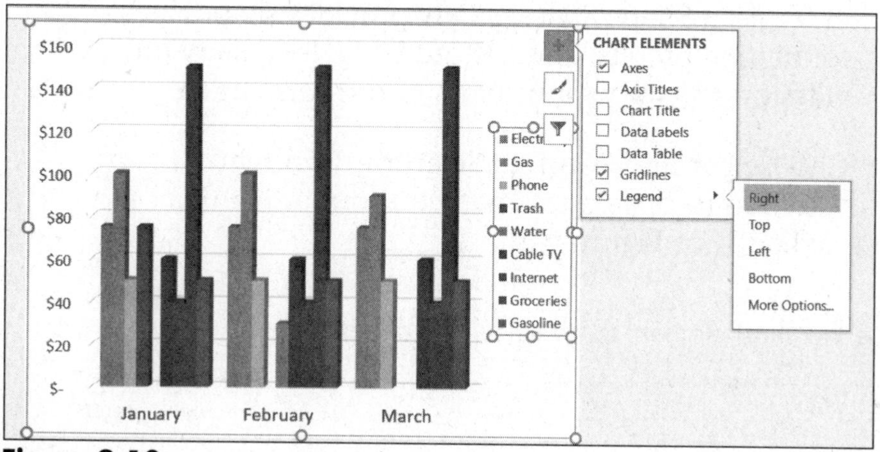

Figure 9-18

Each element of the chart is also selectable for formatting. For example, you can click the legend and then apply formatting to only that.

Sometimes it's difficult to select a tiny element of a chart — and difficult to tell what you selected — so Excel offers some assistance. On the Chart Tools Format tab, the leftmost group is called Current Selection. It has a drop-down list from which you can select a chart element, as an alternative to clicking a chart element to select it.

After you select a chart element, use the tools on the Chart Tools Format tab (shown in **Figure 9-19**) to apply formatting:

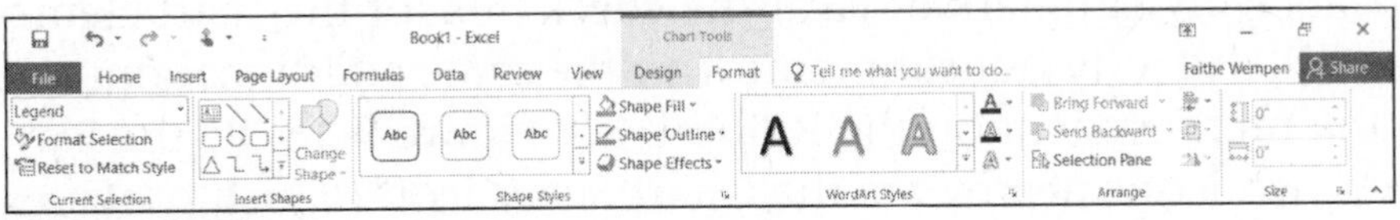

Figure 9-19

- Use any of the controls here to apply a color, border, special effect, or other formatting option to it. For example, a Shape Styles gallery provides shapes and formatting presets, and a WordArt Styles gallery provides presets for various types of text formatting.
- Choose Format ➪ Current Selection ➪ Format Selection to open a task pane for formatting that element. See **Figure 9-20**.

Choose the chart element to be selected from this menu

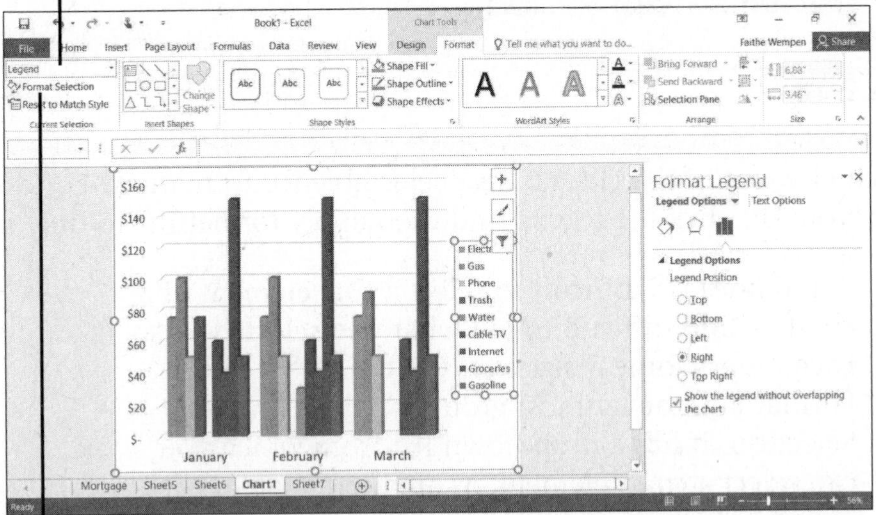

Click Format Selection to open the task pane for that element

Figure 9-20

Alternatively, you can right-click the selected element and choose the format command from the menu that appears. The exact name of the command varies; for example, when a data series is selected and right-clicked, the command is Format Data Series.

When you open the Format task pane for a particular element (select the element and then choose Chart Tools Format⇨Current Selection⇨Format Selection), the choices depend on the type of element. Click one of the icons at the top of the task pane to select a broad category of options, and then double-click headings to expand the options beneath them. Refer to Figure 9-20.

The changes you make in the Format task pane take effect immediately.

Using Excel as a Database

Chapter

10

Besides calculations, the other main reason people use Excel is to store tabular data. For example, Excel works great to store the names and addresses of the people you send holiday cards to every year, or to store a home inventory that you create for insurance purposes.

Although spreadsheet programs like Excel weren't originally created for this purpose, software designers quickly figured out that a lot of people were using Excel to hold lists of data, so they built in features to help do that more effectively. In this chapter, you can read about several Excel 2016 features — such as tables and filtering — for entering and manipulating data.

Get ready to . . .

Understand Databases

A *database* is an organized collection of information about a subject. Examples of databases include an address book, a telephone book, or a home inventory.

Database data is stored in *tables,* which are row-and-column grids. Although Excel isn't a full database program, the row-and-column format of its worksheets is easily adaptable to a simple database.

Each row is a *record:* a set of details about a specific item. For example, a record for a friend in your address book likely contains his name, mailing address, and phone number. A record about a possession in your home could include a name, description, acquisition date, and retail value. Each piece of information you store for each record is a *field.* Field names always appear in the first row of the table. See **Figure 10-1**.

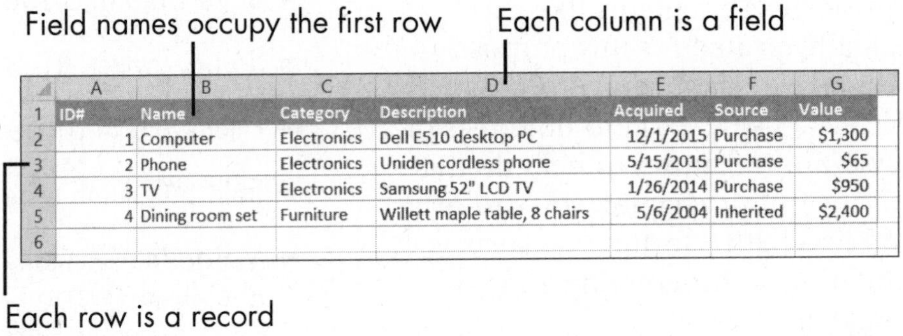

	A	B	C	D	E	F	G
1	ID#	Name	Category	Description	Acquired	Source	Value
2	1	Computer	Electronics	Dell E510 desktop PC	12/1/2015	Purchase	$1,300
3	2	Phone	Electronics	Uniden cordless phone	5/15/2015	Purchase	$65
4	3	TV	Electronics	Samsung 52" LCD TV	1/26/2014	Purchase	$950
5	4	Dining room set	Furniture	Willett maple table, 8 chairs	5/6/2004	Inherited	$2,400
6							

Figure 10-1

Prepare a List for a Mail Merge

One reason why you might create a database in Excel is to store names and addresses for a mail merge — perhaps with a letter you created in Word, for example. (Read all about mail merges in Chapter 6.)

Excel is a great tool for creating such a list. There are just a couple of basic rules:

- The first row (row 1) must contain the field names.
- The data must start immediately beneath the field names (row 2).

When storing lists in Excel, some people like to put a descriptive title in row 1, like "Address Book." That's fine if you're just going to be working in Excel, but it wreaks havoc with a mail merge — so you must delete any such rows in Excel before you use the Excel file for a merge. To delete a row, select it and then choose Home➪Delete.

Store Data in a Table

To create a database in Excel, type the field names in row 1, and then type the records in the subsequent rows. Nothing else is required. You can format the data any way you want it.

However, if you choose to turn a range of cells into a *table* (Excel's term for a database listing), you get some special benefits, such as easy-to-apply automatic formatting and easier sorting and filtering.

A table in Excel is entirely different from a table in Word. In Excel, a table is a range of cells defined as a database structure. In Word, a table is a simple row-and-column grid for holding text.

To convert a range of cells into a table and apply automatic formatting at the same time, follow these steps:

1. Select the range, including the field names in row 1.
2. Choose Home➪Format as Table. A palette of table styles appears. See **Figure 10-2**.
3. Click the desired style. The Format as Table dialog box appears.
4. Confirm the range that appears in the box, and then click OK. Excel applies the formatting, and also sets up the data range as a table.

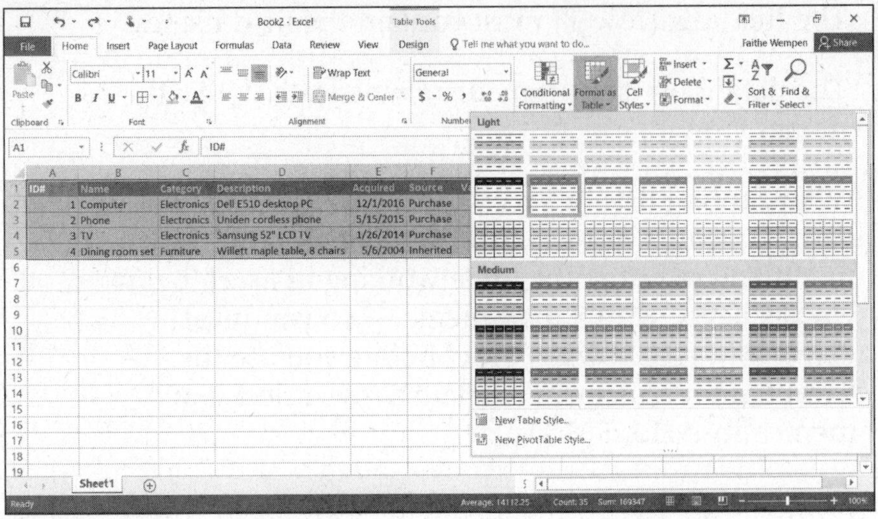

Figure 10-2

If you want just the formatting — and not the other features that a table provides in Excel — choose Table Tools Design ➪ Convert to Range after performing these steps.

Setting up a range as a table has many benefits, including

- **Sorting and filtering:** Click the down arrow that appears next to each field name to open a menu from which you can sort and filter the data easily. (This is covered in more detail later in this chapter.)
- **Automatic table formatting:** Additional records (rows) you add to the table after its initial creation will be automatically formatted in the same way.
- **Other formatting options:** You can apply different formatting at any time with the Table Tools Design ➪ Table Styles gallery. (The Table Tools Design tab is available only when working with a table.)

The drop-down arrow buttons that appear on each field name are for your convenience; you can click one to open a menu for that column for sorting and filtering the data (described later in this chapter). If you don't want to see the arrows, you can turn off their display by choosing Data➪Filter. (That's an on/off toggle; choose that same command again to make the arrow buttons redisplay.)

If you ever want to revert to a regular range (as opposed to a table), you can easily convert the data back to normal cells. Click anywhere in the table and choose Table Tools Design➪Convert to Range.

Sort a Table

Sorting rearranges the order of the records to meet criteria you specify. For example, you might sort an address list on the person's last name or city.

If you convert the range to a table, as in the previous section, each column heading has a drop-down arrow button on it. Click that arrow to open a menu. From that menu, you can choose to Sort A to Z or Sort Z to A on that column. See **Figure 10-3**.

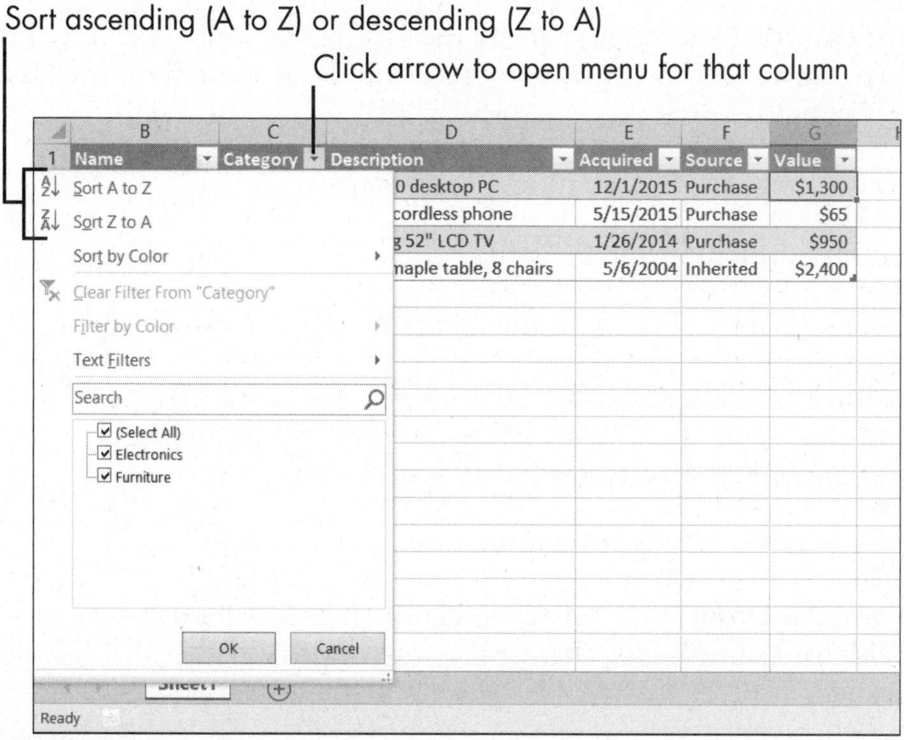

Figure 10-3

If you don't want to use the drop-down menu on the column, you can instead click anywhere in the column and use buttons on the Ribbon:

- Home ⇨ Sort & Filter ⇨ Sort Smallest to Largest (A to Z)
- Home ⇨ Sort & Filter ⇨ Sort Largest to Smallest (Z to A)
- Data ⇨ Sort A to Z
- Data ⇨ Sort Z to A

Not all of these commands are available on every field's menu. Columns with numeric values show Smallest to Largest and Largest to Smallest, whereas columns with text values show Sort A to Z and Sort Z to A.

The method I just showed you works great for single-field sorts. Sometimes, though, you might want a multifield sort, in which you sort the list by one field, and then if two or more records have the same value for that field, another field is the tie-breaker.

For example, you might sort by the Last Name field; and if two people have the same last name, you break the tie by sorting on the First Name field.

To do a multilevel sort, follow these steps:

1. Click anywhere inside the table.
2. Choose Data ⇨ Sort, or Home ⇨ Sort & Filter ⇨ Custom Sort.
3. In the Sort dialog box that opens, open the Sort By list and choose the field by which to sort first. For example, you might sort an address list by Last Name.
4. Leave the Sort On box set to Values.
5. Leave the Order box set to the default (A to Z for a text field, for example), or change it to the opposite order if desired.

The choices in the Order box depend on the type of data. For example, if the field holds dates, your choices are Oldest to Newest or Newest to Oldest.

6. Click the Add Level button to add another set of controls. See **Figure 10-4**.

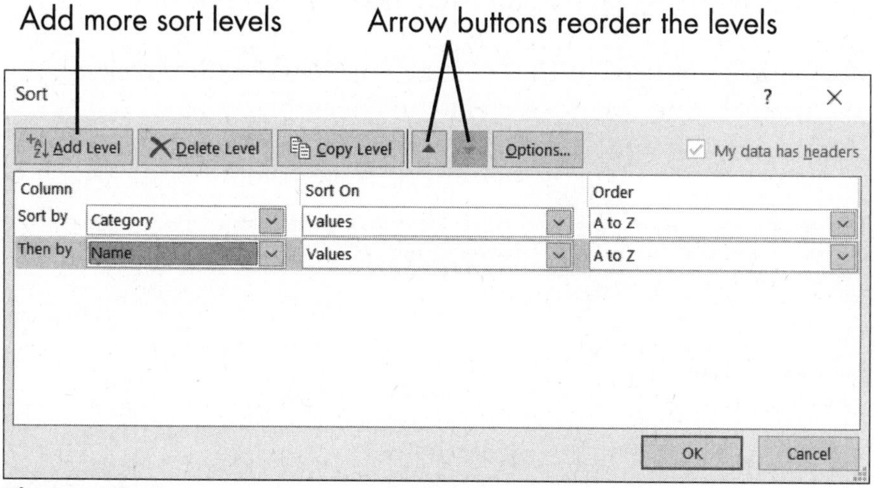

Figure 10-4

7. Repeat Steps 3–5 to complete the second set of controls.

8. Add other levels if needed. When you're finished, click OK.

You can sort a regular range of cells (that is, not a table), but you have to select the entire range before performing the sort. It's much easier if you convert the range to a table first, as I show you how to do earlier in this chapter.

Filter Data in a Table

Filtering data enables you to temporarily hide certain records so that the ones you do want to see become easier to find. Filtering is based on criteria that you specify. For example, you might want to see only items of a certain category or only people who live in a certain state.

The simplest way to filter is to choose which of the existing values for a particular column to include. Follow these steps:

1. Click the down-arrow button to the right of the column name to open its menu.

   If you don't see down-arrow buttons on the column names, choose Data ➪ Filter to make them appear.

2. A list of all the entries in that column appears, with check boxes for each one. Mark or clear the check boxes as needed to choose which values to include. See **Figure 10-5**.

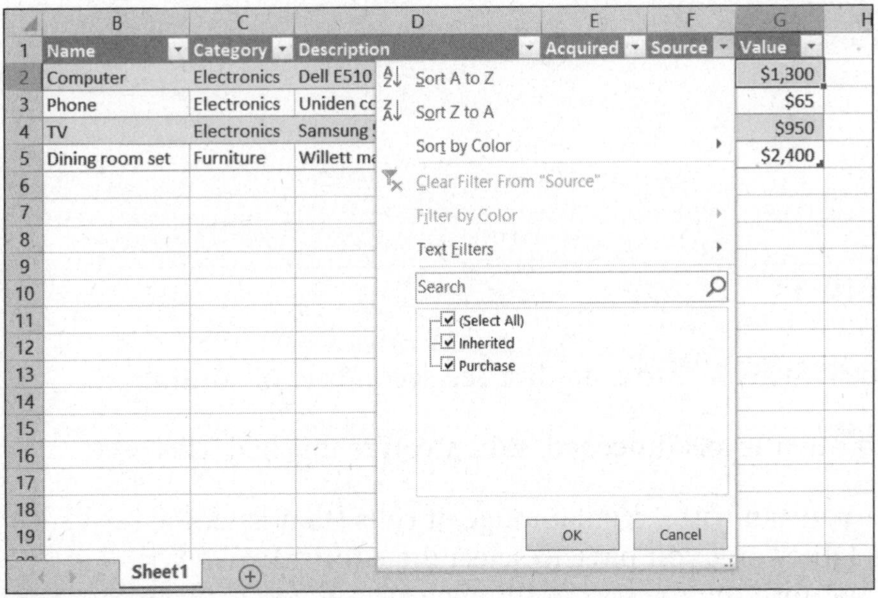

Figure 10-5

3. Click OK at the bottom of the menu. The list is filtered as you specified.

   If you want to turn off the filtering, you can do any of the following:

   - Reopen the menu and mark the Select All check box.
   - Choose Data ➪ Clear.

- Choose Data ⇨ Filter to toggle off the filtering (and also the down-arrow buttons).

Choose Data ⇨ Filter again to turn the button display back on.

If your filtering needs are more complex than a simple inclusion or exclusion, use one of the filters from the Text Filters submenu. (Well, it's Text Filters if that field contains text; otherwise it's Date Filters, Number Filters, or whatever is appropriate for the field type.)

Follow these steps to use a filter from the submenu:

1. Click the down-arrow button to the right of the column name to open its menu.

   If you don't see down-arrow buttons on the column names, choose Data ⇨ Filter to make them appear.

2. Depending on the field type, the command you want next will have different names. To open a submenu, point to the appropriate command:

   - *Text fields:* Text filters
   - *Numeric fields:* Number filters
   - *Date fields:* Date filters

3. Choose the filter that most closely matches what you want to do. For example, if you're working with a Date field, after pointing to Date Filters in Step 2, you might choose Before. See **Figure 10-6**.

4. The Custom AutoFilter dialog box appears for you to finish filling in the desired filter information. For example, if you choose Before in Step 3, it looks like **Figure 10-7**, prompting you to specify the date that all included records must be prior to.

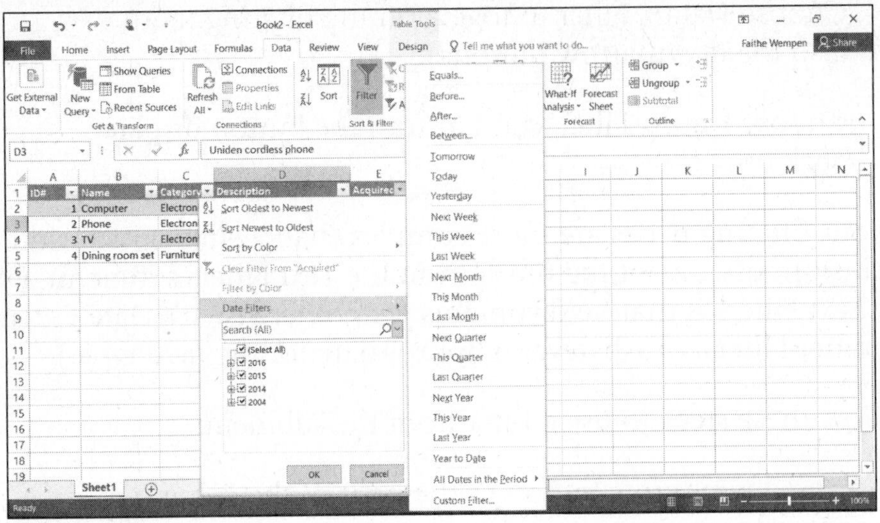

Figure 10-6

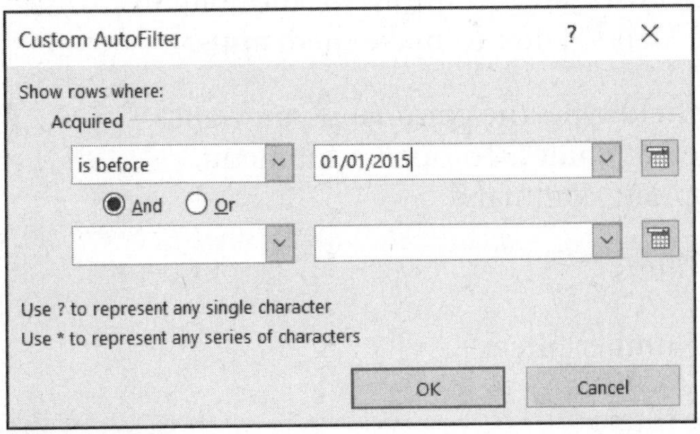

Figure 10-7

5. Type the value you want.

   Depending on the field type, helpers might also be available. For example, in Figure 10-7, you can click the Date Selector button to open a calendar from which you can choose a date.

6. Click OK. The filter is applied to the table.

   To remove the filter, choose Data ➪ Clear, or reopen the field's drop-down list and choose Clear Filter from *fieldname*.

Split a Column's Content

As you're entering data into Excel, you might not give much thought to how that data will be used later. For example, when entering people's names, perhaps you used a Name field that contained both the first and last name of each person, as in **Figure 10-8**.

You can't sort by last name if first and last names aren't in separate fields

	A	B
1	**Name**	**Phone**
2	Sidney Rhoades	317-555-8882
3	Pamela Shelton	317-555-2828
4	Michelle Brick	309-555-1112
5	Roger Findlay	309-555-4422
6		

Figure 10-8

Suppose that you then decide that you want to sort the list by the last name of the person. You can't do that with the data shown in Figure 10-8 because sorting takes place according to the first characters in the cell, and that's the *first* name.

Your best bet is to split the content into two separate cells, so that every field you want to sort or filter on is in its own separate cell. If there are only a few names, like in Figure 10-8, you could easily retype them. But what if there were hundreds?

Excel offers a feature called Text to Columns that can do a split for you automatically. It requires there to be a consistent indicator of where the split should occur, though: a *delimiter*. For example, in Figure 10-8, each first and last name are separated by a space, so the space is the consistent delimiter (separator) character.

The Text to Columns feature doesn't work on data that's in a table in Excel. If your data is in a table (from previous work in this chapter), convert it back to a range with the Table Tools Design ⇨ Convert to Range command before you go any further.

Have a look at the column you want to split, and decide what the delimiter character is. Then follow these steps:

1. Make sure there is an empty column to the right of the one you are going to split. Insert a new column if needed (by choosing Home ⇨ Insert ⇨ Insert Sheet Columns). For example, in Figure 10-8 you would insert a new column between columns A and B.
2. Select the range containing the data you want to split. In Figure 10-8, for example, the range would be A2:A5.
3. Choose Data ⇨ Text to Columns. The Convert Text to Columns Wizard Step 1 of 3 dialog box opens.
4. Leave the Delimited option selected and then click Next.
5. In the next page of the wizard, select the appropriate check boxes to indicate what delimiter character(s) to use. (For example, in **Figure 10-9**, Space is chosen as the only allowed delimiter character.) Then click Next.
6. In the final page of the wizard, leave the default choices for field types and destinations, and then click Finish. Excel splits the data into the adjacent blank column. **Figure 10-10** shows the split data from Figure 10-8.
7. Type a new field name in the first row of the new column, and change the field name for the split column if needed. For example, in Figure 10-10, I might change the text in cell A1 to *First,* and I might type *Last* in A2.

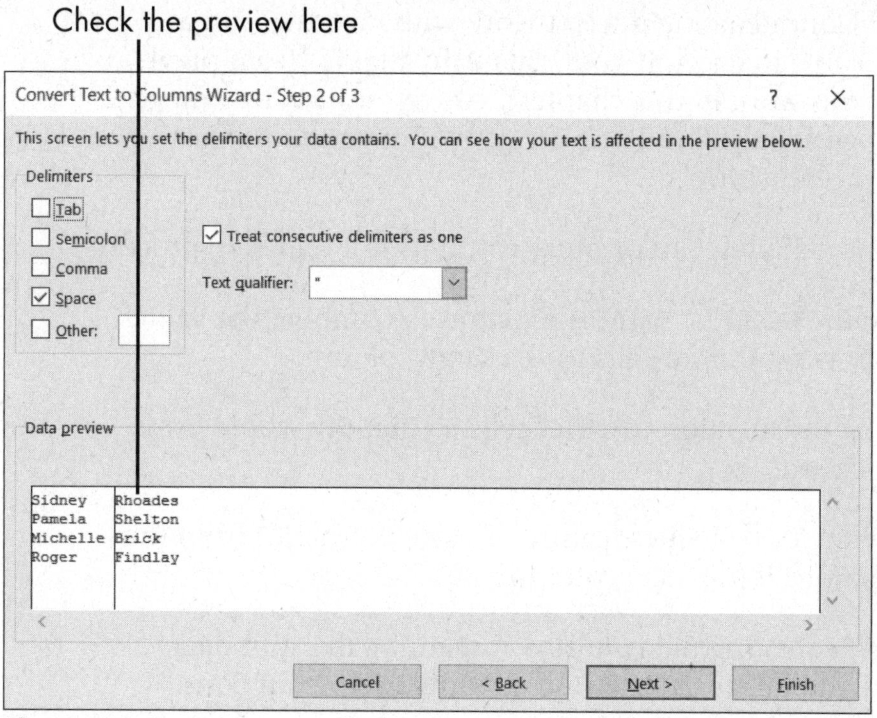

Figure 10-9

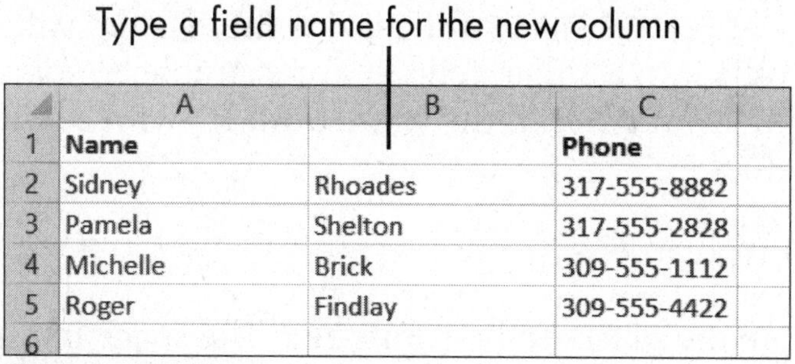

Figure 10-10

Merge the Contents of Columns

You can start with data in two columns (first and last names, for example) and then combine all the data in one column. The process of combining the columns is *merging,* or *concatenating*.

Concatenating doesn't work with data that's in a table in Excel. If your data is in a table (from previous work in this chapter), convert it back to a range with the Table Tools Design ➪ Convert to Range command.

Concatenating two or more columns is a four-step process:

1. Use the =CONCATENATE function to combine the values from two or more cells in the same column.
2. Copy the function to other cells so that the whole list is processed.
3. Use the Paste Values feature to paste the values from the functions into a new column.
4. Delete the original columns containing the split data, and you delete the column containing the functions.

Here's the process in detail.

In the first step, the =CONCATENATE function combines the values from two or more cells into a single cell. So, for example, if you want to combine the value from A2 with the value from B2 with a space between the two values:

```
=CONCATENATE(A2," ",B2)
```

The commas separate the pieces to be combined. The space in quotation marks (" ") creates the space between the two values.

After creating the function, copy it into the other cells in that column. You can use any of the standard copying methods to do this, including the Copy and Paste buttons on the Home tab, the Copy and Paste shortcut keys (Ctrl+C and Ctrl+V), or dragging the fill handle (the black square in the bottom-right corner of the selected cell).

Now you have a concatenated column, but you also have a problem: You can't delete the original two columns because the functions are based on their contents. You could hide them, but that would make it awkward later when you added new records.

To work around this problem, you can use the Paste Values feature to copy the value (that is, the result) of the formula to yet another new column. Then you can delete both the original columns and the column containing the function. Follow these steps:

1. If the column to the right of the one containing the functions is not empty, insert a new blank column there.
2. Select the range of cells that contain the `CONCATENATE` functions.
3. Copy them (press Ctrl+C or choose Home⇨Copy).
4. Click in the first cell where you want to begin pasting the values.
5. On the Home tab, click the down arrow under the Paste button, opening a menu.
6. Click the first icon in the Paste Values section.
7. Select and delete the columns that contained the original data and the column that contained the `CONCATENATE` functions. (Choose Home⇨Delete.)

Part IV
Outlook

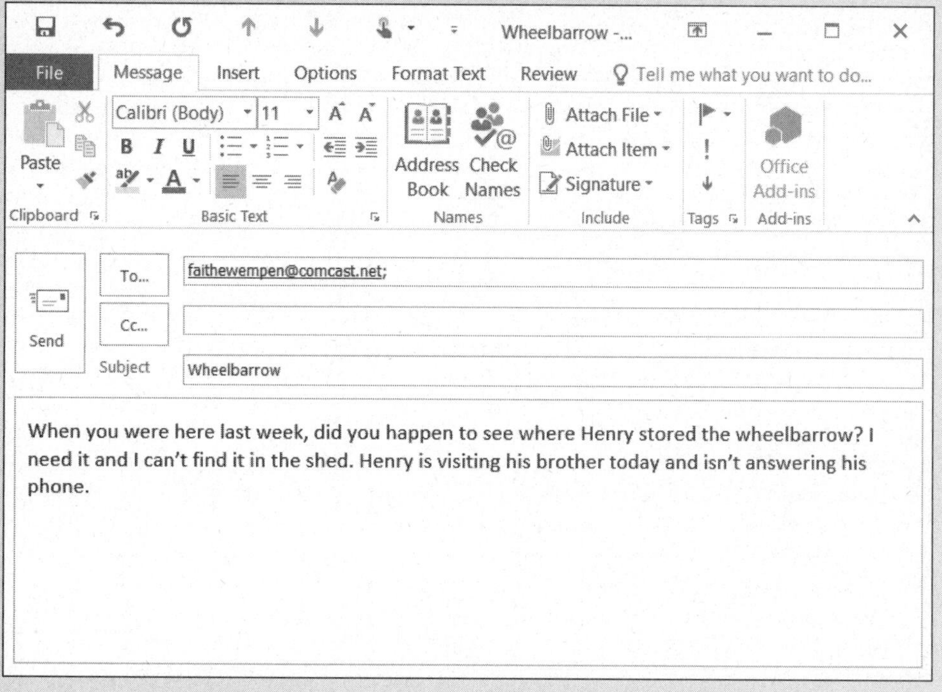

web extras

For a guide to organizing your mail in Outlook, visit `www.dummies.com/extras/office2016forseniors`.

Managing Email with Outlook

Chapter 11

Get ready to . . .

Outlook is a multipurpose program. It's an address book, a calendar, a to-do list, and an email-handling program, all in one.

The most popular Outlook feature, of course, is email. Millions of people use Outlook as their primary email-handling program, and for good reason! Outlook is fast, full-featured, and easy to use and customize.

In this chapter, I show you how to set up an email account in Outlook and then how to use it to send and receive email. I also explain some common email pitfalls and scams and tell you how you can avoid them.

Set Up Outlook for the First Time

The first time you start Outlook, you're prompted to set up your email account. The following steps walk you through the process.

1. Start Outlook. (Open the Start menu, type Outlook, and then click Outlook 2016 in the search results.)
2. If this is the first time you started Outlook, the Welcome to Microsoft Outlook 2016 dialog box opens. Click Next.

If you don't see that dialog box, someone might have already started Outlook on this PC before. Just skip to the next section.

3. At the E-Mail Accounts screen, you're asked whether you want to configure an email account. You do, so click Next.

4. In the Add Account dialog box that opens (see **Figure 11-1**), fill in your details, and then click Next. (You are not really creating a new account; you are just setting up your existing email account in Outlook.)

Passwords appear as asterisks for better security

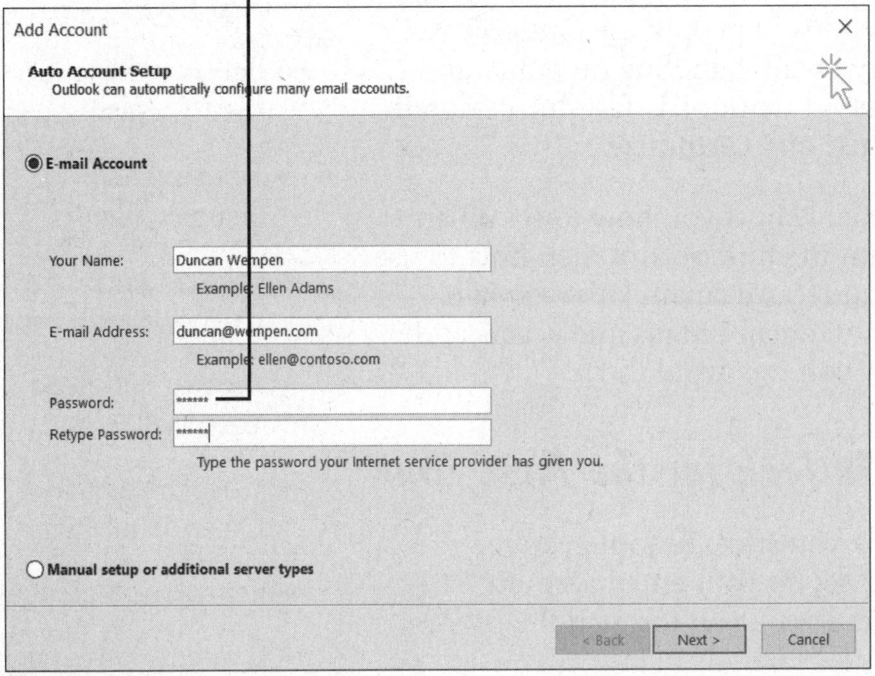

Figure 11-1

Outlook attempts to determine the name of your mail server and then contact it to set up your accounts, using an encrypted connection.

- *If the encrypted connection works,* a message appears telling you so.

- *If the encrypted connection doesn't work,* a message to that effect appears. Click Next, and it tries to connect unencrypted.

If Outlook can determine the right settings (and it does in most cases), it logs into the mail server and sends a test message to you. Wait while all this goes on.

5. Check to make sure Outlook correctly detected the account type. You should see a message like "Your *account type* account has been successfully configured."
6. Click Finish.

If the test message fails, see the upcoming section, "Troubleshoot Mail Setup Problems."

Set Up Additional Mail Accounts

If you have other email accounts, you can set them up in Outlook, too. If you have a separate account for a home-based business or hobby, for example, you might want to be able to get the mail for that address at the same time you retrieve the mail for your main account.

To set up another mail account (or to set up your first one, if you didn't do that when you started Outlook for the first time), follow these steps:

1. Choose File⇨Account Settings⇨Account Settings. The Account Settings dialog box opens.
2. On the E-Mail tab, click New. The Add Account dialog box appears. It is the same as the one shown in Figure 11-1.
3. Fill in the information for the account. Then click Next.
4. Complete the setup by following the prompts that appear.

If you have any trouble with the setup, or the test message doesn't go through, see the next section.

5. When you finish setting up the account, click Close to close the Account Settings dialog box.

Troubleshoot Mail Setup Problems

Each email service has its own quirks in how the account has to be set up in Outlook (or any mail program) to properly send and receive. Outlook can automatically detect the settings in many cases, but it can't always detect every service correctly.

If Outlook wasn't able to successfully send a test message, you need to do some troubleshooting. Don't panic, though. It's not that difficult. If you get stuck, you can always call your ISP's tech support line and get help.

If you're using a Web-based email provider, it might not work with Outlook. Some services have work-arounds that you can follow to make them work in Outlook; check the tech support section at the Web site where you get your Web-based mail to see whether there is anything you can do.

To troubleshoot mail problems, make sure you have the following information handy. If you don't have it, contact your ISP. It might also be available on the ISP's Web site.

- **Your email address and password:** You probably have this already from your earlier attempt.
- **The incoming and outgoing mail server addresses:** They both might be the same.

The *server address* is usually whatever comes after the @ sign in your email address, preceded by the word *mail*. For example, if your email address is `tom@myprovider.com`, the mail server might be `mail.myprovider.com`. If there are separate servers for incoming and outgoing mail, the incoming one might be `pop.myprovider.com`, and the outgoing one might be `smtp.myprovider.com`. Those are just guesses, though; you will need to get that information from your ISP.

- **Information about whether an encrypted connection should be used.**
- **Information about whether your outgoing mail server requires authentication:** And if so, whether the outgoing server requires a different username and password than your regular one.

Armed with all that information, do the following to troubleshoot:

1. Choose File➪Account Settings➪Account Settings. The Account Options dialog box opens.
2. Double-click the email account you want to troubleshoot. The Change Account dialog box opens.
3. Check all the information in the dialog box to make sure that it matches the information you have about your mail account. In particular, check the Account Type, Incoming Mail Server, and Outgoing Mail Server (SMTP).

   You might not be able to change the account type. If you can't, and it's wrong, you will need to delete that account from Outlook and set it up again, as if it were a new account.

4. Mark or clear the Require Login Using Secure Password Authentication (SPA) check box, whichever is different from the current setting. Then click Test Account Settings to see whether that fixed the problem. If it didn't, go back to the original setting.

5. Click More Settings. On the Outgoing Server tab, mark the My Outgoing Server (SMTP) Requires Authentication check box. See **Figure 11-2**. Click OK and then click Test Account Settings to check whether it helped.

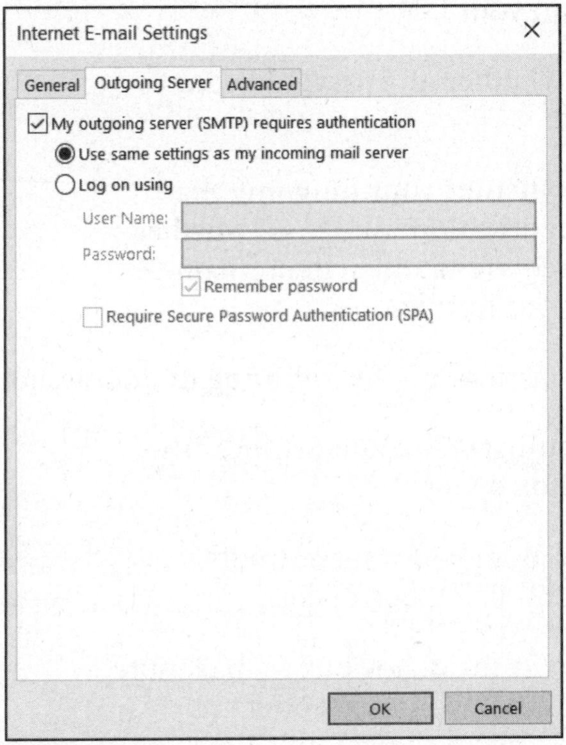

Figure 11-2

For the username, use your complete email address. If that doesn't work, try using only the part of your email address before the @ sign. Try it with the Require Secure Password Authentication (SPA) check box cleared, and then try it with that check box marked.

6. Click More Settings again. On the Outgoing Server tab, choose Log On Using, and then enter your user name and password in the boxes provided. Click OK and then click Test Account Settings to try again.

7. Click More Settings again. On the Advanced tab, check the Incoming server and Outgoing server port numbers

to make sure they match the port numbers recommended by your ISP for your account.

8. On the Advanced tab, drag the Server Timeouts slider closer to the word *Long* (that is, farther to the right). This can help give more time to a mail server that is slow to respond. A timeout delay of more than two minutes isn't usually needed. Then click OK, and click Test Account Settings.

9. If you got Outlook to successfully complete a test message, great. Close all dialog boxes.

   If not, contact your email service provider's tech support and find out what setting you need to change to make it work.

Take a Quick Tour of Outlook's Mail Feature

After you configure Outlook for email, take a quick look around the Outlook interface as it pertains to email. **Figure 11-3** points out the following features:

- **Navigation pane:** This pane shows different things, depending on the part of Outlook you're working with. When working with mail, it shows the Mail Folders list. (See Figure 11-3.) You can move to a different folder by clicking its name here.

- **Inbox:** Whatever folder is selected on the Mail Folders list appears here. In Figure 11-3, that's the Inbox. New mail arrives in the Inbox, so it's the folder you work with most of the time.

- **Reading pane:** Whatever email message is selected in the Inbox appears here in preview. That way, you don't have to open each message (by double-clicking it) to see what it contains.

By default, the Reading pane appears to the right of the Inbox. You can have it appear below the Inbox window, though; choose View➪Reading Pane➪Bottom.

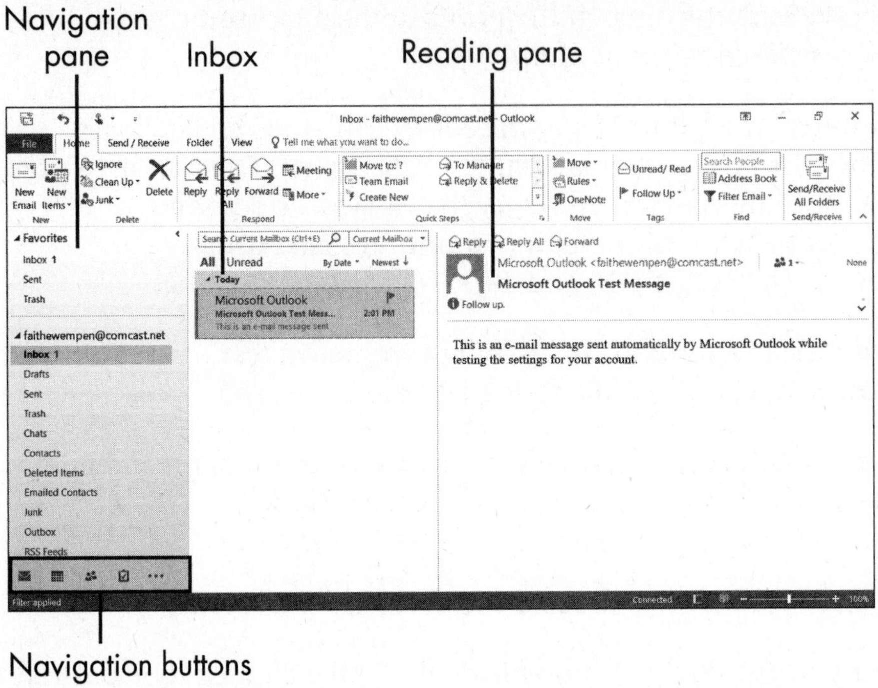

Figure 11-3

The Navigation pane and Reading pane can be turned on or off from the View tab. Also on the View tab you can turn the To-Do bar or the People pane on and off. (Neither of these are on by default.)

- **Navigation buttons:** At the bottom of the Navigation pane are a series of buttons for moving to different parts of the Outlook program. The left-most one (the envelope) represents Mail, in which you are now working. The others shown in Figure 11-3, from left to right, are Calendar, People, and To-Do List. To access additional icons, click the ellipsis (. . .) for a pop-up menu of the other areas: Notes, Folders, and Shortcuts.

Receive and Read Your Mail

After you configure your email account(s) in Outlook, receiving mail is an automatic process. Outlook automatically sends and receives mail when you start it, and also at 30-minute intervals whenever Outlook is running. Your incoming mail comes automatically into the Inbox folder.

You can also initiate a manual send/receive operation at any time. Just click the Send/Receive All Folders button on the Quick Access toolbar (Directly above the File tab) or press F9.

Here's how to change the interval at which Outlook automatically sends and receives mail.

1. Choose Send/Receive ➪ Send/Receive Groups ➪ Define Send/Receive Groups; or press Ctrl+Alt+S.
2. In the text box next to the Schedule an Automatic Send/Receive Every check box (which should be marked), change the number of minutes for the interval. See **Figure 11-4**.
3. Click Close.

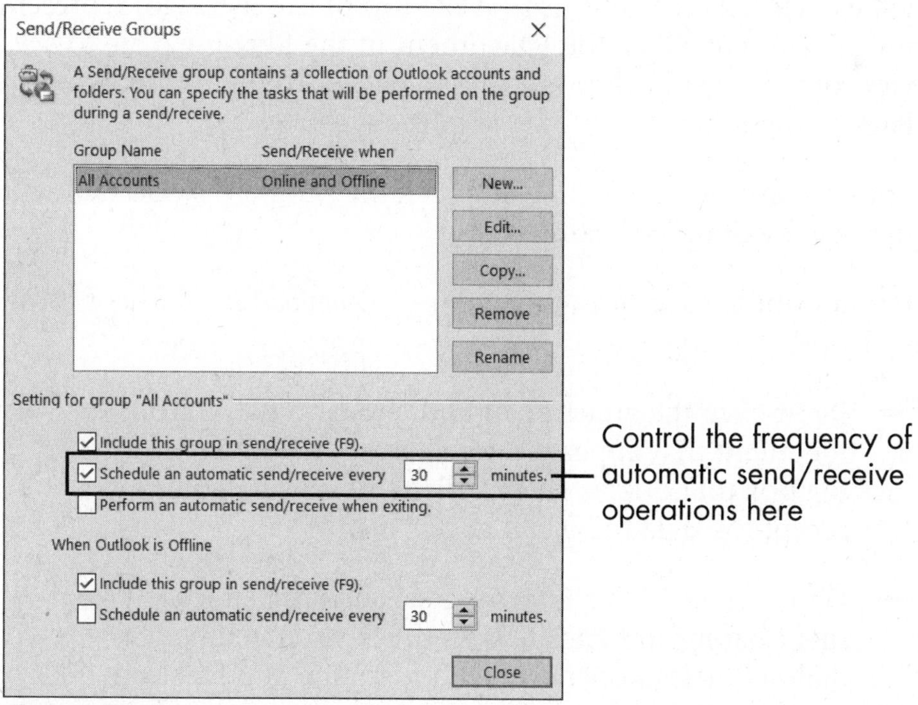

Figure 11-4

To read a message, click it in the Inbox. Its content appears in the Reading pane. Many people read their mail exclusively in the Reading pane, and never "open" a message formally. To open a message (that is, to display it in its own window), double-click it.

View Photos and Other Attachments

Email messages can contain file attachments. The most common type of attachment is a photo; family members can send you photos that they took with their digital cameras, for example.

Some types of attachments can carry viruses. (Pictures are generally safe, though.) If you have any doubts about the safety of any file you receive, *do not open it.* At the end of this chapter are some tips for discerning which attachments are risky.

You can tell that a message has an attachment by the paper clip icon next to it in the Inbox, as shown in **Figure 11-5**. Then in the Reading pane, note the icon and text (at the top of the message) representing the attachment. Click the attachment in the Reading pane to see a preview of it. To get back to the message itself in the Reading pane, click Back to message.

You can also open the attachment in the program associated with its file type by double-clicking it.

If you want to save the attachment — *download it* — any of these ways will work:

- Right-click the attachment and choose Save As from the menu that appears. In the Save Attachment dialog box that opens, enter a filename and location, or accept the defaults. Then click Save.

- Choose File⇨Save Attachments, click the attachment name, and click OK. In the Save Attachment dialog box that opens, enter a filename and location, or accept the defaults. Then click Save.

- Double-click the attachment to open it in the program associated with its file type. Then save the file from there, using that program's Save command (probably File➪Save As or some variation of that).

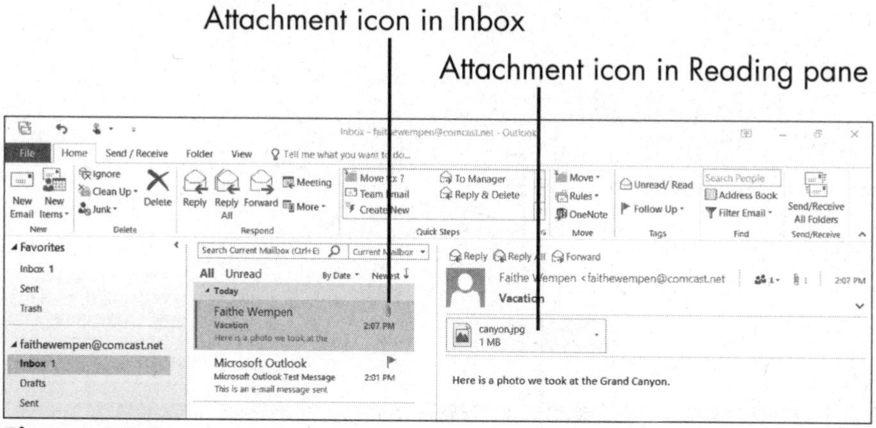

Figure 11-5

Reply to a Message

Replying to a message is quick and easy because you don't have to look up the recipient's email address. It's already filled in for you.

To reply to a message, click the Reply button (either the one at the top of the Preview pane or on the Home tab), or press Ctrl+R. A reply draft is generated in the Preview pane, with the original message quoted in the body of the message and the original sender's email address in the To field. See **Figure 11-6**. Type your reply, and then click Send to send your reply.

Clicking the Reply All button sends the reply to the original sender plus any other original recipients (other than you).

Using Reply All is useful for an ongoing email discussion with a group of people. Be careful, though, that you don't accidentally use Reply All and send a sensitive message to a wider audience than you intended.

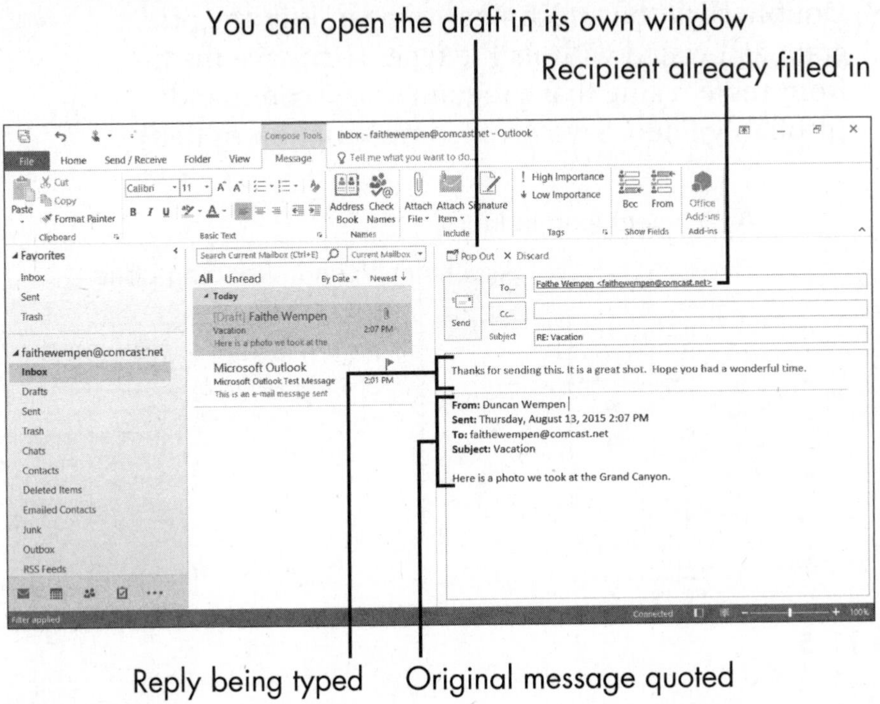

Figure 11-6

Earlier versions of Outlook opened a separate window when composing a reply. If you want to work in a separate window instead of the Preview pane, click Pop out at the top of the Preview pane.

Compose a Message

When you compose a new email message, you (not Outlook) fill in every piece of information: the recipient(s), the subject, and the body. Unlike with replying (see the preceding section), none of that information is filled in for you automatically.

- **Recipient:** This is the information in the To field. You need the email address of each person you want to send your message to. The Contacts section of Outlook provides storage for email addresses; Chapter 12 addresses the Contacts list. For now, though, assume that you know the address and will type it in.

- **Subject:** You can type anything you want as the subject (or nothing at all), but your recipients will be appreciative if you keep the subject descriptive and to the point.

- **Body:** This is the main part of the message. It can be plain or formatted text.

You can format the text in the message using the formatting controls on the Ribbon. These are the same as the formatting controls in Word. Read all about Word formatting in Part II of this book.

To compose an email message, follow these steps:

1. Click the Home tab and then click the New E-Mail button, or press Ctrl+N.

2. In the new message window that appears, type the email address(es) for the recipient(s) in the To field.

   If you have more than one recipient, separate the addresses with a comma.

3. (Optional) To send a courtesy copy to someone other than a main recipient, type the email address in the Cc (carbon copy) field.

   You can also send a blind carbon copy (Bcc) to someone. A Bcc differs from a regular Cc in that none of the other recipients see the Bcc person's name listed. To send a Bcc, click the To or Cc button, opening a Select Names box. At the bottom of that box is a Bcc line. Type the cloaked recipient's address there.

4. (Optional) If you have more than one email account set up in Outlook, click the From button and select the account from which you want to send. The From button isn't present unless you have more than one email account set up.

5. Type a subject in the Subject line.

6. Type the message body in the body area (below the Subject line). **Figure 11-7** shows a message ready to send.

7. Click Send to send the message.

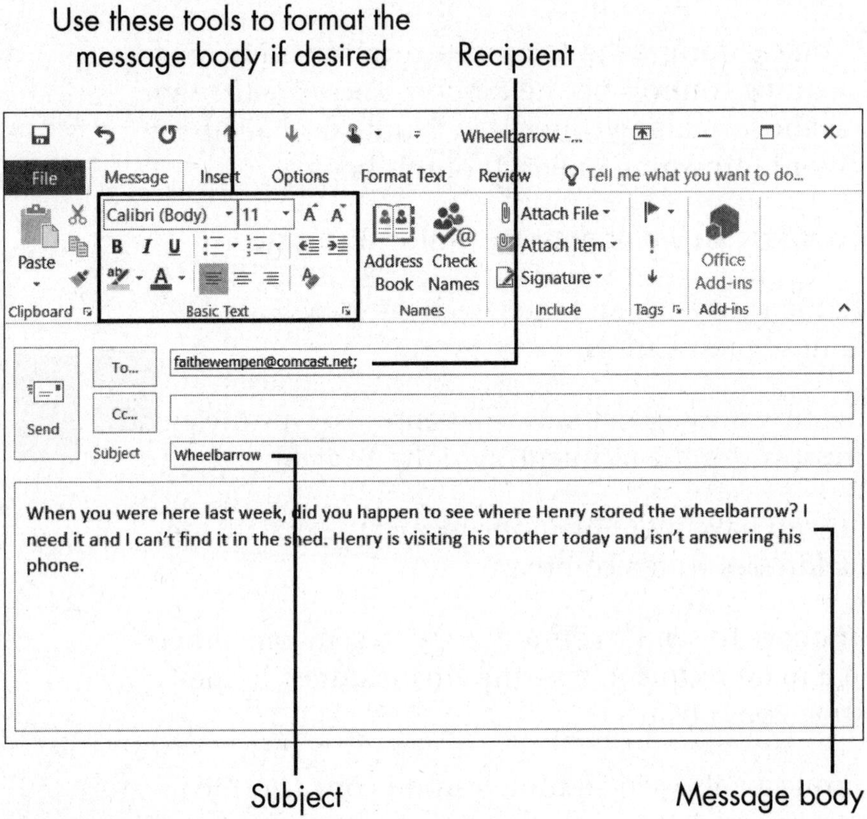

Figure 11-7

To apply basic text formatting to the message body, use the tools in the Basic Text group on the Message tab. For more advanced formatting tools, see the Format Text tab.

When you send a message, it's immediately moved to your Outbox folder. There it waits until the next Send/Receive operation. You can send it immediately by clicking Send/Receive on the toolbar, or let it go out during the next scheduled Send/Receive.

If you click Send and then immediately realize you made a mistake and want to call back the message, here's the fix:

1. Double-click the Outbox folder in the folder list at the left.
2. Immediately double-click the unsent message to open it. As long you have the unsent message open, it won't be sent. With the unsent message open, you can edit it or delete it.

If Outlook won't let you open it because it already started transmitting, do the following:

1. Click the Send/Receive indicator in the bottom-right corner of the Outlook window to open a menu.
2. From that menu, choose Cancel Send/Receive as quickly as you can.

Another workaround is to quickly exit from Outlook. A prompt will appear that you still have messages in your Outbox; click Yes to exit anyway. Then disable your Internet connection before you reopen Outlook.

Attach a File to a Message

You might sometimes want to send files from your own computer to other people via email attachment, such as a photo, a document, or a spreadsheet. It's easy to do!

As you compose the email message (or reply to a message), click the Attach File button to open a menu, and then click Browse This PC (to browse locally) or Browse Web Locations and then click OneDrive (to browse your OneDrive).

Either way, the Insert File dialog box opens. From here, you can navigate to the file you want and then click Insert. The attachment appears on the Attached field in the message composition window. See **Figure 11-8**.

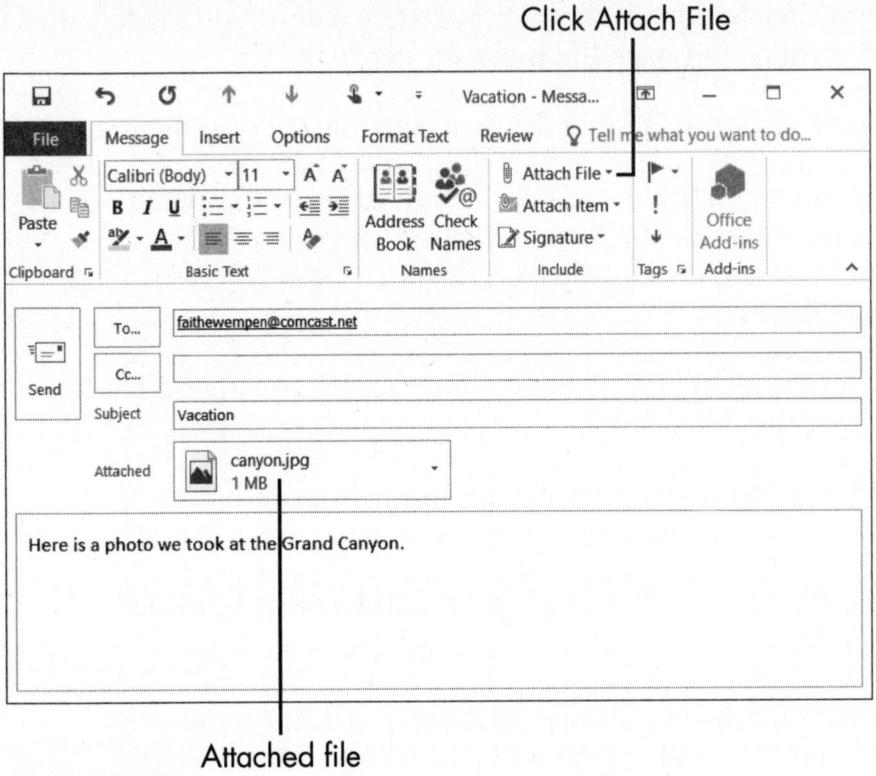

Figure 11-8

If you change your mind about sending that attachment, you can delete it from the message by selecting it and pressing the Delete key.

Avoid Frauds, Scams, and Viruses

You might have heard horror stories about people whose computers became infected with viruses, worms, and all sorts of other nasty things, and who had to pay a lot of money to get it cleaned up — if they could. These stories are real, and so is the threat. However, you can do some very basic things to minimize your exposure to such risks.

First, look at what the threats are:

- **Spoofing/phishing:** These legitimate-looking email messages contain bogus links to Web sites that can trick you into providing confidential information, such as passwords and bank account data. Thieves then use this information to steal your identity and empty your bank accounts.

- **Viruses:** These *executable* files (that is, program files) do destructive things to your computer, such as delete files or corrupt a disk. Watch out for files with an `.exe` extension.

- **Worms:** These program files or scripts use your computer to send out mass-mailings of spam without your knowledge or consent.

- **Exploits:** These program files or scripts target weaknesses in your computer's security to use it to send out spam or do other harmful things. These usually come from hidden utilities built into some Web sites.

- **Spyware:** These hidden programs spy on your usage habits (including passwords you type, in some cases) and report them back to their owner via the Internet.

- **Adware:** These hidden programs pop up ads on your screen, or change the behavior of your Web browser to display its own ads.

- **Unwanted search toolbars:** These add-on toolbars replace your default search tools with the search database sponsored by a certain company, so that the results of your searches bring up their sponsored sites.

Those are the threats you face. Now, look at how to face them down. Here are my top ten tips:

- Windows comes with a basic antivirus program (Windows Defender), but you might want to get a more full-featured one that includes email scanning. Two of the most popular are Symantec (Norton) Antivirus and McAfee VirusScan.

- Most full-featured antivirus programs include incoming and outgoing email scanning. Keep that feature turned on. It will protect you from most viruses and worms attached to emails.
- If you get an email with an attachment, be suspicious of it. Do not open the attachment until you verify the following:
  - Is the attachment from someone you know?
  - Were you expecting a file from that person?

  If the answer to either question is No, contact the person who sent it to you and find out what it is before you open it.
- Never open any attachments that have any of these extensions (file types): EXE, COM, BAT, VBS.
- If you get an email with an attachment with a ZIP extension, be extra suspicious. (A ZIP file contains other files.) One common worm infection distributes itself in a ZIP file that's marked as an online greeting card, for example.
- If you get an email message that appears to be from your bank or a government office, be very suspicious. Most banks and government offices don't do important business via email. Instead, go directly to the organization's Web site by typing its address into your Web browser. Whatever you do, *do not click the link in the message.*
- If you get an email message that appears to be from PayPal or eBay, be suspicious. These companies do sometimes send out legitimate emails, but phishing sites often impersonate those sites. Go directly to PayPal or eBay via your Web browser; *do not click the links in the emails.*

If a message from PayPal or eBay doesn't address you by name, it's more likely to be a fake. However, this isn't a reliable way to tell.

- If you're not sure about a link in an email, point the mouse pointer to the link. A ScreenTip appears showing the actual address that the link is pointing to. If it doesn't match the text on the link, it's probably a fake.

- Some unwanted search toolbars trick you into installing them as you install other software. You can usually get rid of them via Control Panel in Windows. (Right-click Start and click Control Panel and then under the Programs heading, click Uninstall a program. Scroll through the list of installed programs there and look for anything with *toolbar* in the name — and remove it.

The Yahoo! and Google toolbars are okay to keep; these are legitimate.

Managing the Details: Contacts, Notes, and Tasks

Chapter

12

Get ready to . . .

Outlook has a lot more to offer than just email! Outlook is a full-fledged, personal information management program. It does a great job as an address book, a to-do list, and a storage cache for all the miscellaneous info that you might have "organized" on sticky notes all over your desk. Whatever information you need to organize, Outlook can help.

In this chapter, I show you how to use the Contacts part of Outlook to store and look up names and addresses, both email and postal mailing addresses. It's a handy substitute for a standard paper address book. I also introduce you to the Tasks list (which helps you prioritize and manage your responsibilities) and the Notes database (where you can store everything from confirmation numbers for your next vacation to passwords for the Web sites you visit).

Store Contact Information

Outlook refers to the information you store about people and organizations as *contact information,* and stores it in a folder called Contacts. To access the Contacts folder, click the Contacts icon (which looks like two people) in the bottom-left corner of the Outlook window.

The Contacts folder, shown in **Figure 12-1**, shows each contact that you've entered.

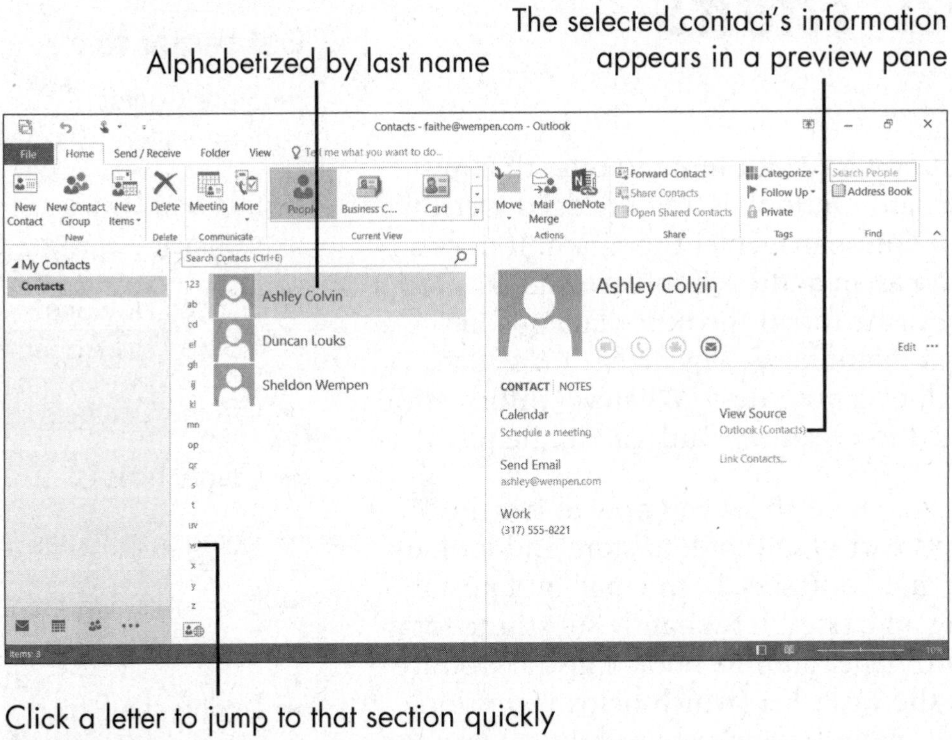

Figure 12-1

Although Figure 12-1 shows several contacts, you don't have any when you start out. You must enter each one individually.

To store someone's contact information, follow these steps:

1. From the Contacts window, click the New Contact button in the upper-left corner. A new Untitled – Contact window appears.

   In step 1, you can also choose Home ➪ New Contact or press Ctrl+N to start a new contact.

2. Fill in the information you want to store for the person or organization. You can fill in as much or as little as you like. **Figure 12-2** shows an example.

File As determines how it will be alphabetized

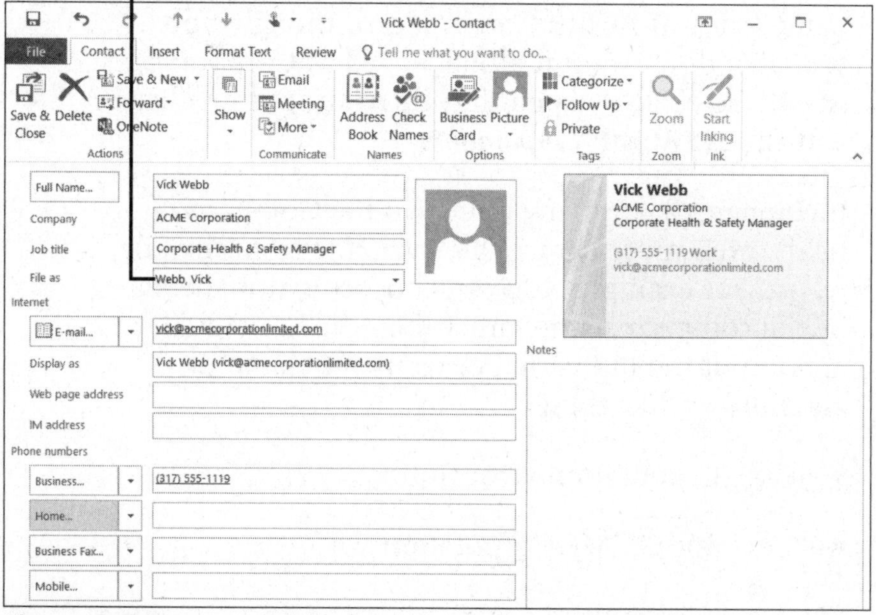

Figure 12-2

The more complete you make an entry for a person, the more helpful Outlook can be. However, it takes more time to enter all the details required for a complete record than to just enter a name and email address. None of the fields are mandatory.

3. Click the Save & Close button on the Ribbon. The contact is added to your Contacts list.

Here are some tips to consider when you're entering contact information:

- Whatever you type in the Full Name field replaces *Untitled* in the dialog box's title bar immediately.
- In the File As field, specify how this entry is alphabetized. The default is by last name, so it reverses whatever you put in the Full Name field. For example, if you enter **John Doe** in the Full Name field, the File As appears as *Doe, John*. For people's names, this is usually the best way to go. For a company name (such as ACME Corporation), though, you probably don't want it alphabetized as Corporation, ACME. To fix that, open the File As drop-down list and choose *ACME Corporation*.
- If you enter a company name (in the Company field), even more choices are available from the File As list. For example, you can choose to alphabetize by the company name rather than the individual, and to put the individual or company name in parentheses, like these:
  - ACME Corporation (Doe, John)
  - Doe, John (ACME Corporation)
- You can store multiple email addresses for the same person. Notice that E-mail isn't just a field label, but also a drop-down list. Open the list and choose E-mail 2, E-mail 3, and so on for additional addresses.
- All Phone Numbers fields also have drop-down lists associated with their labels. You can store four phone numbers for a person, and you can choose which labels each of those will carry. For example, you could assign the label Mobile to one of the phone numbers.

- You can have three addresses for a person: Business, Home, and Other. Switch between them with the drop-down list in the Addresses section.
- When you enter an address but don't enter it in proper mailing format (address, city, state, and zip code), a dialog box will prompt you to fill those in. This is for your own protection: to make sure every address you enter is usable.
- Use the Notes pane to store any additional information about the person that doesn't match up with any of the fields.
- To customize how your Contacts appear, choose from sets of fields other than the defaults. The ones in Figure 12-2 are the General fields.

Edit and Delete Contacts

People move, get new phone numbers, and change email providers. In a paper address book, you have to cross out the old address and write new information. (That sloppy look is a big part of what I hate about paper address books!) With Outlook, though, you can simply edit the stored information onscreen.

Editing a contact is a snap.

1. Double-click the Contact.
2. When that Contact's window opens (refer to Figure 12-2), make any changes, and then click the Save & Close button.

To delete a contact from the list, do the following:

1. Select the contact.
2. Press the Delete key on the keyboard, or right-click it and choose Delete, or choose Home⇨Delete.

If you delete a Contact by mistake, you can retrieve it from the Deleted Items folder. To restore an accidentally deleted contact:

1. Click the Mail icon (the envelope) in the bottom-left corner of the Outlook window. (No, it's not really mail you're after, but the Mail area provides easy access to the Deleted Items folder.)

2. In the Navigation pane, click Deleted Items.

3. Locate the deleted contact in the list of items. See **Figure 12-3**.

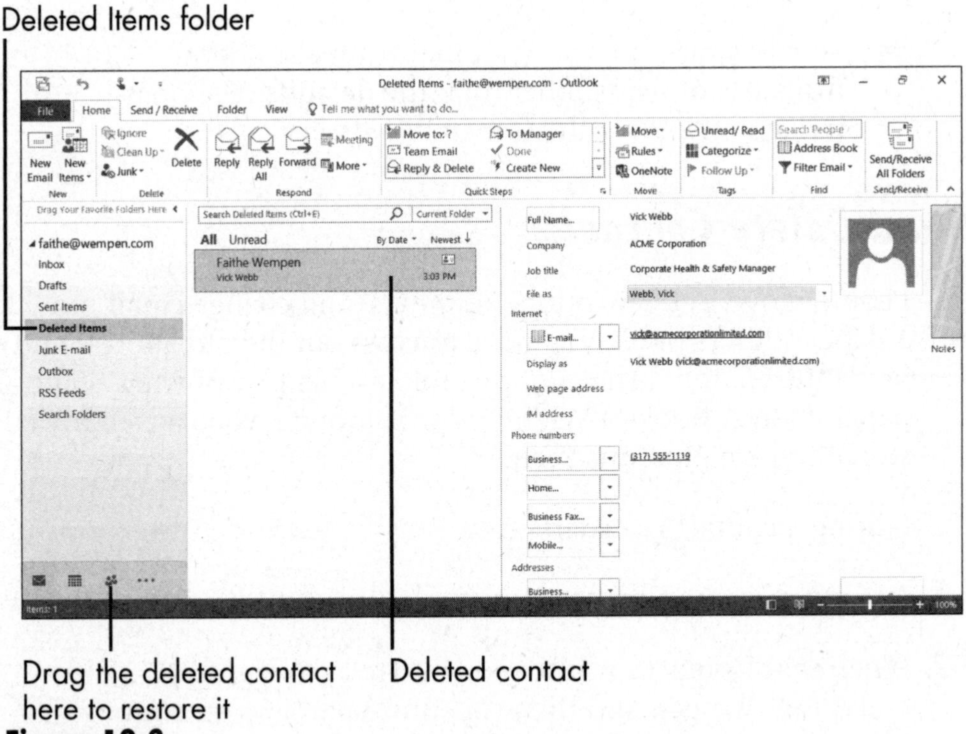

Figure 12-3

4. Drag and drop the deleted contact onto the Contacts icon in the lower left corner of the Outlook window. It's restored.

If you want to completely delete a contact so that it is irretrievable, delete it from the Deleted Items folder.

If you don't see the item in the Deleted Items folder, look in the Trash folder, if you have one. The name may vary depending on your email account type.

Choose How the Contact List Appears

Usually, the default view of the Contacts list is People; refer to Figure 12-1. You can easily switch to other views whenever you like, such as Business Cards view, as shown in **Figure 12-4**.

Click here to choose a different view

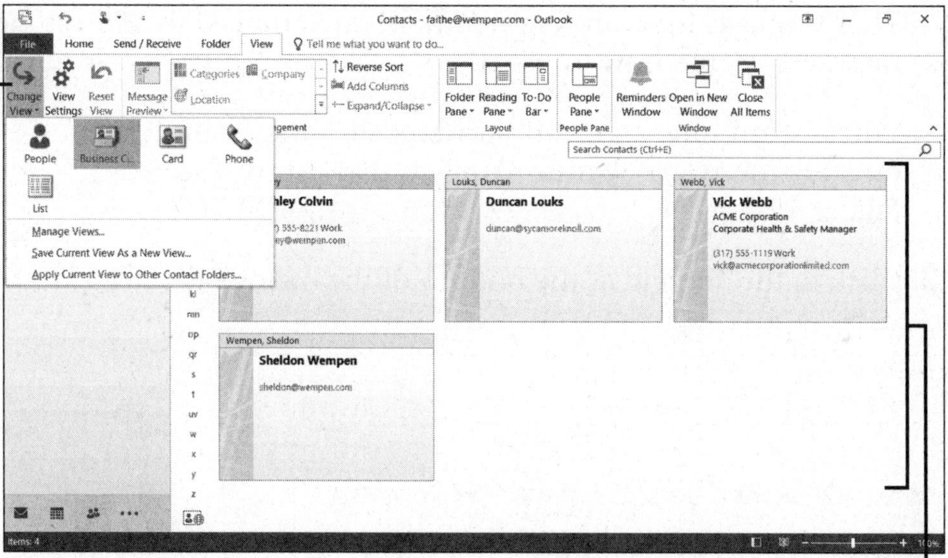

Current view is Business Cards

Figure 12-4

To switch to a different view, choose View ➪ Change View and then click the view you want. For even more control, choose View ➪ Change View ➪ Manage Views.

Use the Contacts List

After you get your Contacts list set up, it's good for lots of things other than a substitute for your paper address book.

To quickly locate a specific contact by filtering, follow these steps:

1. Click in the Search Contacts field (upper-right corner).
2. Type a word that the contact information contains. (It doesn't need to be the person's name. For example, you could enter a town to find everyone who lives there.) The Contacts list is temporarily filtered to show only entries that contain that word.

To clear the filter, click the Clear Search (X) button to the right of the Search Contacts field.

Your Contacts list comes in handy when you need to address email messages. Here's how to use it:

1. When composing an email message, click the To button, opening the Select Names: Contacts dialog box. (See **Figure 12-5**.)
2. Click in the To field at the bottom of the dialog box.

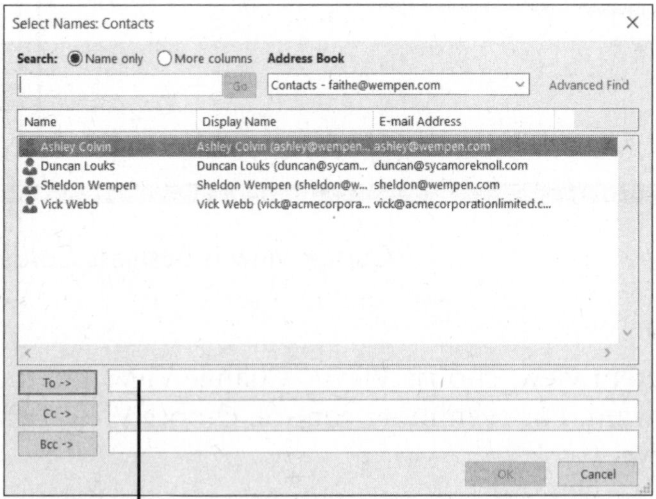

First, click here. Then double-click one of the names above

Figure 12-5

3. Double-click a contact to add that person as a recipient.

   You can do the same thing with the Cc and Bcc fields.

4. Click OK when you're finished.

To start an email from the Contacts folder

1. With the Contacts folder displayed, select a contact.
2. Choose Home ⇨ E-Mail. A new message composition window opens with that person's email address pre-filled in the To field.

If your PC uses a dialup modem connected to a live phone line, you can use Outlook to dial the phone for you. To place a phone call

1. Select the contact and then click Home ⇨ More ⇨ Call and then click the desired phone number for that contact, such as Business or Home.
2. In the New Call dialog box that opens, confirm the contact name and address and then click Start Call. See Figure 12-6.
3. Lift the phone receiver, click Talk, and begin your call.

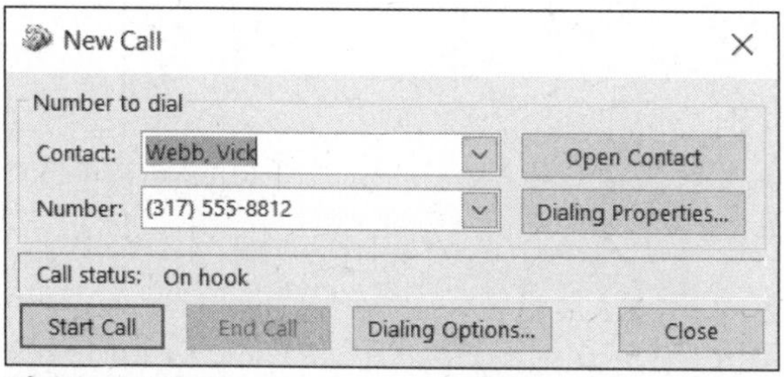

Figure 12-6

Dialing a telephone isn't a big chore, so why use Outlook to dial? For one thing, Outlook doesn't make any dialing mistakes. That can be a great help if you have a disability. Another reason is that if you let Outlook manage the call, it adds a record of the call (and its length) to the Journal area of Outlook. The Journal is a tool for tracking your activities in Outlook. It's used frequently by people who bill customers by the hour.

Create Notes

Lots of people use sticky notes to create reminders for themselves of bits of information: everything from Web site passwords to memorable quotations. Outlook includes *Notes,* which are the electronic equivalent of these sticky notes. You can store anything you want on a note, but they are best used for small bits of data, like reservation confirmation codes or membership ID numbers. You can leave a note open (as long as Outlook is open) so that you will be reminded every time you see it, or you can close the note so that it isn't in your way. **Figure 12-7** shows one open note, with the rest of them closed.

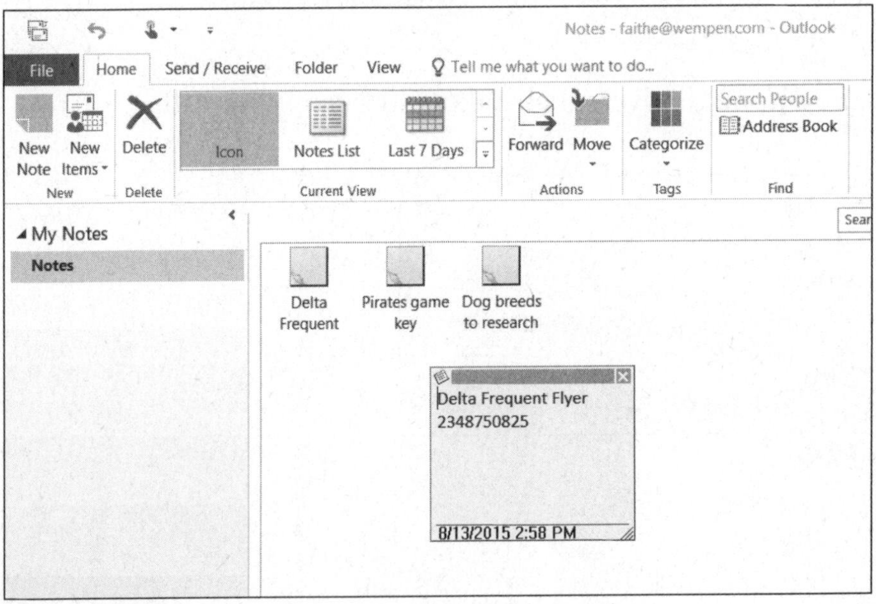

Figure 12-7

To create a note, follow these steps:

1. Display the Notes section of Outlook. To do so, click the More icon (. . .) in the lower-left corner of the window, and on the menu that appears, click Notes. See **Figure 12-8**.

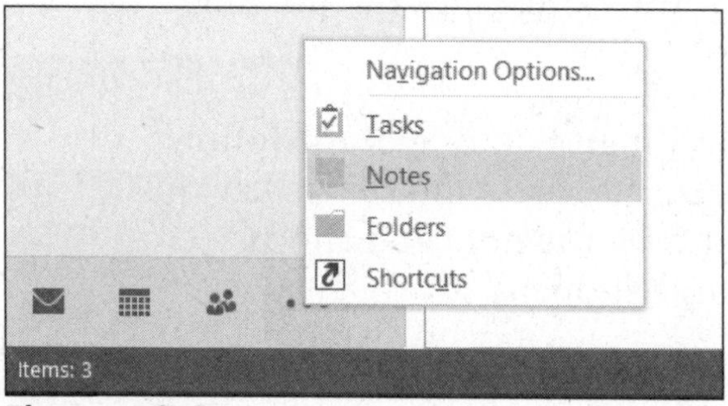

Figure 12-8

2. Choose Home➪New Note or press Ctrl+N. A new blank note appears.
3. In the new blank note that appears, type whatever you want.

   The first few words of the first line will appear as an icon title, so try to be descriptive there. Unless, of course, you're trying to camouflage information, like a password; then you might want some misleading text as the first line. I have a friend who keeps her passwords in a note that is titled Family Birthdays, thinking that someone snooping to steal her passwords would not care about family birthdays and would pass that by.

4. Close the note by clicking the X button in its upper-right corner. It's saved automatically.

Here are some handy Note tips:

- **To reopen a note:** Double-click it. It remains open until you close it, or until you exit Outlook.

- **To move a note:** Drag it around by its title bar (the colored bar at the top of it), placing it anywhere onscreen, even outside boundaries of the Outlook window. It stays there until you close Outlook.
- **To edit a note:** Open it and edit away.
- **To change the size of the note:** Click on and drag its lower-right corner.
- **To delete a note:** Select it and do one of the following: Choose Home⇨Delete, press the Delete key on the keyboard, or right-click the note and choose Delete from the menu that opens.

Just like with a deleted contact, a deleted note is moved to the Deleted Items folder.

To retrieve a deleted note, open the Mail section of Outlook, display the contents of the Deleted Items folder, find the note, and drag it onto to the Notes icon in the lower-left corner of the window. You can also right-click it, choose Move to Folder, and then specify where you want to move it.

Categorize Notes

Because a note is such a multipurpose item, you might find it useful to create categories to differentiate one type of note from another.

By assigning a color to a note, you can indicate what type of information it contains. For example, you might choose to make financial notes green and make family notes blue.

To assign a color category to a note

1. Right-click the note and choose Categorize. A menu of color choices appears.
2. Click the desired color.

If you have used this category before, you are done at this point. The note's icon and background turn that color. However, the first time you use a certain color, the Rename Category dialog box opens, so you can assign a name. Outlook doesn't affix any special meaning to a color; you do that on your own. If prompted, change the name in the Name box. See **Figure 12-9**. Then click OK.

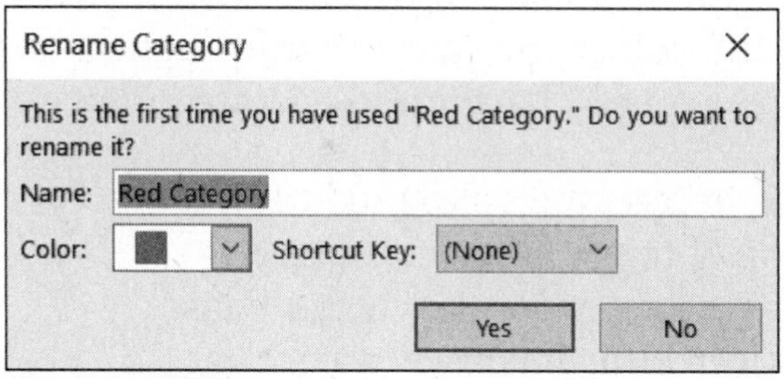

Figure 12-9

If you want to rename a category, you can do so by following these steps:

1. Choose Home➪Categories➪All Categories. The Color Categories dialog box opens. See **Figure 12-10**.

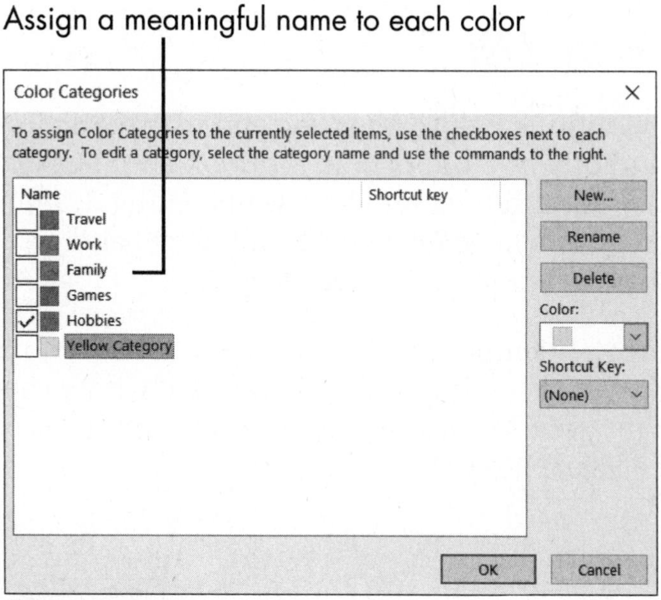

Figure 12-10

2. Click the desired category and click Rename. The name becomes editable.

3. Type the new name and press Enter.

Notice in Figure 12-10 that you can also create and delete categories and change the color assigned to a category. (This might be useful, for example, if you wanted to change the color used to represent a certain category but you didn't want to lose the category information already assigned to existing notes.) You can have up to 25 categories.

A note can have multiple categories assigned to it. Each category is an on/off toggle for each note. A note's icon shows only the color for the category last assigned to it, but it still retains its other categorization too. To remove a category from a note, select the note, click Home⇨Categorize, and click the category to toggle off for that note.

The categories are also shared by the Calendar and Tasks features in Outlook. As you are creating categories, think about how you might like to categorize appointments and events too.

Use Tasks and the To-Do List

The Tasks feature in Outlook helps you create and manage action items for yourself and others. Not only can Outlook keep track of what you need to do, but it can remind you of upcoming deadlines, record what percentage of a large job you've completed, and even send emails out that assign certain tasks to other people.

To view the Tasks area of Outlook, click Tasks in the lower-left part of the Navigation pane. (The icon looks like a clip board with a check mark on it. You might need to click the More icon to find it, as you did with Notes.) See Figure 12-11.

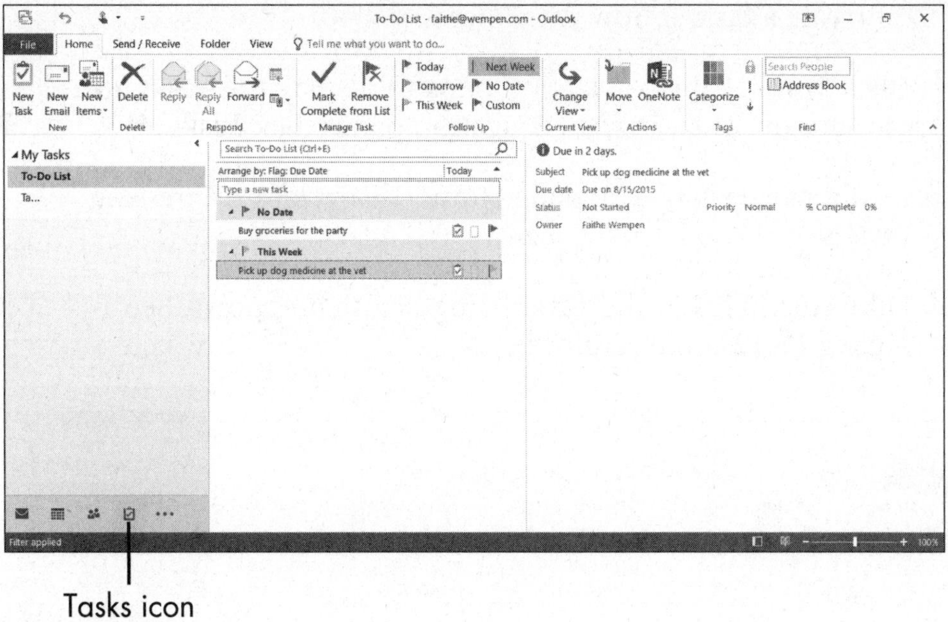

Figure 12-11

Notice that under the My Tasks heading in the navigation pane, there are two sub-headings: To-Do List and Tasks. There is a subtle difference in Outlook between them:

- **Tasks** are specific items you created in the Tasks section of Outlook. Something isn't technically a *task* unless it was created in the Tasks section.
- **The To-Do list** contains everything from the Tasks list, plus other items you have marked for action, such as email messages you flag for follow-up.

In the Inbox section of Outlook, you can flag a message for follow-up by selecting it and then clicking the red flag button on the toolbar.

You can click either To-Do List or Tasks to specify which set of activities you want to look at. For the purposes of this book, I assume that you choose Tasks. I describe how to work only with to-do items that are true tasks, not other items for follow-up.

To create a task, follow these steps:

1. Click Tasks in the Navigation pane to display the Tasks area of Outlook. Then in the Navigation pane, click Tasks.
2. Start a new task by choosing Home ➪ New task or pressing Ctrl+N.
3. Fill in the fields in the Task dialog box that appears. See **Figure 12-12** for an example.

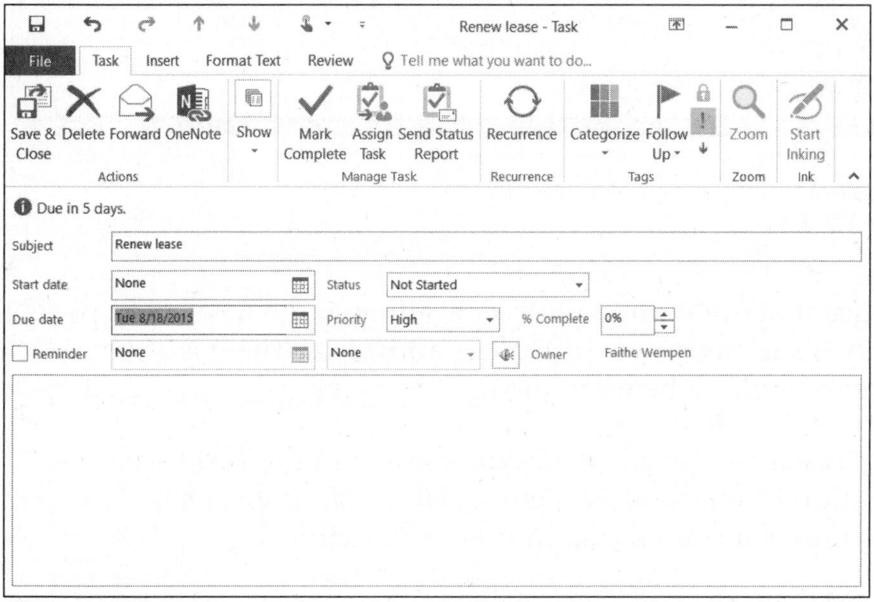

Figure 12-12

4. Click the Save & Close button. The task appears on the Tasks list.

Tasks might appear differently on the list, depending on their statuses and due dates. For example, overdue tasks appear in red. Tasks that are 100-percent complete appear in gray with strikethrough in some views, and do not appear at all in other views (because they're no longer active). Choose View ➪ Change View and choose the view you want.

To reopen a task, double-click it. The list of tasks looks different depending on which you chose (from the View➪Change View command). **Figure 12-13** shows the Detailed view with the reading pane set to Bottom (View➪Reading Pane➪Bottom).

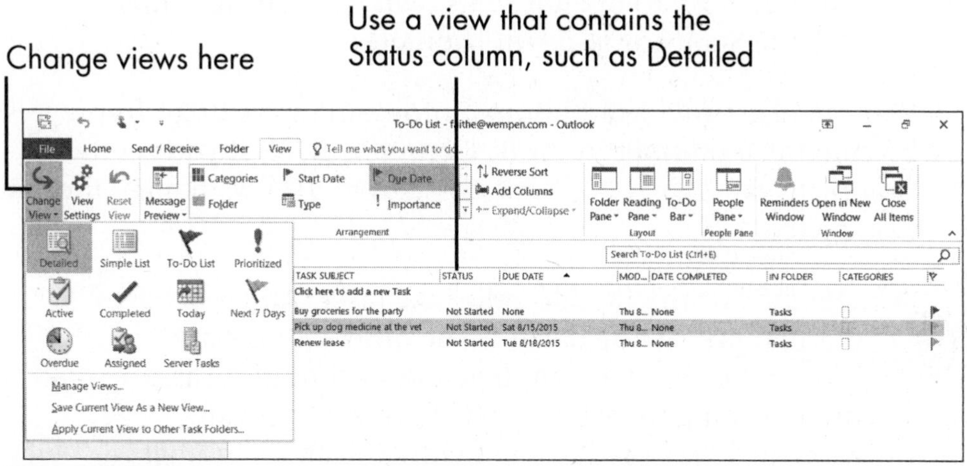

Figure 12-13

Any notes you typed when you created the task appear in the reading pane if it is displayed.

Completing a task does *not* automatically delete it. Depending on the view, a completed task might disappear from the Tasks list, but it's not gone. Switch to another view, such as Detailed, and it will reappear.

To delete a task — say, one that you completed — select the task and press Delete. (Or choose Home➪Delete, or right-click the task and choose Delete from the menu that appears.)

Update the Status of a Task

As you make progress on a task, you can update its status in Outlook to reflect that.

- **If the view you're using contains a Status field (column), as in Figure 12-13:** Click the task's current status to open a drop-down list, and then select a new status from there. Your choices are Not Started, In Progress, Waiting on Someone Else, Deferred, or Completed.

- **If the view doesn't contain a Status field:** Double-click the task to open it in its own window, and then use the Status drop-down list there.

You can also provide additional information about an in-progress task by entering a number in the % Complete field. If you set the % Complete value to 100%, Outlook automatically changes the Status to Completed.

Use the Priority field to prioritize tasks. All tasks have Normal priority by default. The other choices are Low and High. You can then sort or filter the Tasks list according to task priority if the view you are using includes the Priority field. (Switch to another view if it doesn't.) The Priority field's symbol is an exclamation point. High-priority tasks appear with a red exclamation point in that column; low-priority tasks show a blue down-pointing arrow there.

Set a Task Reminder

To help you remember to work on a task, you can set an alarm for it: a *reminder.* A reminder pops up onscreen at a certain date and time you specify.

To set a reminder for a task, follow these steps:

1. Double-click the task to open it.
2. Mark the Reminder check box.
3. Set the date and time for the reminder.

A default-assigned sound plays when the reminder occurs. To change the sound, click the Sound button (it looks like a speaker) and browse for a different sound file.

4. Click the Save & Close button.

   Figure 12-14 shows a reminder being set for 8 a.m. on the task's Due Date, for example.

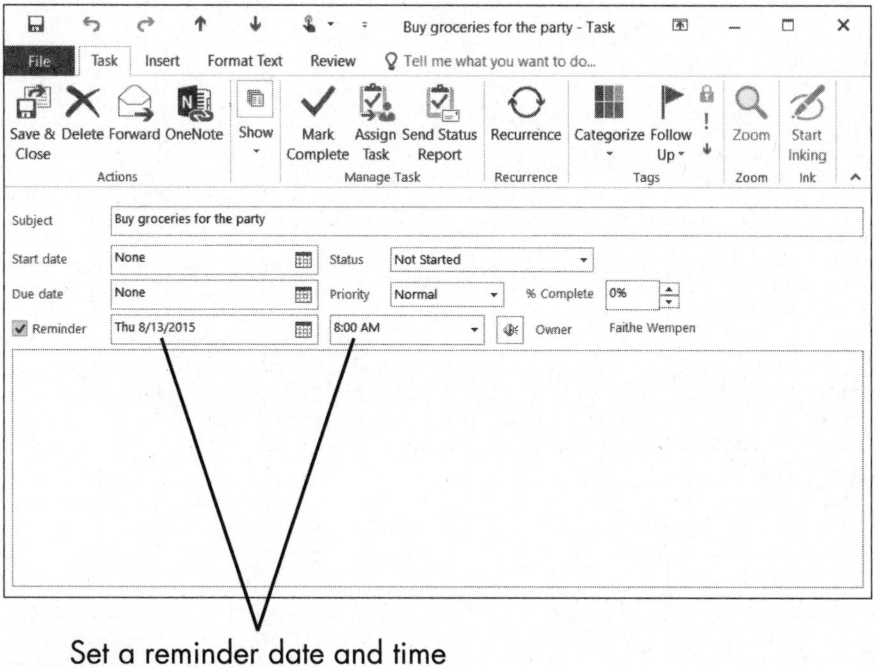

Figure 12-14

Set your reminder to occur before the task's actual due date to give yourself some time to work on it. For example, set a budget's reminder for two weeks prior to the date.

When the date and time come for the reminder, it pops up in a box within Outlook (if Outlook is running) and a sound plays, if assigned.

If Outlook isn't running at that date/time, it pops up the next time Outlook starts.

In the Reminder box that appears (see **Figure 12-15**), click the Dismiss button to dismiss the reminder, or click the Snooze button to temporarily turn off the reminder but have it pop up again later. (You get to define "later" by specifying that from the drop-down list to the left of the Snooze button.)

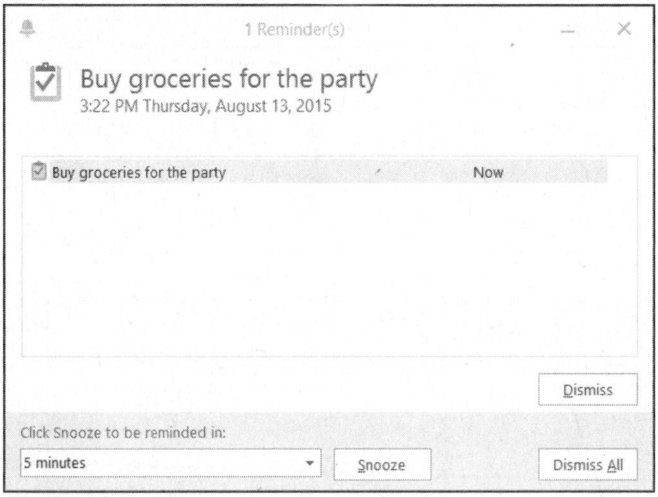

Figure 12-15

Your Busy Life: Using the Calendar

Chapter 13

Get ready to . . .

You probably have a paper calendar you use to keep track of your appointments, meetings, and events. The problem with a paper calendar, though, is that it's, well, *paper.* It's limited.

The Calendar in Outlook offers everything a paper calendar does, and much more. You can easily switch between different views (daily, weekly, or monthly), and you can edit and delete calendar items without any messy pencil edits. You can even set up Outlook to remind you of an event shortly before it occurs. This chapter covers all that and more.

View Your Calendar

To view Calendar in Outlook, click the Calendar icon at the bottom of the Navigation pane.

The default view of the calendar is Month view, as shown in **Figure 13-1**.

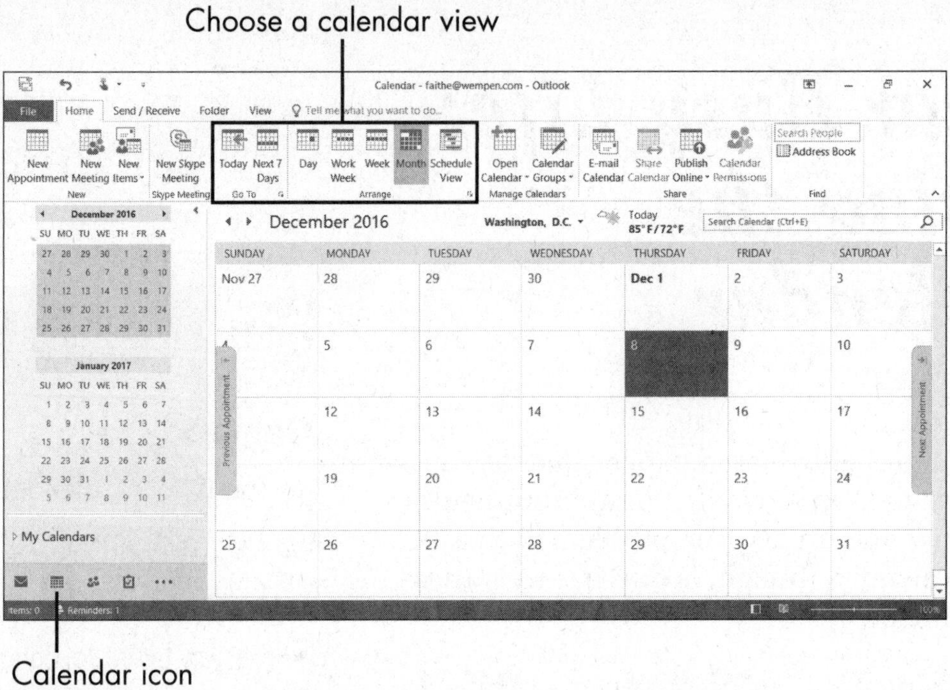

Figure 13-1

To switch to a different calendar view, click the Day, Work Week, Week, or Month button on the Home tab.

- **Month view:** Shows the entire month at a glance. Only the titles of the appointments/events are shown, and sometimes these are truncated.
- **Week view:** Shows one week at a time. Each day is represented by a large box, with all its appointments and events in it. Your Tasks list appears at the bottom.
- **Work Week view:** Shows one week at a time, but only the workdays (Monday through Friday).
- **Day view:** Shows one day at a time. An hour-by-hour grid appears, with the appointments and events slotted at their appointed times. Your Tasks list appears at the bottom.

Choose File ⇨ Options ⇨ Calendar for access to many options you can set that fine-tune calendar behavior. Here are a few things you might want to do in the Outlook Options dialog box (see **Figure 13-2**):

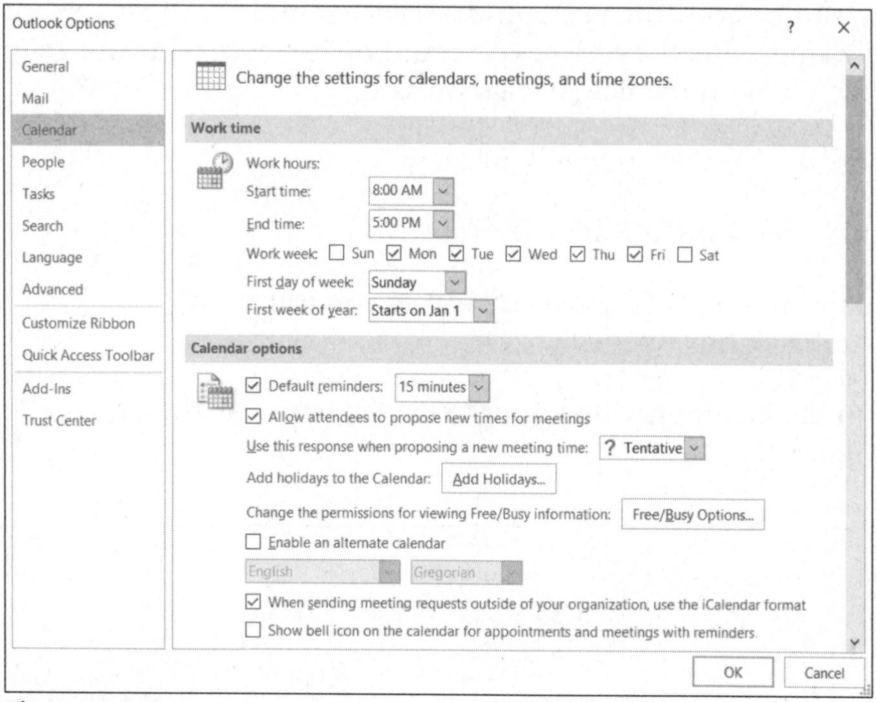

Figure 13-2

- Under the Work Time heading, mark or clear the check boxes for the days of the week you consider your "work week." These are the days that will appear when you choose to view the calendar in Work Week view.
- Under the Work Time heading, set the First Day of Week setting to the desired day. Most calendars start with Sunday, and that's the default.
- Under Display Options, click the Default Calendar Color button and choose a color for the calendar accents.

Create and Delete a Calendar Event

Outlook calls all calendar items *events*. In reality, events can be anything date-related: meetings, birthdays, parties, and even reminders of things to be done on a certain date. For example, if there's a show that you want to buy tickets for, you could put an event on your calendar to buy them on the day they go on sale.

To create an event, follow these steps:

1. Display the calendar (any view).

2. Double-click a blank spot on the date you want. An Event dialog box opens.

3. Fill in the boxes provided to describe the event, as shown in **Figure 13-3**.

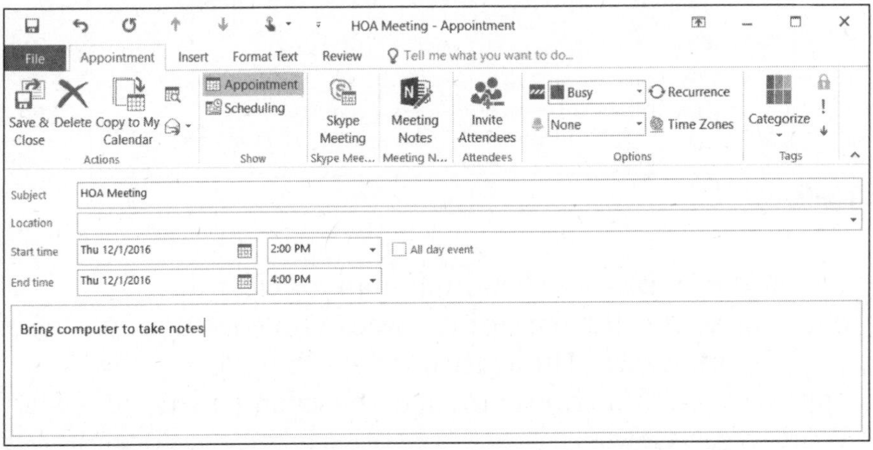

Figure 13-3

- *Subject:* Type a brief title for the event. Whatever you enter here will appear on the calendar and in the title bar when the event is open in its own window.
- *Location:* This is optional. Indicate where the event will occur, if relevant.

- *All Day Event:* This check box is marked by default. Clear it if you want to enter a start time and/or end time. See the following bullet.
- *Start Time, End Time:* Enter start and end times for the event if applicable. If not applicable, mark the All Day Event check box (if it's not already marked).
- *Notes:* This is optional. Enter any additional information you want to record about the event. This might include names of meeting attendees, a list of things you need to bring, or information about the type of dress expected.

4. Click the Save & Close button to add the event to the calendar.

If you want to edit the event's settings, double-click it in Calendar to reopen this same dialog box. Then make your changes and click Save & Close.

To delete an event from Calendar, select it and press Delete, or right-click it and choose Delete, or choose Home➪Delete.

Set an Event to Recur

Some events happen on a regular schedule. For example, birthdays come every year (whether we like it or not!), organizations have monthly meetings, and religious services happen the same day and time every week.

Rather than setting up each occurrence as a separate event, you can create a *recurring event.* Outlook then puts all the occurrences on the calendar for you automatically.

To set up recurrence for an event, follow these steps:

1. Open the event, if it's not already open, by double-clicking it in Calendar. The event window opens. (Refer to Figure 13-3.)

2. On the Ribbon, click Recurrence. (If you don't see Recurrence, click the Options button.) The Appointment Recurrence dialog box opens.

3. In the Recurrence Pattern area, select a radio button that best represents the type of recurrence you want. For example, in **Figure 13-4**, I chose Monthly.

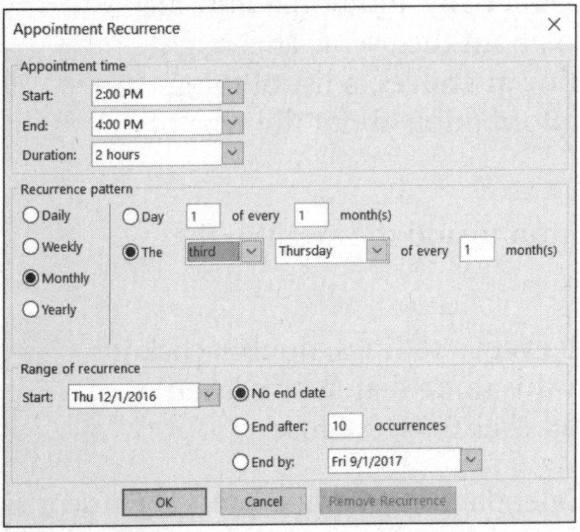

Figure 13-4

4. Use the controls to the right of the option you just chose to specify the details of the pattern. For example, in Figure 13-4, the event recurs the third Friday of the month.

A Weekly event can actually occur on multiple days of the week, and does not have to occur every week. If you set it to occur every four weeks, that's basically once per month, but it's different from choosing Monthly because it determines the next occurrence by counting weeks, not by counting months. In some months that have five weeks, an event that occurs every four weeks would happen twice, for example.

5. In the Range of Recurrence area, specify how many times, or for how long, the recurrence will continue. In Figure 13-4, there is no end date specified, so the recurrence will continue indefinitely.

6. Click OK to accept the recurrence settings.

7. Click the Save & Close button to save your changes to the event.

   From this point on, when you double-click the event on the calendar, a dialog box asks whether you want to open that one occurrence or the series. If you choose to open the series, the changes you make to the event affect all occurrences.

   If you want to edit or remove the recurrence, reopen the event, and then click the Recurrence button again. In the Appointment Recurrence dialog box that reopens (refer to Figure 13-4), you can make any changes you like. To remove the recurrence entirely, click the Remove Recurrence button.

Configure Event Reminders

Outlook can remind you of an event by popping up a Reminder box. The default lead time is 15 minutes, but you can set any amount of lead time you want. For example, if it takes you 45 minutes to drive to the meeting place, you might set the reminder for one hour prior to the meeting time.

To set a reminder for an event, follow these steps:

1. If the event isn't already open, double-click to open it.

2. In the Options group on the Appointment (or Appointment Series) tab of the event window, open the Reminder drop-down list and choose a time interval. See **Figure 13-5**. Or, to turn off the Reminder feature, choose None.

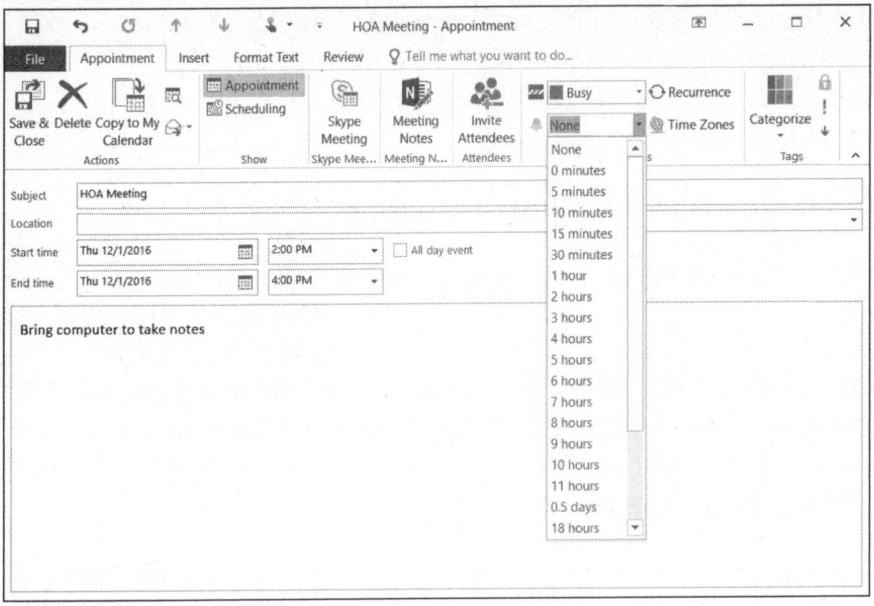

Figure 13-5

At the bottom of the drop-down list is a Sound command, which you can use to change the sound that plays when the reminder occurs. The default sound is reminder.wav, which is a simple chime.

3. Click the Save & Close button to save the changes to the event.

Here's how to change the default reminder time, or set it to None so that no reminders are used:

1. Choose File⇨Options⇨Calendar.

2. Do either of the following:

- Clear the Default Reminders check box if you don't want to use reminders by default.
- Enter a different amount of time to use as the default.

Add Holidays

One of the nice things about a paper calendar is that the major national holidays are already printed on it. When is Easter this year? When is Thanksgiving? You never have to wonder.

You can achieve this same effect by adding holidays to the Outlook Calendar. Here's how:

1. Choose File ➪ Options ➪ Calendar.
2. In the Calendar options section, click Add Holidays. The Add Holidays to Calendar dialog box opens. See **Figure 13-6**.

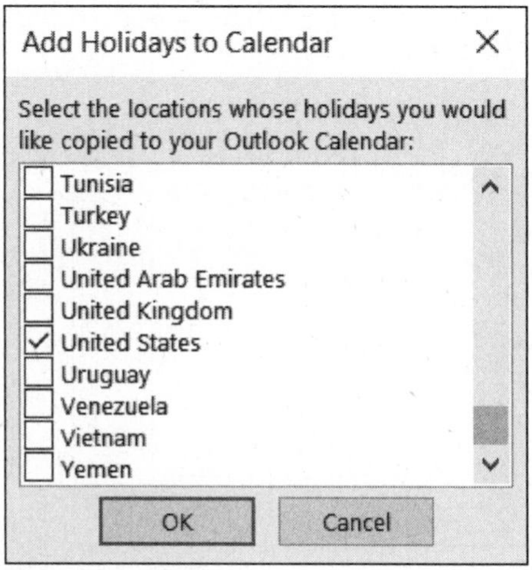

Figure 13-6

3. Mark the check boxes for each country's holidays that you want. By default, only the United States is marked.
4. Click OK. Outlook adds holidays to your calendar.
5. Click OK to close the confirmation box.
6. Click OK to close the Outlook Options dialog box.

Print a Hard Copy of Your Calendar

With an Outlook calendar, you can have your cake and eat it, too. You can not only have an electronic calendar, but also a paper one. Just print it yourself! You can print your calendar in Day, Week, Work Week, or Month view, for whatever date ranges you like.

To print your calendar, follow these steps:

1. Display the calendar.
2. Choose File⇨Print or press Ctrl+P. The Print options appear. See **Figure 13-7**.

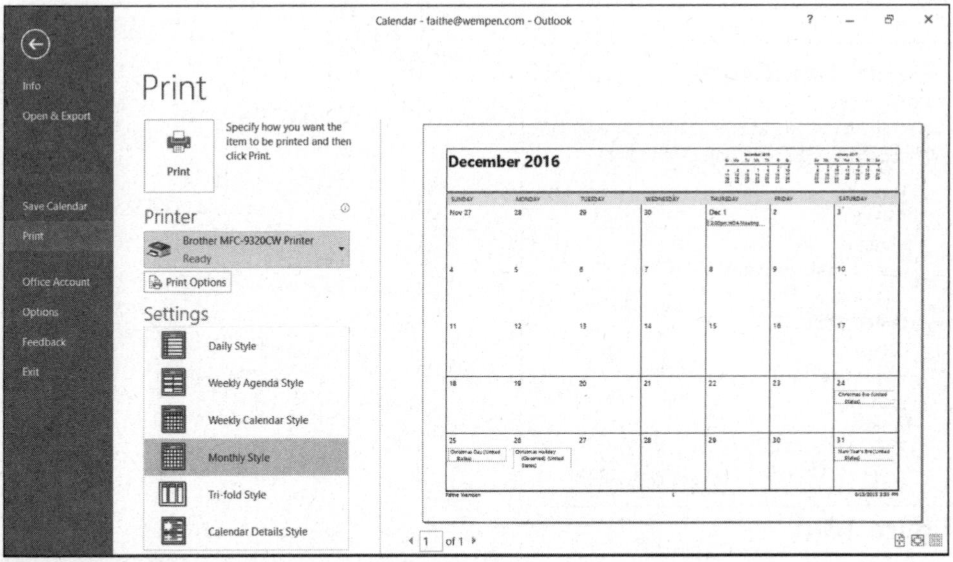

Figure 13-7

3. Check the printer name under the Printer heading. If it's not correct, click the current printer name to open a list of available printers and choose a different printer.
4. In the Print What area, click the style you want. Not only can you choose from a variety of daily, weekly, and monthly calendars, but you can choose from a couple of other views that are for printing only:

- *Tri-fold Style:* Creates a compact calendar that shows your daily calendar, your Tasks list, and your weekly calendar, all in a format that you can easily fold for carrying in a pocket or envelope.
- *Calendar Details Style:* Creates a listing of all the events on your calendar for the day, including all details stored about each one.

5. Click Print Options. The Print Options dialog box opens (as shown in **Figure 13-8**).

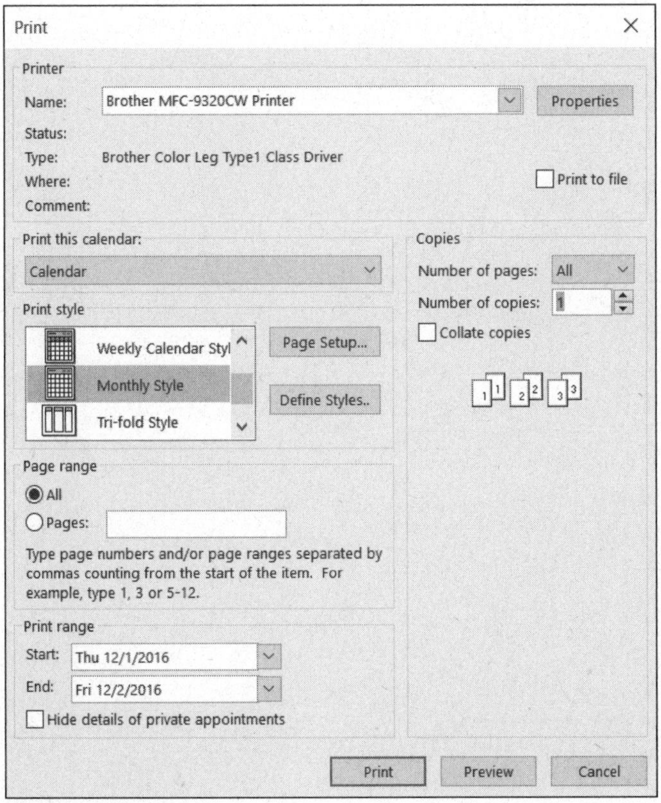

Figure 13-8

6. In the Number of Copies field, enter the number of copies you want. (1 is the default.)

7. In the Print Range area, enter the starting and ending dates for the printout.

If you specify that you want to print only a few days, but you choose Month view to print, Outlook prints the entire month (or months, if the chosen dates span two months). The same goes for weeks. If you specify only one day to print but print Week view, Outlook prints the entire week.

8. Click Print. The calendar prints.

Part V

PowerPoint

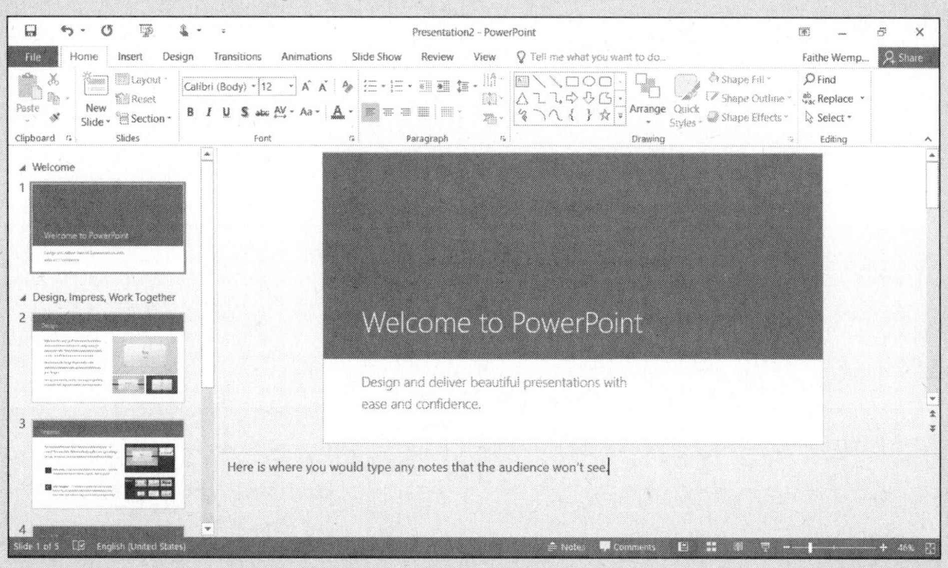

For five great PowerPoint tricks, visit `www.dummies.com/extras/office2016forseniors`.

Getting Started with PowerPoint

Chapter 14

PowerPoint is best known for creating business presentations — slide shows, if you will — but it's actually a much more versatile tool. PowerPoint is a great tool for almost any situation where you need to convey a visual message. For example

- An overview of an organization or club for new members
- Posters and signs with large lettering, such as *Please Help Yourself* or *Sign In Here*
- A photo tribute for an anniversary celebration or memorial service
- Lyrics for a group sing-along
- Information about meeting rooms and activities at a seminar

This chapter offers you some basics for working with PowerPoint, including how to use slide layouts and content placeholders that make it easy to create all these types of materials and more.

Get ready to . . .

Explore the PowerPoint Interface

In PowerPoint, you work with slides and presentations rather than documents (as in Word) or worksheets (as in Excel). A *slide* is an individual page of the presentation. The term *page* isn't a perfect descriptor, though, because PowerPoint slides are designed to be displayed on a computer screen or with a projector rather than printed. A *presentation* is a collection of one or more slides saved in a single data file.

At a big-picture level, PowerPoint's interface is very similar to that in Word and Excel: It has a Ribbon, an Office button, and a status bar. The default view of the presentation, called *Normal view*, consists of three panes, as shown in **Figure 14-1**.

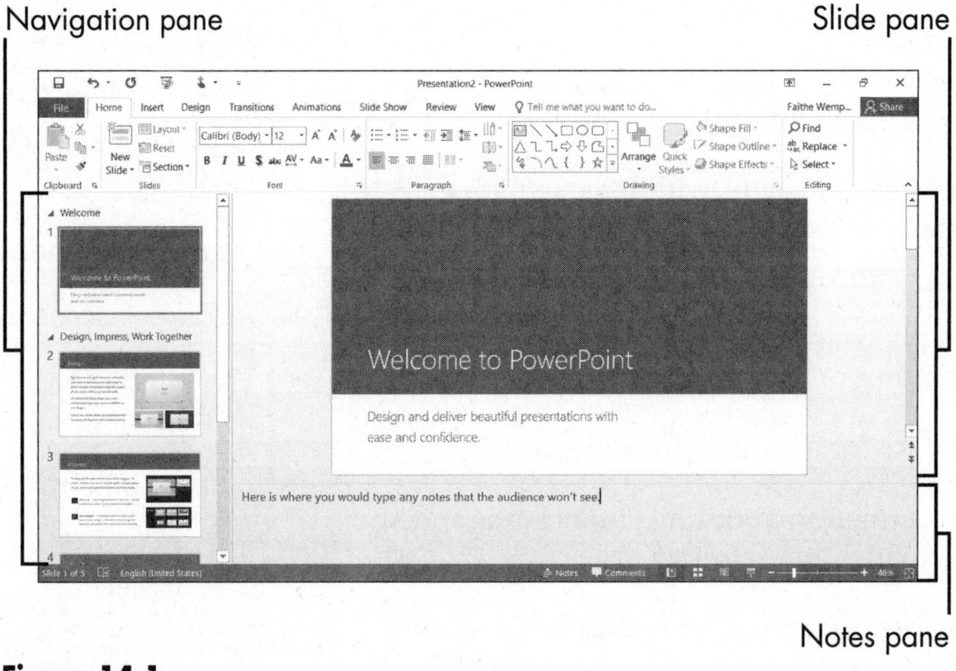

Figure 14-1

- The **navigation pane** is the bar along the left side. Thumbnail images of the slides appear here.

Outline view is just like Normal view except it shows a text outline instead of thumbnails in the navigation pane. To change views, use the View tab.

- The **Slide pane** in the middle shows the active slide in a large, editable pane. Here's where you do most of your work on each slide.
- The **Notes pane** runs along the bottom of the screen. Here you can type any notes to yourself about the active slide. These notes don't show onscreen when you display the presentation, and don't print (unless you explicitly choose to print them). By default the Notes pane is minimized, but you can drag upward from the bottom of the Slide pane to bring it into view, as shown in **Figure 14-1**.

Work with PowerPoint Files

When you start PowerPoint, the Start screen appears, just like it does in Word and Excel. Press Esc or click the Blank Presentation button to start a new presentation with a single slide in it. You can work with this presentation, and then save it in any of these ways, the same as in Word and Excel:

- Choose File⇨Save.
- Press Ctrl+S.
- Click the Save icon on the Quick Access toolbar.

Or, if you prefer, you can open an existing presentation file, just like in other Office applications:

- Choose File⇨Open.
- Press Ctrl+O.
- Choose File⇨Open and then choose one of the recently opened files on the right side of the File menu.

You can also start PowerPoint and open an existing file at the same time by double-clicking the filename from any location in File Explorer (such as This PC or Documents).

Understand PowerPoint Views

Like other Office applications, PowerPoint provides several different views for you to work with. Each view is useful for a different set of activities. Normal view (refer to Figure 14-1) — the default — is the most commonly used view. You can choose between the other views in either of these ways:

- Click one of the View buttons in the bottom-right corner of the PowerPoint window. (Not all the views are represented there.)
- On the View tab, click a button for the view you want.

Figure 14-2 shows Slide Sorter view, and also points out the two places where you can switch views.

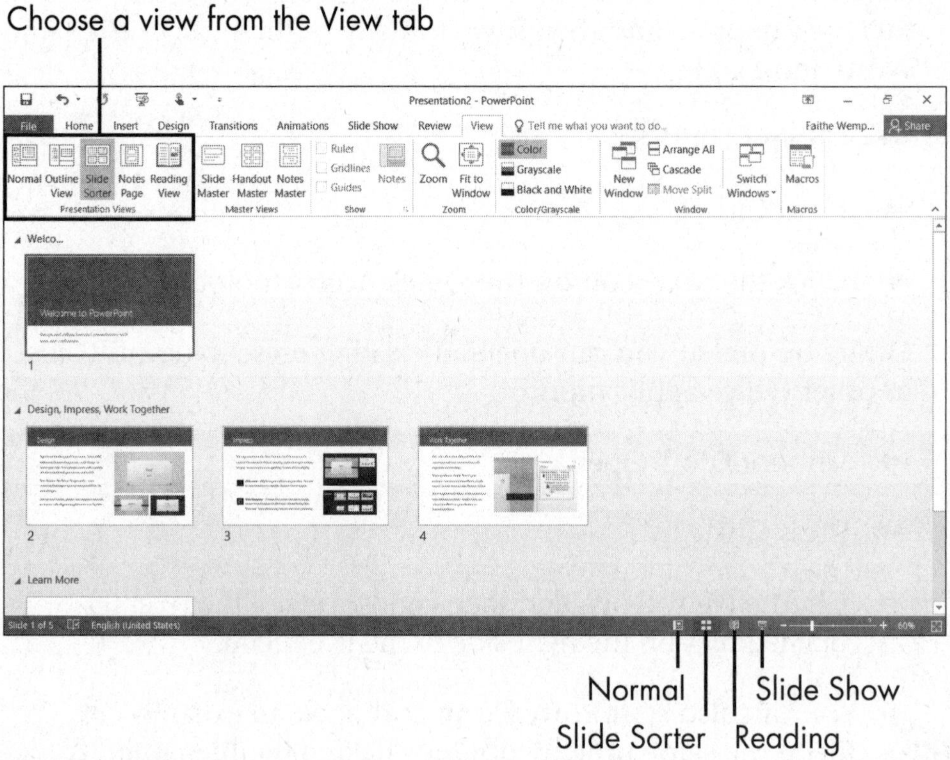

Figure 14-2

Table 14-1 summarizes the available views and tells what each view is good for. I show you many of these views in more detail later, when I discuss how to do activities that these views are well suited for.

Table 14-1 PowerPoint Views

View	*How to Select*	*Useful For*
Normal	Click the button in the bottom-right corner; or choose View⇨Normal	Editing slide content of any kind
Outline	Choose View⇨Outline View	Viewing and editing text in slide placeholders
Slide Sorter	Click the button in the bottom-right corner; or choose View⇨Slide Sorter	Viewing all slides in the presentation at a glance, rearranging slide order
Notes Page	Choose View⇨Notes Page	Editing the speaker notes for each slide
Reading View	Click the button in the bottom-right corner; or choose View⇨Reading View	Showing a presentation in a window
Slide Show	Click the button in the bottom-right corner; or choose Slide Show⇨From Beginning, or Slide Show⇨From Current Slide	Showing the presentation full-screen
Slide Master	Choose View⇨Slide Master	Making global changes that affect all slides in the presentation
Handout Master	Choose View⇨Handout Master	Making changes that affect the design of the handouts you print
Notes Master	Choose View⇨Notes Master	Making changes that affect the design of the speaker note pages you print

Create New Slides

Each new presentation begins with one slide in it: a title slide. You can easily add more slides to the presentation in any of these ways:

- Select the slide that the new slide should come *after* and then choose Home⇨New Slide.

- In the navigation pane in Normal view click the slide that the new slide should come *after*, and then press Enter.
- In the navigation pane in Outline view, click at the beginning of the title of the slide that the new one should come *before*, and then press Enter.

When you add a new slide in any of these ways, you get the Title and Content layout. This is the default slide layout for all slides in the presentation except the first one. (The first slide's default layout is Title Slide.) The next section covers slide layouts in more detail.

If you want a different slide layout when inserting a new slide, click the down arrow under the Home⇨New Slide button. A palette appears showing various layouts. Click the one you want. See **Figure 14-3**.

To duplicate an existing slide, including all its content, select it and then choose Duplicate Selected Slides from the New Slide button's menu.

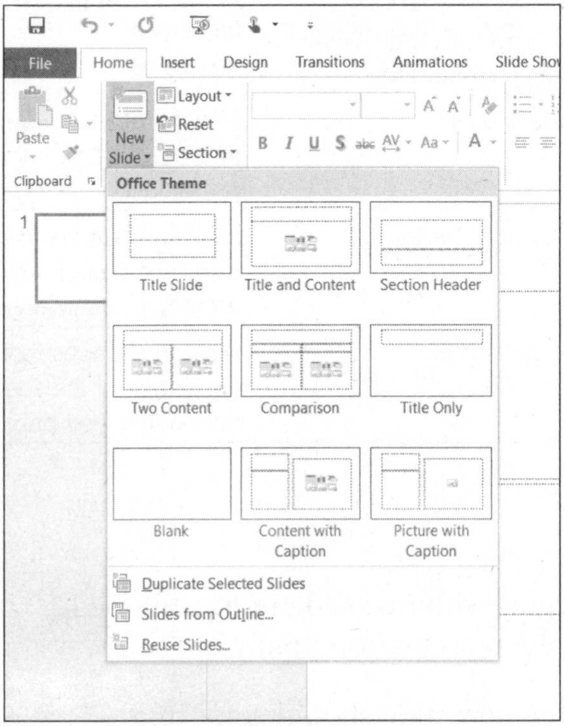

Figure 14-3

Use Slide Placeholders

A *slide layout* is a combination of one or more content placeholders. For example, the default slide layout — Title and Content — has two boxes: a text box at the top for the slide's title, and one multipurpose content placeholder in the middle that can be used for text, a graphic, or any of several other content types. See **Figure 14-4**.

Some placeholders are specifically for text. For example, the placeholder for each slide's title is text-only. Click in such a placeholder and type the text you want. A content placeholder, such as the large placeholder on the default layout, can hold any *one* type of content: text, table, chart, SmartArt graphic, picture, clip art, or media clip (video or sound). Later chapters explain some of these other types of content in more detail.

Text placeholder

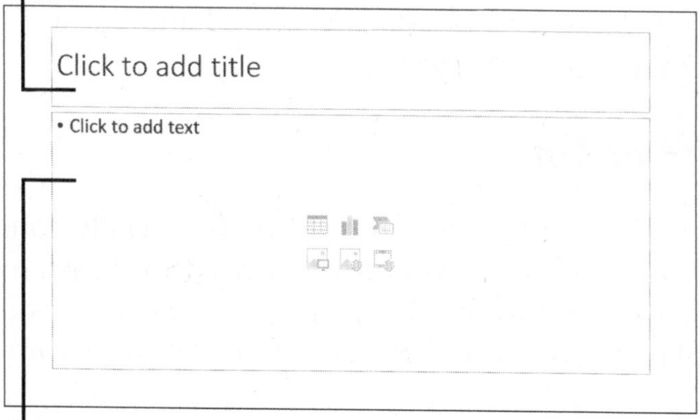

Content placeholder

Figure 14-4

To add text to a content placeholder, click the Click to Add Text area and type what you want. To add any other type of content, click the icon in the placeholder for the type you want. These are identified in **Figure 14-5**.

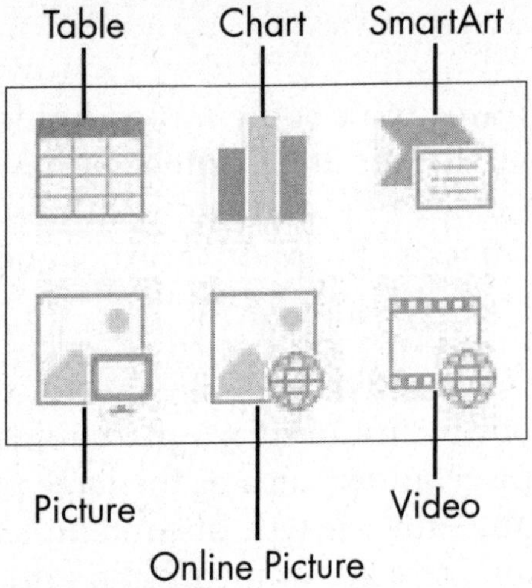

Figure 14-5

Use placeholders whenever possible rather than manually placing content on a slide. If you change the presentation's design (covered in Chapter 15), any content in placeholders is automatically shifted and reformatted to match the new design.

Turn Text AutoFit Off or On

If you type more text than will fit in that text box (especially common for a slide title, for example), the text automatically shrinks itself as much as is needed to allow it to fit. This feature — *AutoFit* — is turned on by default. AutoFit is very useful because it prevents text from being truncated.

Sometimes, however, you might not want text to AutoFit. For example, it might be important to you that all the titles on your slides be exactly the same font size, for consistency.

To control whether AutoFit is in effect in a particular text placeholder, follow these steps:

1. Right-click the text box and choose Format Shape from the menu that appears.

2. In the Format Shape task pane that appears, click Text Options, and then click the Textbox icon.

3. In the AutoFit section, select the Do Not AutoFit radio button. See **Figure 14-6.**

4. Close the task pane.

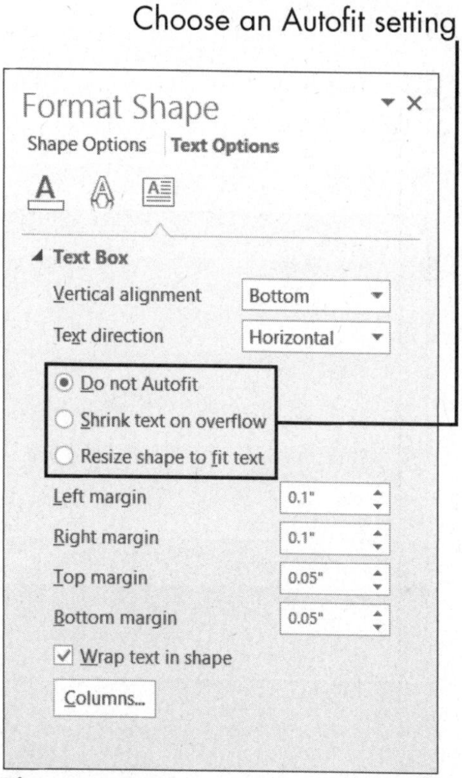

Figure 14-6

If you don't want to use AutoFit at all, you can turn it off at a global level. To do so, do the following:

1. Choose File⇨Options.

2. Click Proofing (on the left).

3. Click the AutoCorrect Options button. The AutoCorrect dialog box opens.

4. Click the AutoFormat as You Type tab.

5. In the Apply as You Type section (see **Figure 14-7**), clear the following check boxes:

   - AutoFit Title Text to Placeholder
   - AutoFit Body Text to Placeholder

6. Click OK.

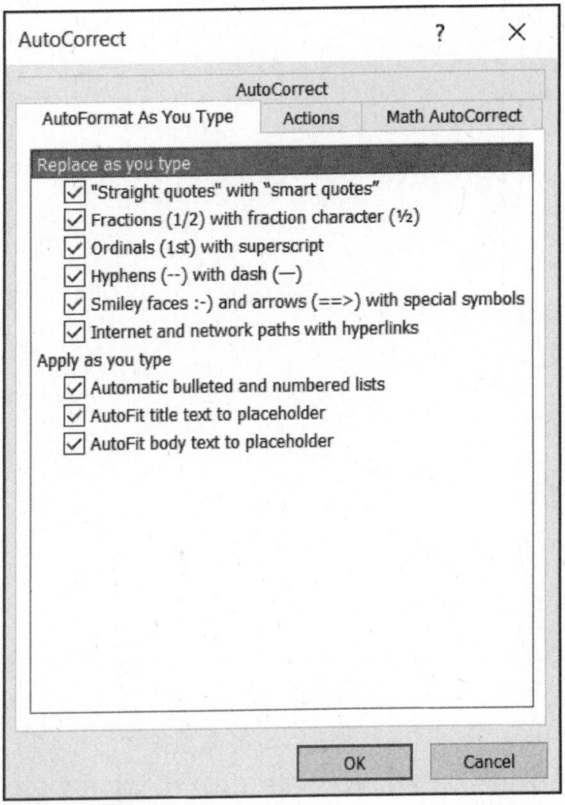

Figure 14-7

Change Slide Layouts

The Title and Content layout is very versatile. You can place any one type of content on the slide, in addition to a text title. Sometimes, though, you might want something different: for example, two different content types on the same slide (like a bulleted list on one half and a picture on the other) or just a title with an empty space underneath it (for manually inserted content).

To change a slide's layout, follow these steps:

1. Select the slide for which you want to change the layout.
2. Choose Home➪Layout. A palette of the available layouts appears.
3. Click the layout you want.

Move or Resize Slide Content

Each placeholder box on a slide is a separate object. It can be moved or resized freely.

To resize a box, select it and then drag a selection handle. A *selection handle* is a circle or square on the border of the box. Each box has eight selection handles: one in each corner, and one on each side. To maintain the height-width proportion for the box — its *aspect ratio* — hold down the Shift key while you drag one of the corner selection handles.

To move a placeholder box, position the mouse pointer over the border of the box, but not over a selection handle. The mouse pointer changes to a four-headed arrow. Click and drag the box to a new location.

If you resize the placeholder(s) on a slide and then apply a different layout or design to the slide, everything snaps back to the default size and location. So make sure you have the right layout and design chosen before you spend a lot of time resizing or moving placeholders.

If you want to move or resize a certain placeholder on every slide in your presentation, do so from Slide Master view (covered in Chapter 15). That way, you can make the change to the layout's template, and the change is applied automatically to every slide that uses that layout.

Manually Place Text on a Slide

Whenever possible, you should use the layout placeholders to insert slide content. However, sometimes you might not be able to find a layout that's exactly what you want. For example, maybe you want to add a caption or note next to a picture, or you want to create a collage of text snippets arranged randomly on a slide.

The text in such a text box doesn't appear in Outline view, and doesn't export when you save the presentation as an outline, so use this type of text box sparingly.

Here's how to create a manual text box on a slide:

1. Display the slide.
2. Choose Insert⇨Text Box. The mouse pointer turns into a vertical line.
3. Click where you want the text to appear, and then start typing.

Manually placed text boxes behave somewhat differently from placeholder text boxes.

- **The text box widens as you type.** The text doesn't automatically wrap to the next line. You can press Enter to create a new paragraph, or press Shift+Enter for a line break within the same paragraph.
- **Manually placed text boxes aren't resizable.** The box resizes itself to fit whatever text is inside it.

If you want a manual text box to behave more like a placeholder, adjust its AutoFit setting:

1. Right-click the text box and choose Format Shape from the menu that appears.

2. Click Text Box.

3. In the AutoFit section, select one of these options:

   - *Do Not AutoFit:* Turns off all AutoFit properties, which allows you to manually resize the text box. Text doesn't resize if it doesn't fit in the box.

   - *Shrink Text on Overflow:* Turns on AutoFit. You can manually resize the text box. Text resizes if it doesn't all fit in the box.

Navigate and Select Text

As in Word and Excel, you might find using keyboard shortcuts more convenient than using the scroll bar (shown in Chapter 1).

The function of some PowerPoint keyboard shortcuts depends on whether you're editing in a text box or navigating in a presentation.

Table 14-2 lists the most common navigation shortcuts in PowerPoint.

Table 14-2 Navigation Keyboard Shortcuts

Press This	***PowerPoint Text Box***	***PowerPoint Presentation***
Up arrow (↑)	One line up	Previous slide
Down arrow (↓)	One line down	Previous slide
Right arrow (→)	One character to the right	Next slide
Left arrow (←)	One character to the left	Previous slide
Tab	Next tab stop	Next placeholder box on this slide
Shift+Tab	Next tab stop	Previous placeholder box on this slide

(continued)

Table 14-2 *(continued)*

Press This	***PowerPoint Text Box***	***PowerPoint Presentation***
Ctrl+arrow key	→ or ←: one word to the left or right; ↑ or ↓: one paragraph up or down	→ or ←: one word to the left or right; ↑ or ↓: one paragraph up or down
Home	Beginning of the line	First slide
End	End of the line	Last slide
Ctrl+Home	Beginning of the text box	First slide
Ctrl+End	End of the text box	Last slide
Page Down	Next slide	Next slide
Ctrl+Page Down	Next slide	Next slide
Ctrl+Page Up	Previous slide	Previous slide

Select Content

To select text in PowerPoint, you can either

- Drag the mouse pointer across it (holding down the left mouse button)

  or

- Click where you want to start and then hold down Shift as you press the arrow keys to extend the selection.

When text is selected, its background changes color. The color depends on the color scheme in use; with the default color scheme, it's light blue.

Table 14-3 shows keyboard shortcuts to help you select text.

Table 14-3 Keyboard Text Selection Shortcuts

Press This	***PowerPoint Extends Selection This Much***
Shift+← or →	One character in arrow direction
Shift+↑ or ↓	One line in arrow direction
Ctrl+Shift+←	The end of the word
Ctrl+Shift+→	The beginning of the word
Ctrl+Shift↓	The end of the current paragraph (if in a text box)
Ctrl+Shift+↑	The beginning of the current paragraph (if in a text box)
Ctrl+Shift+End	The end of the current text box (if in a text box)
Ctrl+Shift+Home	The beginning of the current text box (if in a text box)
Ctrl+A	All slides

Dressing Up Your Presentations

Chapter 15

Get ready to . . .

In this chapter, I show you a variety of techniques for adding attractive and interesting formatting to your PowerPoint presentation slides. You see how to apply consistent formatting across multiple slides, and also how to format individual objects on individual slides.

In this chapter, I also show you how to insert digital photos in a presentation. Finally, stay tuned to see how to create photo albums in PowerPoint.

Understand and Apply Themes and Variants

A *theme* is a design set that you apply to a PowerPoint presentation to change several elements at once, including background, color scheme, fonts, and the positions of the placeholders on the various layouts. Word and Excel also use themes, but in PowerPoint, the theme feature is exceptionally strong and full featured.

All presentations have a theme, but the default theme — literally named Blank — is so plain that it's almost like it's not there at all. Blank uses a white background, black Calibri Light and Calibri text, and no background or design graphics.

To switch to a different theme, display the Design tab and then do one of the following:

- Click one of the themes in the Themes group. See **Figure 15-1**.
- Open the Themes menu (by clicking the More arrow pointed out in Figure 15-1) and then click the one you want.

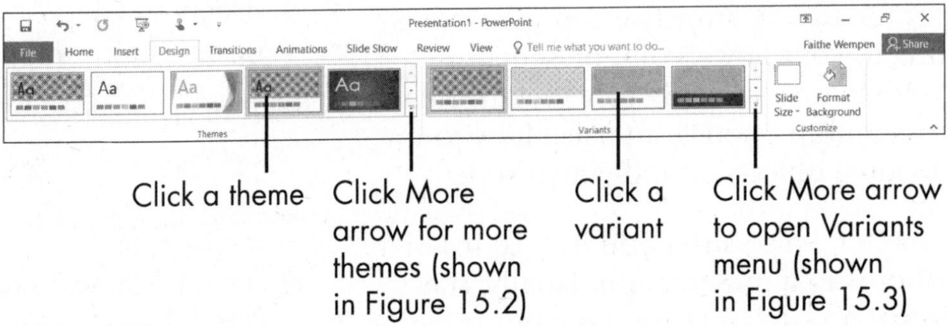

Figure 15-1

Notice the several categories on the Themes menu. (See **Figure 15-2.**) The Built-In themes — the ones that come with PowerPoint — are always available. The theme under This Presentation is the one in use. The Custom section contains any themes you created yourself.

To create your own theme, set up a presentation's formatting how you want by formatting the Slide Master (covered later in this chapter), and then use the Save Current Theme command on the Themes menu (see Figure 15-2) to save it.

A *variant* is an alternate version of a theme. Depending on the theme, a variant may include a different background, different colors, and/or different accent graphics. To choose a different variant, click it in the Variants group on the Design tab (see Figure 15.1). The Variants group also has a More arrow that opens additional choices (if available), and also a menu. You'll use this menu in the next section.

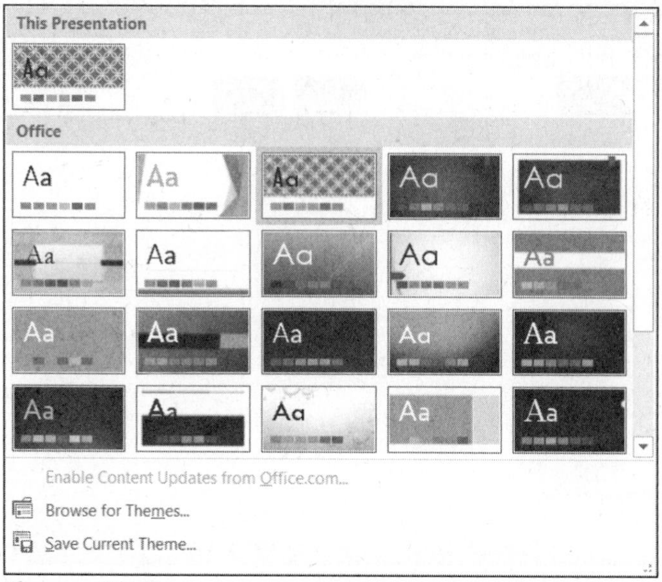

Figure 15-2

Change the Presentation Colors

Each theme can be applied in a variety of color combinations, so you don't have to choose between a theme that has the right style and one that has the right colors.

When you apply a theme, it appears with its default colors. One way to change those is to choose a different variant, as you learned in the previous section. Another is to select a specific color scheme.

Here's how to choose a color scheme:

1. On the Design tab, click the More button in the Variants group, opening a menu.
2. Point to Colors, opening a submenu.
3. Click the color combination you want. See **Figure 15-3**.

If none of these color combinations appeal to you, create your own combination. At the bottom of the Colors menu, click Customize Colors, and then choose the exact colors you want from the Create New Theme Colors dialog box that appears.

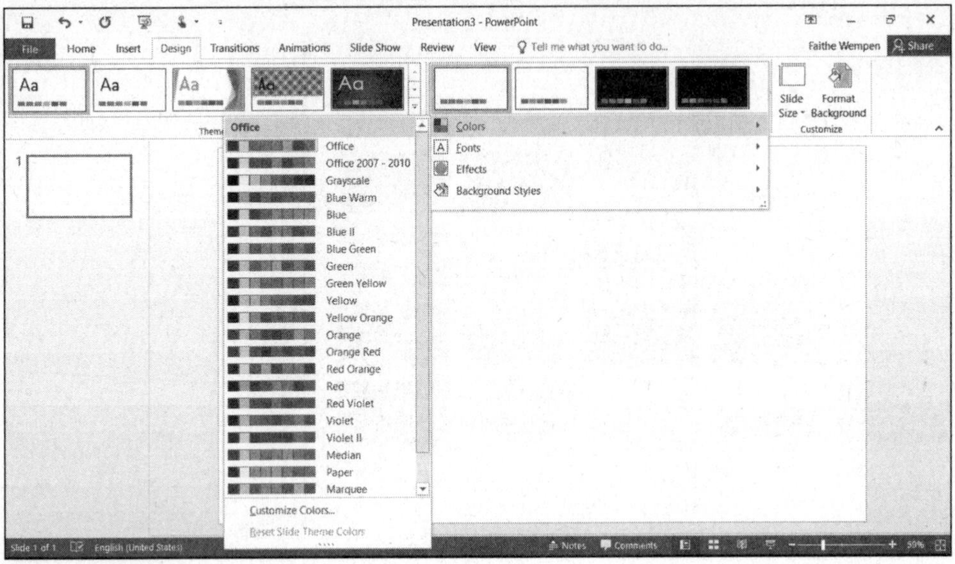

Figure 15-3

Edit Slide Masters

When you choose a theme, the theme is applied to the *Slide Master*, which is a template that affects the look of all slides in the presentation. Formatting the Slide Master automatically formats every slide, and that's a big bonus because a presentation looks more professional when all the slides match.

After applying a theme, if the appearance isn't exactly the way you want it, you could change the formatting on each individual slide, but it's much more consistent and easy to simply make the change once to the Slide Master and let that change trickle down to the individual slides.

To edit the Slide Master, choose View➪Slide Master. The slide that appears isn't an actual slide in your presentation, but rather a template. Or, more precisely, it's a series of templates: one for each of the different layouts. You can make changes in these two ways, depending on the scope of change you want to make:

- **To make a change that affects every slide, regardless of its layout:** Click the top-left slide in the left pane. This top slide is the master for the entire presentation.

- **To make a change that affects only a certain layout:** Select that layout's thumbnail image from the left pane. **See Figure 15-4.**

Select the topmost slide to affect all slides

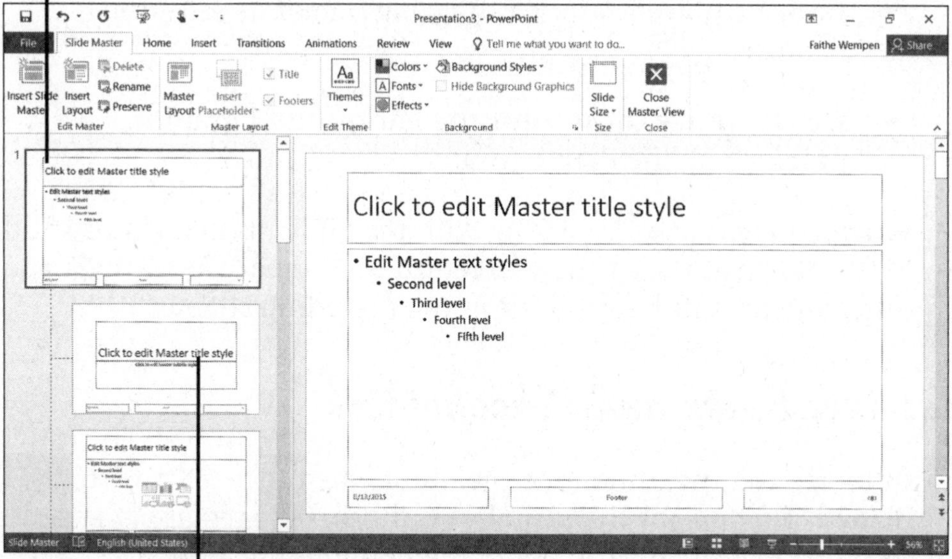

Select one of the individual layouts to affect only slides with that layout

Figure 15-4

Here are some of the edits you might want to make:

- **Select a different set of fonts** from the Slide Master ⇨ Fonts list.
- **Change the font used for an individual bullet level** by selecting the text sample representing that level and then choosing a different font from the Home tab's Font drop-down list.
- **Apply a different bullet type to each line of sample text** (from the Home tab) to change the bullet characters used at each level.

- **Move a placeholder** on the slide by dragging its border.

To move a placeholder, drag its border — not the selection handle. See the next bullet.

- **Resize a placeholder** by dragging one of its selection handles.

- **Delete, resize, or recolor the background graphic** provided by the theme (if any).

When you're finished working with the Slide Master, choose Slide Master⇨Close Master View to return to Normal view. (I talk about the different views in PowerPoint in the preceding chapter.)

Format Text Boxes and Placeholders

In most cases, presentations look best when they're consistently formatted. That means that usually your best bet is to apply formatting to the Slide Master, as I discuss in the preceding section.

Sometimes, however, you might want to format an individual text box or object differently from the rest, to make it stand out.

The easiest way to apply formatting to an object is with the Shape Styles command. *Shape Styles* are formatting presets that use the theme colors in the presentation. Depending on the style you choose, a Shape Style can include a border, a fill color, and special effects that make the shape look shiny, matte, or raised.

To apply a Shape Style to an object:

1. Select the object. If it's a text box, click its outer border to select the box itself (not text inside it).

2. Click the Drawing Tools Format tab.

If you don't see a Drawing Tools Format tab, you don't have an object selected.

3. Open the Shape Styles palette by clicking the More arrow in the Shape Styles group. See **Figure 15-5**.

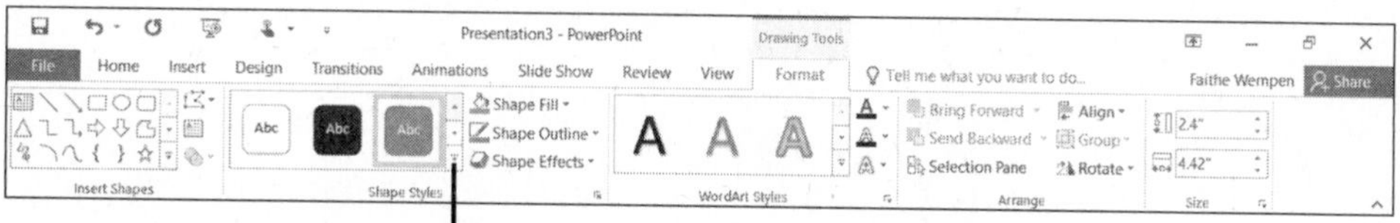

Click here for a palette of Shape Styles

Figure 15-5

4. Click the desired shape style.

   If none of the Shape Styles is what you want, you can also choose the background and an outline for an object separately. Use the Shape Fill, Shape Outline, and Shape Effects button menus on the Format tab. (Refer to Figure 15-5.)

To quickly change text formatting within a text box, use the WordArt Styles palette, also on the Format tab. It works just like the Shape Styles feature except that it applies to text.

Insert Pictures

One of the most common uses for PowerPoint is to display digital photos. There are a couple of ways to do that.

- **Insert individual photos into presentations.** I show you how in this section.
- **Create a special Photo Album presentation.** I explain this in the next section.

First, look at how to put an individual photo on an individual slide:

1. To insert the picture into a layout placeholder, click the Pictures icon on the placeholder. See **Figure 15-6**.

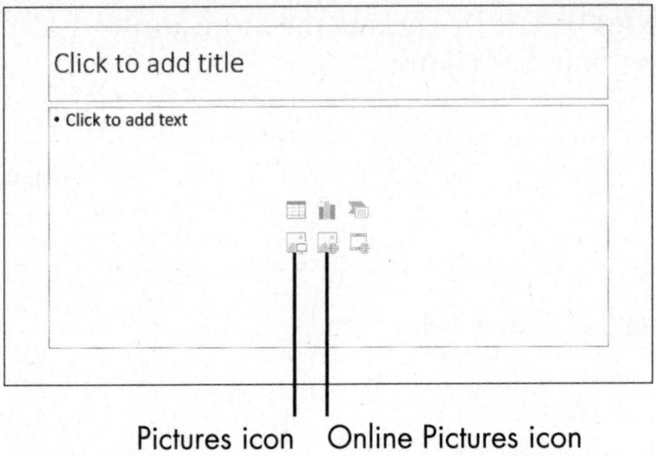

Figure 15-6

If you want the picture to be independent of any placeholder, choose Insert⇨Picture when no placeholder is selected.

2. In the Insert Picture dialog box that appears, select the picture you want to insert. Change the location if needed.

3. Click Insert. The picture appears on the slide.

4. (Optional) Move or resize the image as desired.

- *To move the image:* Drag it by its center.
- *To resize the image:* Drag a selection handle around the edge.

In addition to your own photos, you may sometimes want to use decorative or generic artwork from other sources. Office applications include a means of performing a Bing image search from within the applications themselves, so you can find an image without having to exit out to a web browser. Bing is Microsoft's web search engine.

Follow these steps to find and insert an image with Bing:

1. Click the Online Pictures icon in the content placeholder on the slide (refer to **Figure 15-6**) if you want to use a placeholder. Or, to insert a free-floating picture, choose Insert ⇨ Online Pictures.

2. In the search box next to Bing Image Search, type one or more keywords that define what you are looking for, and then press Enter. An assortment of images appear. **Figure 15-7** shows an example.

3. Scroll through the images, select the one you want, and click Insert.

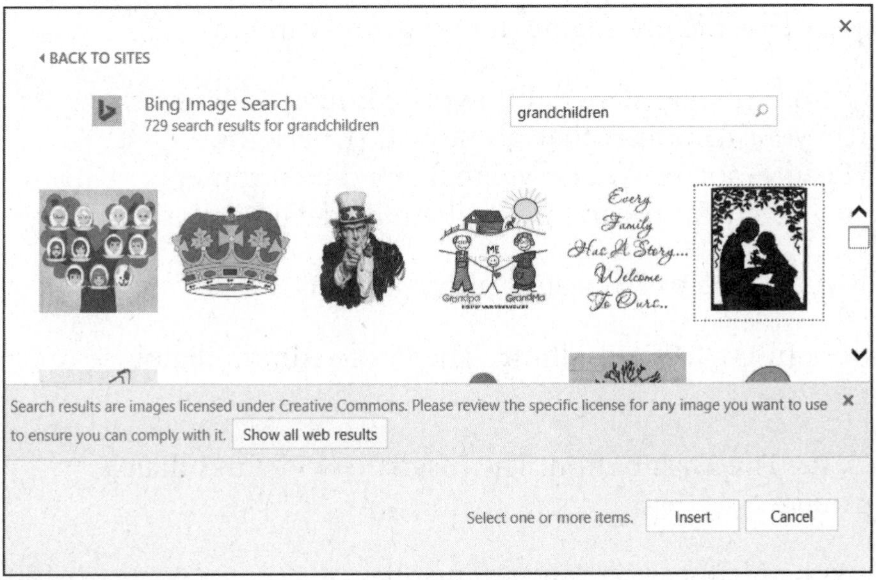

Figure 15-7

As the note overlaid on the search results shows in Figure 15-7, the images that Bing finds within Office are licensed under Creative Commons. This means they are royalty-free images that are okay to use for non-commercial projects. However, don't count on an image being free to use just because it shows up in the Bing search results. If you are creating a publication that will be widely distributed, or sold, you should research the images selected to make sure the owners have not placed any restrictions on their use. When you select an image in the dialog box, a hyperlink appears in the bottom left corner of the dialog box; you can follow it to the original image source, and from there you can glean information about its usage restrictions, if any.

Create a Photo Album Presentation

If you want to create a presentation that is primarily (or exclusively) photos, there's a special feature just for you! The Photo Album feature makes it easy to create photo-centric presentations with special features such as picture edging, framing, and captions.

Before you get started, find your photos. Know where on your computer they are stored. (Check the Pictures folder! That's where many digital camera management programs put them by default.)

Follow these steps to create a photo album:

1. Choose Insert ⇨ Photo Album. The Photo Album dialog box opens.

2. Click the File/Disk button. The Insert New Pictures dialog box opens.

3. Select the pictures you want to include.

   To select more than one picture at a time, hold down the Ctrl key while you click each one.

4. Click Insert. The pictures you select appear in the Pictures in Album list of the Photo Album dialog box. See **Figure 15-8.**

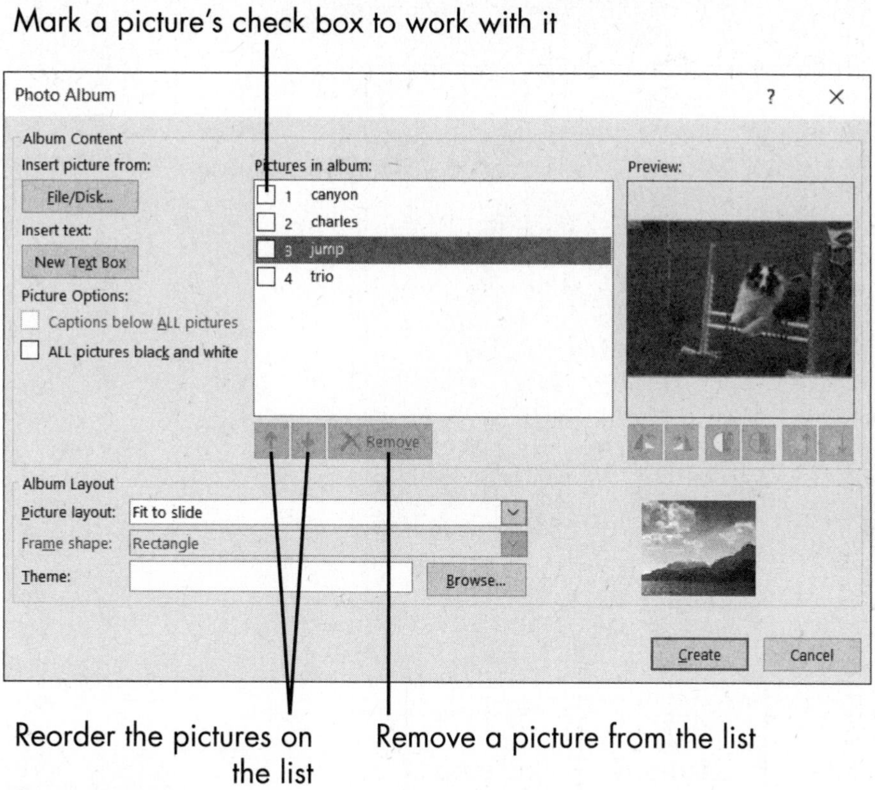

Figure 15-8

5. (Optional) Reorder the pictures.

a. Select the picture that's not in the right place in the order.

b. Click the up-arrow or down-arrow button below the list to reposition it.

6. (Optional) Rotate a picture or adjust its brightness or contrast (see **Figure 15-9**):

a. Select the picture's name.

b. Use the buttons under the Preview pane to adjust the picture's appearance as needed.

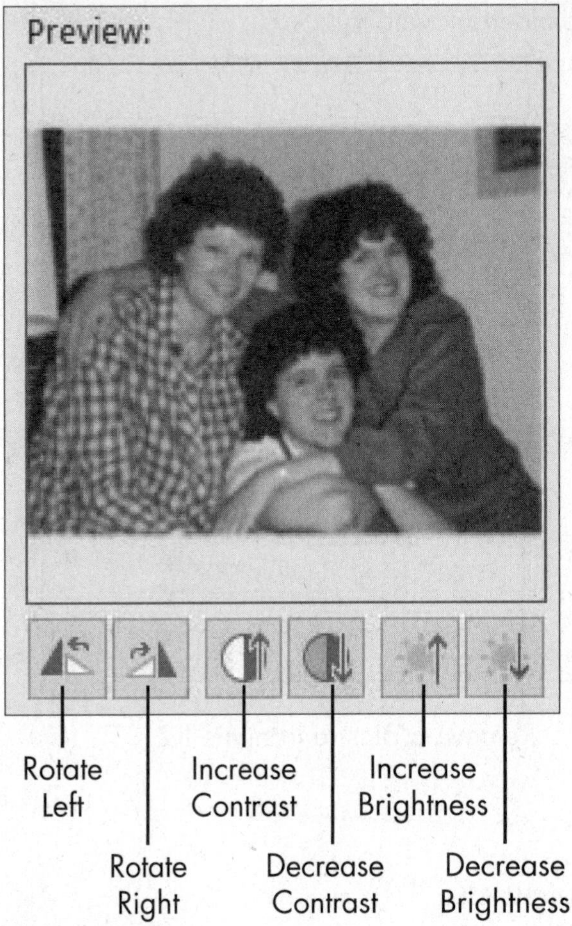

Figure 15-9

7. In the Album Layout section of the Photo Album dialog box, select the following options:

- *Picture Layout:* Choose how many pictures you want per slide.
- *Frame Shape:* Choose a frame shape/style for each photo.
- *Theme (optional):* Click the Browse button and then select a presentation theme to apply to the photo album.

You don't have to choose the theme now; you can apply a theme change to the presentation after its creation. (Choose Design➪Themes.)

8. Click the Create button. A new presentation is created using your photos.

   The resulting presentation is like any other presentation, except for one small extra: Because it is a photo album, you can return to the Photo Album dialog box at any time to manage the photos and effects. To do so, on the Insert tab, click the down arrow below the Photo Album button, and then choose Edit Photo Album from the menu that appears.

Adding Movement and Sound

Chapter 16

Get ready to . . .

Remember slide projectors? Maybe you still even have one in the back of your closet. They show one slide after another on a screen, with a *ker-chunk* sound as the next slide pushes the previous one out the chute. Not very glamorous or exciting.

In PowerPoint, though, because your slides are electronic, a presentation can have much more exciting animation. You can assign any sounds or music you want, and you can create interesting animations when one slide replaces another or when content appears on a slide. A bulleted list can appear one line at a time, a graphic can "fly" in separately from the text, or a trumpet sound can announce an important slide's appearance.

In this chapter, I show you how to create animation and transition effects on slides. I also show you how to add a musical soundtrack from an audio CD to a presentation.

Animate Objects on a Slide

By default, all the objects on a slide appear at once. Say you have a title, some text, and perhaps a graphic on a slide: They all show up together.

To add more visual interest to the presentation or to reveal bits of information at a time, you can use animation in PowerPoint. For example, you can pose a question in the title of the slide and then provide the answer in the body. Or you can have each item in a bulleted list appear one at a time.

You can control when the delayed content shows up by setting

- A **time delay:** The additional content appears after a certain number of seconds. This technique is good for autonomous presentations (without human interaction).
- **A mouse click delay:** Additional content appears only when you click the mouse or press a key on the keyboard. This technique is good for presentations with a live speaker because if someone asks a question or you get off-schedule, the animation won't occur at the wrong time — you control its timing.

For simple entrance animation, pick an animation preset from the Animation tab's Animation gallery. Follow these steps:

1. Select the object to be animated on its entrance. For example, if you want to animate a bulleted list on a slide, select the text box that contains those bullets. Or if you want to animate a graphic, select the graphic.
2. On the Animations tab, click the More arrow to open the palette in the Animate group. A selection of animation effect presets appears. See **Figure 16-1**.
3. Choose one of the effects from the Entrance section.

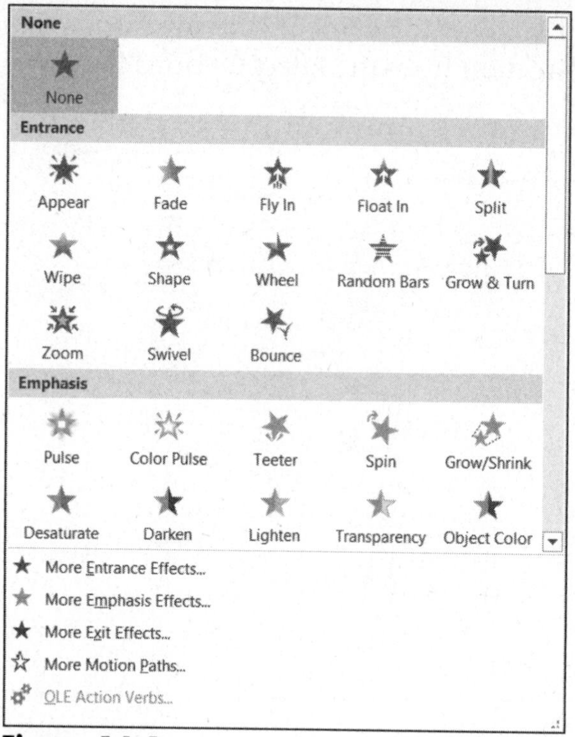

Figure 16-1

4. Click the Effect Options button on the Animations tab and select the options to fine-tune the effect. The choices depend on the type of object you are animating and the animation preset you chose in Step 2. **Figure 16-2** shows the choices for a text box that has the Float In animation applied, for example.

   If the object you chose is a text box, these are the choices for Effect Options:

   - *As One Object*: The entire content of the text box is animated as a single unit.
   - *All at Once:* Each paragraph is animated separately, but their animations occur simultaneously.
   - *By Paragraphs:* The first paragraph of the text appears when you click the mouse, and the next paragraph appears when you click again, and so on.

If the animation you chose involves the content entering from a direction, you can choose the direction from the Effect Options list, as in Figure 16-2.

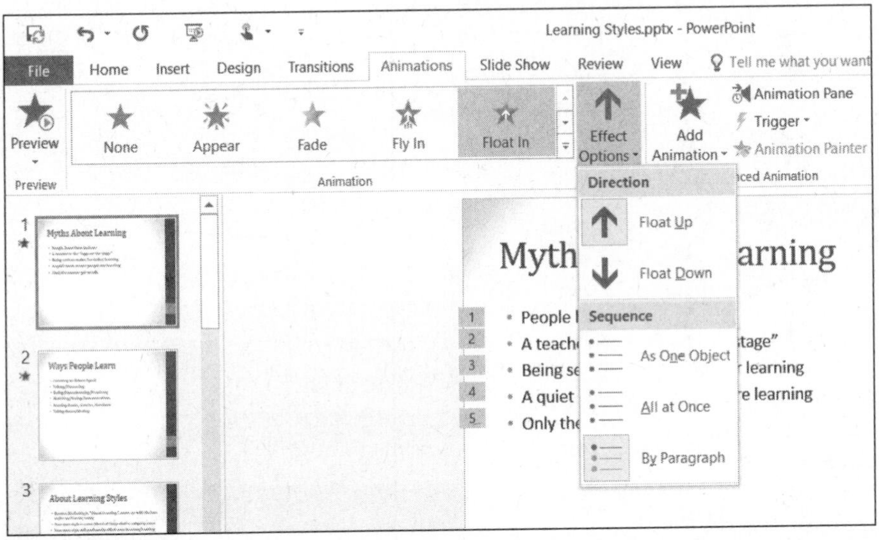

Figure 16-2

5. (Optional) To see a preview of the animation you chose, choose Animations ⇨ Preview.

   If you did not like any of the choices for animation effects, choose More Entrance Effects from the palette shown in Figure 16-1. This opens the Change Entrance Effect dialog box (shown in **Figure 16-3**). Click any of the effects there and click OK.

   After setting up an animation, there are a number of settings you can adjust for it. The most common change is to set the animation to occur automatically on a time delay rather than having it execute on mouse click. To make this change, do the following:

1. Select the object.
2. On the Animation tab, open the Start drop-down list and choose After Previous.

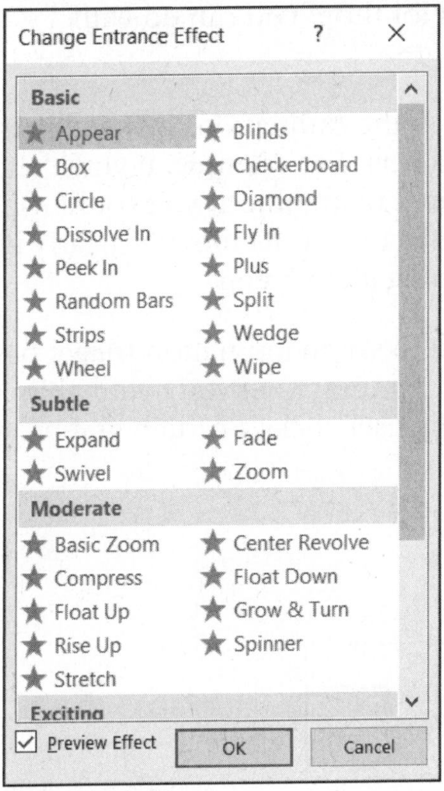

Figure 16-3

3. (Optional) If you want a delay between the previous event (such as the slide appearing) and this animation, enter it in the Delay box.

(Optional) If you want to adjust the speed at which the animation occurs, increment the value in the Duration field. (Clicking the up arrow makes it slower; down makes it faster.) See **Figure 16-4**. The Delay setting delays the animation from starting by a certain amount of time.

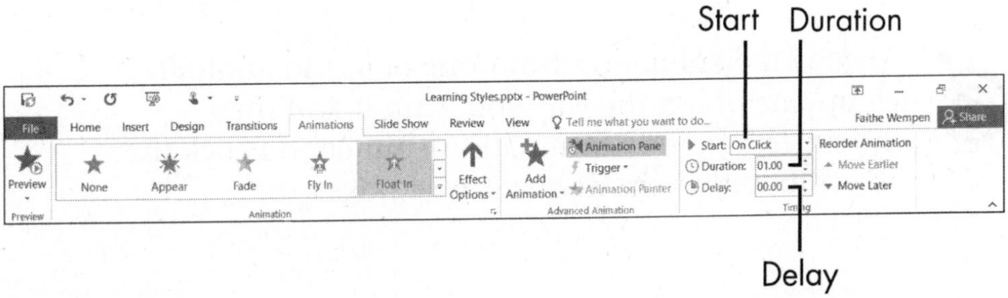

Figure 16-4

That's the basic stuff, but there's a lot more you can do with animation.

The Add Animation button, also on the Animations tab, enables you to assign more animations to an object. For example, if you already have an entrance animation assigned to an object, you could use Add Animation to also assign an exit effect for it. Its menu is nearly identical to that of the Animation group's gallery menu.

The Trigger command enables you to set an animation trigger based on some other object on the slide. For example, you could animate a text box so that it appears when the user clicks a certain graphic object on the slide, as in **Figure 16-5**.

Trigger an animation by clicking some other object

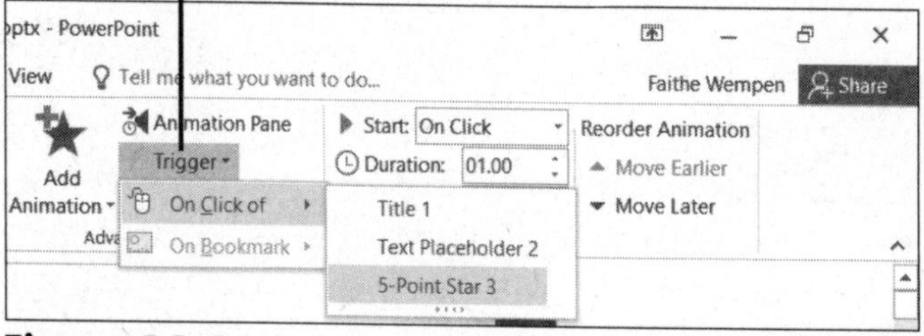

Figure 16-5

Animations play out in the order in which they are created by default. The current animation order is indicated by numbers on the slide, as shown in **Figure 16-6**.You can use Reorder Animation buttons to change the order. If you have a hard time visualizing the order from the numbers, click Animation Pane to show the animations in a list. There are also Move Earlier and Move Later arrow buttons on the Animation Pane, too.

To copy the animation from one object to another, set up one object the way you want it and then choose Animation ⇨ Animation Painter and click the object to receive the animation settings.

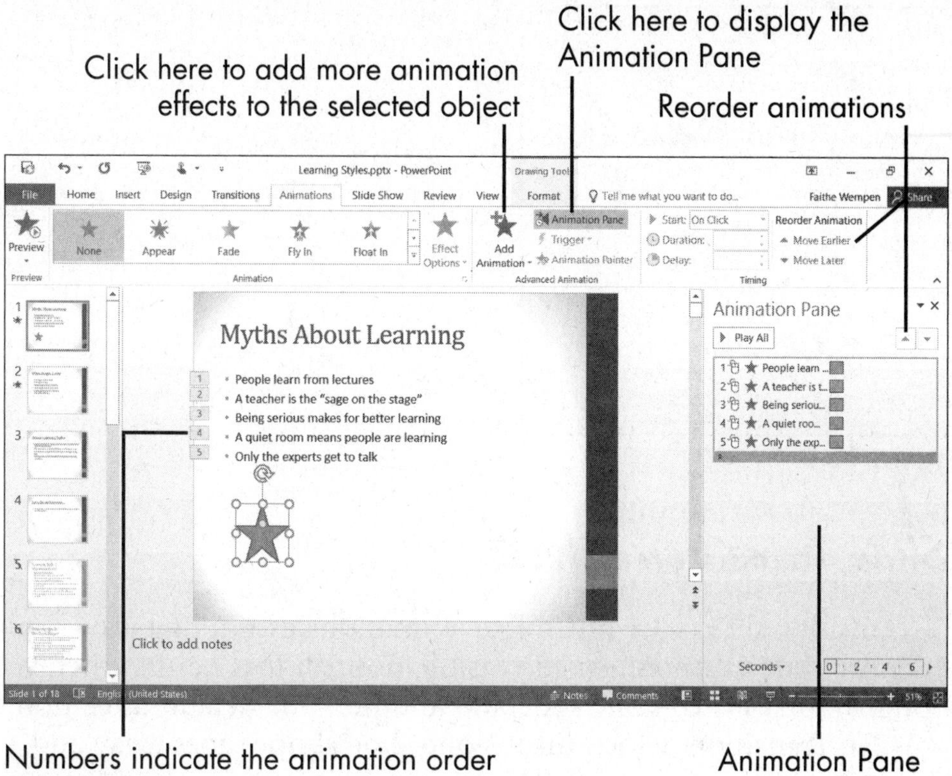

Figure 16-6

For even more control, right-click an animation event on the Animation Pane and then use one of the following commands to further fine-tune:

1. *Effect Options:* Opens a dialog box where you can choose whether sound will occur with the animation and how the object will appear after the animation has finished. See **Figure 16-7**.

2. *Timing:* Opens a dialog box where you can set the start, duration, delay, triggers, and other timing-related settings.

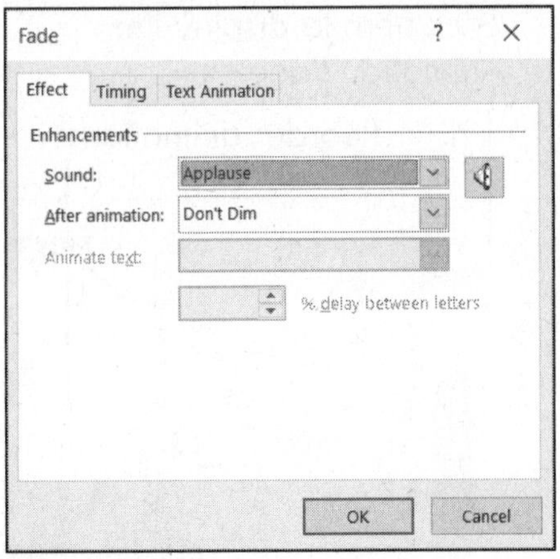

Figure 16-7

Add Slide Transition Effects

Transition effects are much like animations except that they apply to entire slides. A *transition effect* is the flourish that occurs when you transition between one slide and another. The default transition effect is No Transition, which means one slide simply goes away and another appears, with no flourish at all.

The transition effects you can use include fades, cuts, dissolves, and wipes. It's difficult to explain each of these effects, but if you see them, you'll immediately understand them. To try them out, follow these steps:

1. Click the Transitions tab.
2. In the Transition to This Slide group, point at one of the transition effects. A preview of it appears on the active slide. For more choices, click the More arrow to open a palette of more transition effects.
3. When you're ready to select a transition for a slide, click the transition you want (rather than just pointing at it). It's immediately applied to the active slide.

4. If the transition has options, the Effect Options button becomes available. Click it and make your choice. See **Figure 16-8.**

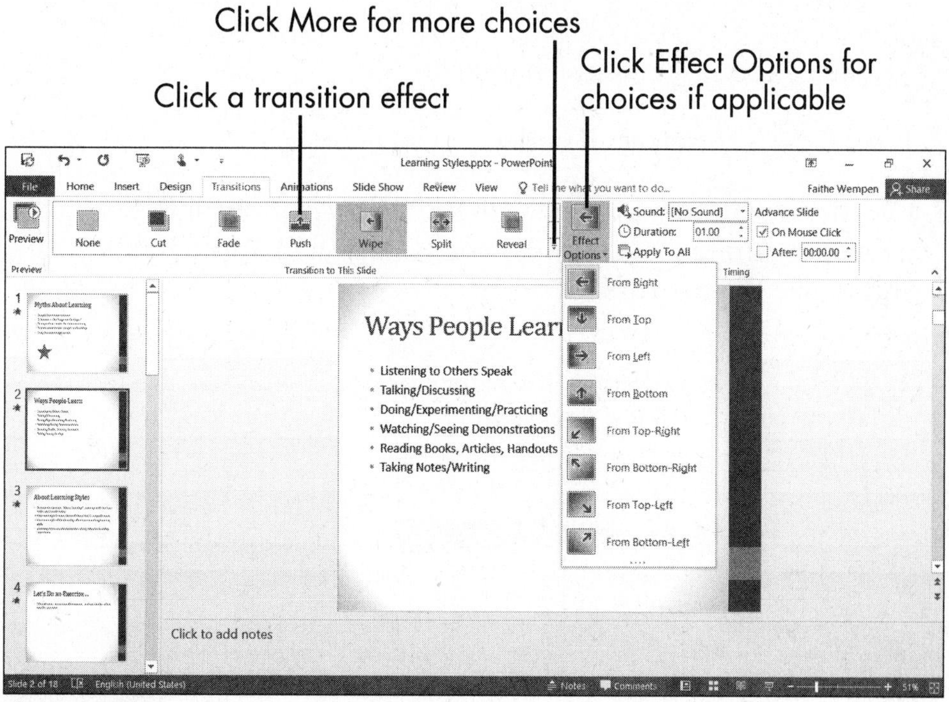

Figure 16-8

Use the Duration field and Sound drop-down list box to the right of the transitions to customize the speed at which the transition occurs and the sound that plays when the transition occurs (if any). Be wary of assigning sounds to transitions, though; in a long presentation, audiences might find them annoying.

Set Slides to Automatically Advance

By default, slides transition from one to another on mouse click, not automatically. If you want the slide show to progress automatically, with a certain amount of pause between slides, on the Transitions tab, mark the After check box, and then enter a number of seconds.

That setting applies only to the active slide, but you can easily apply it to all slides by doing the following:

1. Click in the Slides (left) pane in Normal view, or switch to Slide Sorter view.

   Read about views in Chapter 14.

2. Press Ctrl+A to select all slides.

3. On the Transitions tab, mark the After check box, and enter the number of seconds. The change will apply to all slides. See **Figure 16-9**.

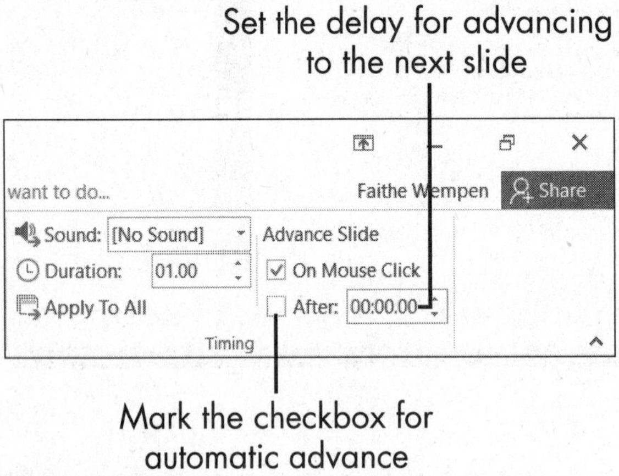

Figure 16-9

At any time, you can test your presentation by going into Slide Show view (choose View⇨Slide Show). Press Esc to return to Normal view.

Add a Soundtrack

As your presentation plays, you might want to have music in the background. PowerPoint enables you to specify a digital audio track, such as an MP3 file, on the PC that's being used to show the presentation and play it in synchronization with the presentation.

Musical soundtracks work best for *self-running presentations:* that is, those presentations where the slides are set to advance automatically after a certain number of seconds. In a presentation with a live speaker manually advancing the slides, that live speaker is probably also speaking to the audience, and the speech can interfere with the music (and vice versa).

To set up a soundtrack, follow these steps:

1. Select the first slide in the presentation, or the slide on which the music should start playing.

2. Choose Insert ➪ Audio ➪ Audio on My PC.

3. Navigate to the location where the audio file is stored. Select it and click insert.

4. Click Audio Tools Playback ➪ Play in Background. See **Figure 16-10**.

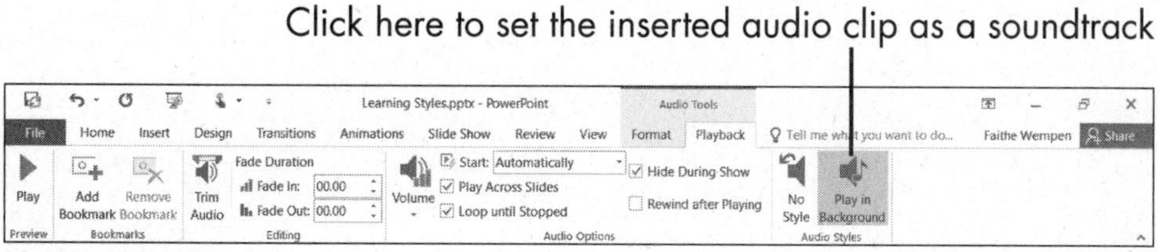

Figure 16-10

5. Check your work by viewing the presentation in Slide Show view (by choosing Slide Show ➪ From Beginning).

Choosing Play in Background in step 4 changes several settings, which collectively give you the effect you want. In earlier versions of PowerPoint you had to configure this combination of settings manually, which made it tricky, but now it's one-click simple.

Presenting the Show

Chapter 17

Get ready to . . .

Presenting . . . *your show!*

The whole point of a PowerPoint presentation is to deliver a show to an audience. That audience might be in the same room with you or a thousand miles away. Folks might watch it simultaneously or pull it up on their own PCs at their convenience.

This chapter explains how to display a presentation on your own computer screen. That's useful if you're going to be there in-person when the audience views the show, like during a club meeting or religious service. I also show you how to package a presentation to move it to a different PC as well as how to make printouts for yourself and your audience.

You also discover here how to make a self-running CD that you can send to people so they can view the presentation on their own computers, and how to make a video of your presentation.

Display a Slide Show Onscreen

Slide Show view is the view that you use when showing the presentation to others. (Read more about PowerPoint views in Chapter 14.)

One slide appears onscreen at a time, completely filling the screen. You might have used this view already — to check your work — while you were creating the presentation.

You can start Slide Show view from the first slide or from the current slide. Table 17-1 summarizes the methods of doing each.

Table 17-1 Methods of Entering Slide Show View

	From First Slide	*From Current Slide*
Shortcut key(s)	Press F5	Press Shift+F5
Slide Show tab	Slide Show⇨From Beginning	Slide Show⇨From Current Slide
View buttons (bottom right of screen)	N/A	Slide Show View button

Then, after you're in Slide Show view, you can show your presentation. Here's how:

- **Move to the next slide** (in any of these ways):
  - Click the mouse.
  - Press any key on the keyboard (except Backspace or the left arrow).
  - Right-click to display a shortcut menu and then choose Next. **Figure 17-1** shows this shortcut menu.
- **Move to the previous slide** (in any of these ways):
  - Press Backspace or the left arrow on the keyboard.
  - Right-click to display a shortcut menu and choose Previous. Refer to Figure 17-1.

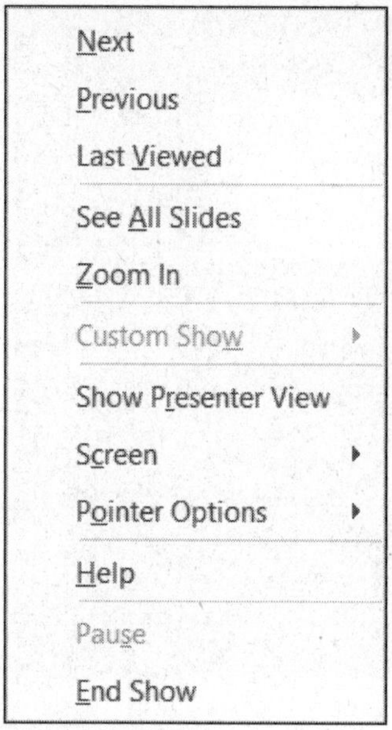

Figure 17-1

- **Jump to a specific slide**:

  a. Right-click to display a shortcut menu and choose See All Slides.

  b. Click the slide you want to display. See **Figure 17-2**.

- **End the show** (in any of these ways):

  - Click through to the end of the slide show (black screen) and then click one more time.
  - Press the Esc key.
  - Right-click to display a shortcut menu and then choose End Show.

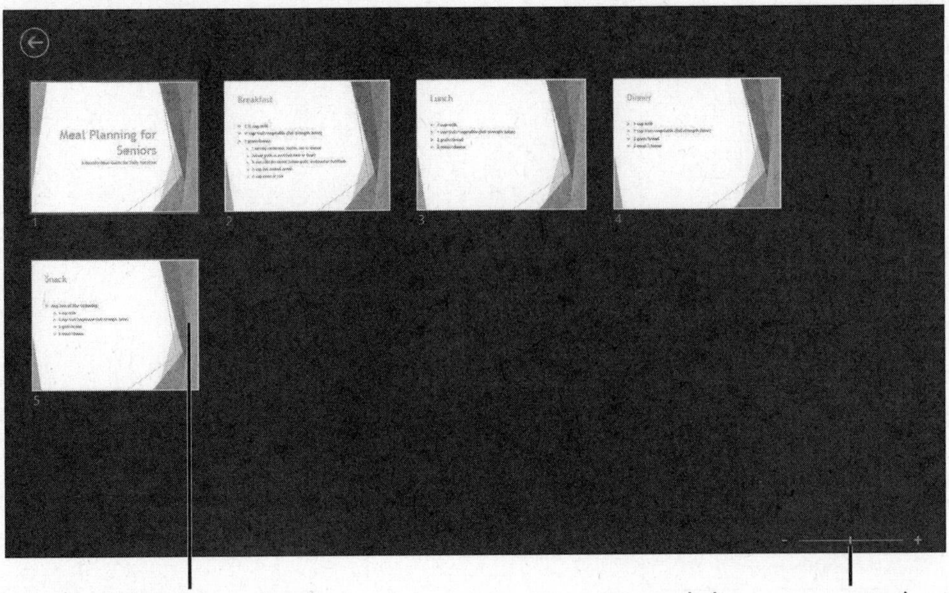

Figure 17-2

Use the Slide Show Tools

When you're working in Slide Show view, a very faint set of buttons appears in the lower-left corner. When you roll your mouse over these buttons, they brighten up so you can see them better. **Figure 17-3** shows the buttons on this toolbar.

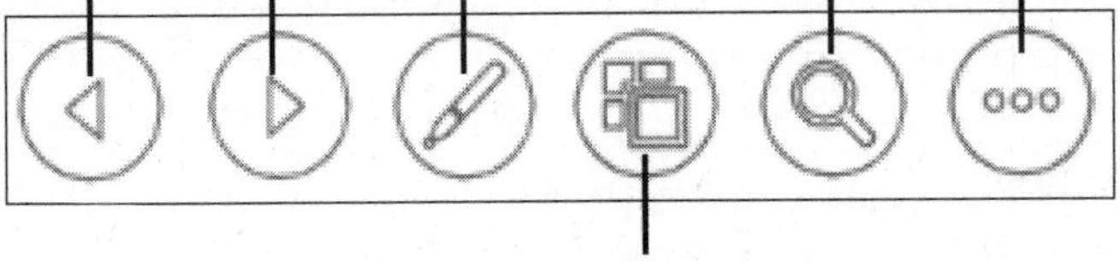

Figure 17-3

I enhanced Figure 17-3 to show all the buttons in their "bright" mode at once, so you can see them better. In reality, a button lights up only when you point at it, and you can point at only one at a time.

The buttons are

- **Previous:** A left-pointing arrow. Use this to go to the previous slide.
- **Next:** A right-pointing arrow. Use this to go to the next slide.
- **Pen:** Opens the Pen menu, which you can use to control a mouse-controlled "pen" that draws on the slides. There are three options: Laser Pointer (does not leave marks on the slide), Pen (leaves a thin line), and Highlighter (leaves thick, semi-transparent line). You can also choose an ink color. See **Figure 17-4**.

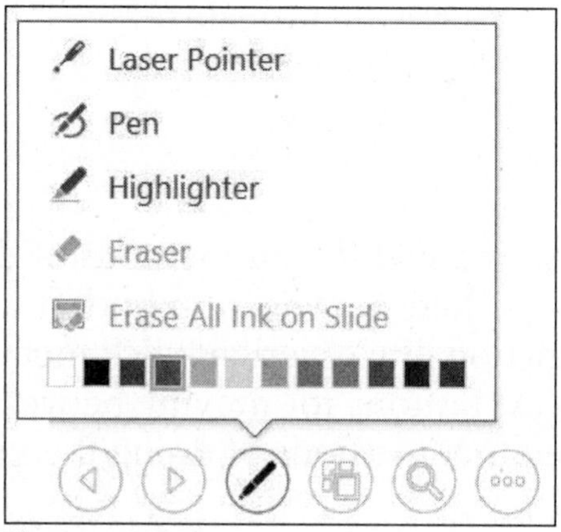

Figure 17-4

- **Show All Slides:** Opens the same pane as in Figure 17-2, showing thumbnails of all slides. Click a slide to jump to it.
- **Zoom:** Changes the mouse pointer to a large rectangular magnifier. Drag it around onscreen to the area you want to magnify and then click. Press Esc to return to regular viewing.

- **Options:** Opens a menu containing several miscellaneous commands for working in Slide Show view. See **Figure 17-5**.

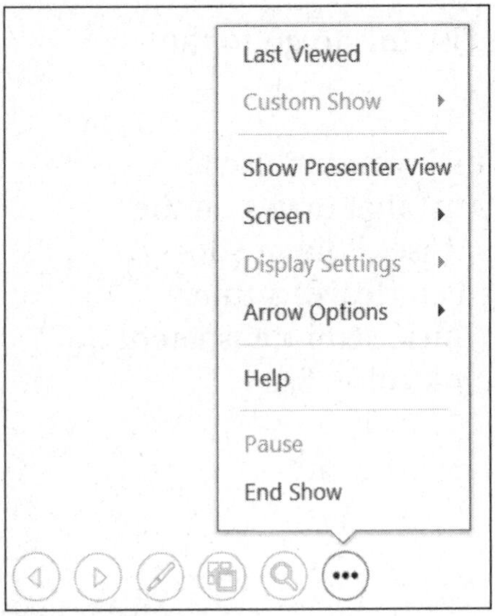

Figure 17-5

You might wonder why there are so many different methods of doing the same things. For example, why is there a navigation button that does nothing but duplicate the functionality of a right-click menu? And why are there Previous and Next buttons for moving between slides when there are at least three other methods of doing the same thing? (Refer to Table 17-1.)

PowerPoint allows you to lock down or disable certain navigation methods in Slide Show view so that people interacting with your presentation at an unattended computer won't inadvertently (or purposely) disable or damage the presentation. When one method is disabled, you might need to rely on another method to do what needs to be done.

One of the choices on the Options menu is Presenter View. If you have two monitors, you can use Presenter View to show the slides full-screen on one monitor while you use a specialized view for managing the slide show on the other monitor.

Print Copies of a Presentation

There are many uses for printouts of a presentation. You might want to print the slides themselves, for example (one big slide per page), to use as a kind of low-tech delivery system. If you don't have a computer or projector available, you can just hold up each slide, one by one! You might also want copies of the presentation to give to your audience, or a copy of the presentation to refer to while you speak.

When you print in PowerPoint, you're given a choice of the type of printout you want. Here are the choices available:

- **Full Page Slides:** A full-page copy of one slide per sheet.
- **Notes Pages:** One slide per page, but with the slide occupying only the top half of the page. The bottom half is devoted to any speaker notes you typed into PowerPoint.
- **Outline View:** A text-only version of the presentation, structured as an outline, with the slide titles as the top-level outline items.
- **Handouts:** Multiple slides per page (two to nine, depending on your choice of settings), suitable for giving to the audience to take home.

Different numbers of slides per page have different layouts. For example, if you choose three slides per page, the layout has lines next to each slide for the audience to take notes on.

To print any of these types of printouts, follow these steps:

1. (Optional) If you want to print only certain slides, select them. The easiest view to do this in is Slide Sorter.
2. Choose File⇨Print. The Print settings appear. See **Figure 17-6**.

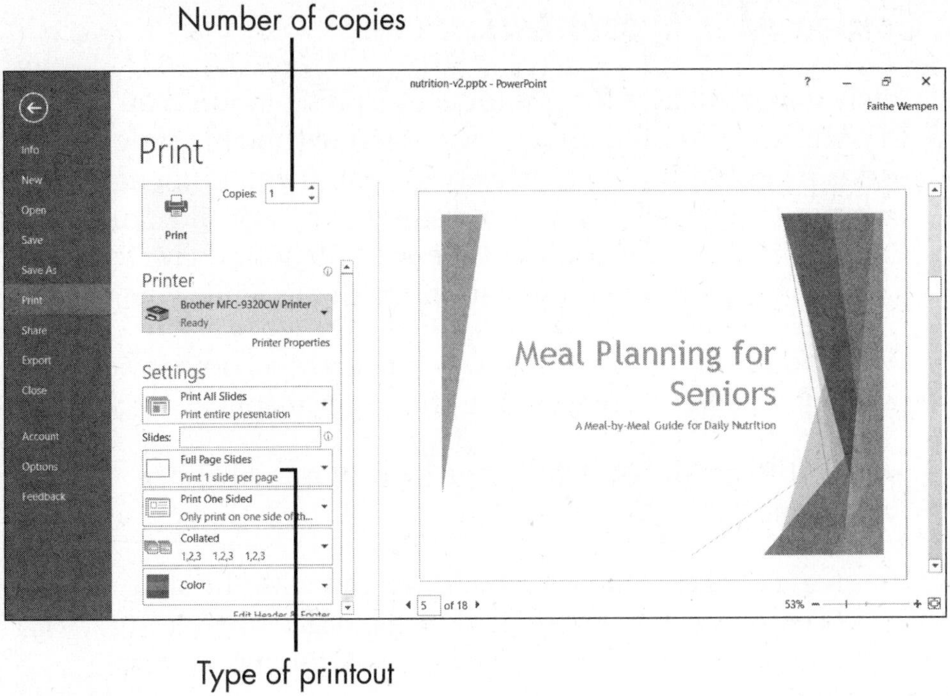

Figure 17-6

3. (Optional) If you want to print more than one copy, change to a higher number in the Copies box. The default number of copies is 1.

4. Under Printer, make sure the correct printer is chosen. Click the selected printer name and make another choice from the menu that appears if needed.

5. In the Settings area, if you do not want to print all the slides, enter the slide numbers in the Slides box. Use a dash for ranges (1-3 selects slides 1, 2, and 3, for example), or use commas to separate individual noncontiguous slides.

6. The default is to print full-page slides. If you want something else, such as handouts or notes pages, click Full Page Slides to open a menu from which you can choose another option. See **Figure 17-7**.

7. Click the Print button. The presentation prints.

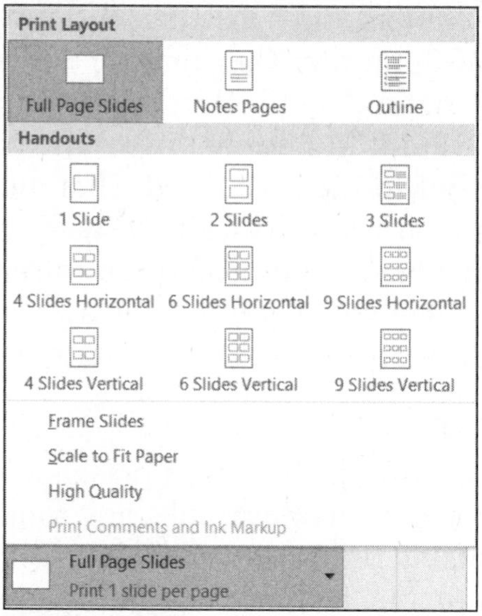

Figure 17-7

If you want to create handouts that can be edited in Word, choose File⇨Export⇨Create Handouts⇨Create Handouts. Then choose a format in the dialog box that appears and click OK. Once they're in Word, you can modify them as needed and then print them from there.

Package a Presentation for Distribution

The PC you play your presentation on might not always be the one you create it on. For example, if you're traveling to different clubs or organizations to give the same speech, each one might have its own computer system attached to its projector. If you have a laptop, you can bring your presentation with you, but you might find it easier to simply bring the presentation on a *flash drive* (a portable device used for storing files) or a CD.

If your presentation consists only of text and pictures, it's self-contained in a single PowerPoint file (with a `.pptx` or `.ppt` extension), so you can just copy that file to your flash drive — or email it to yourself as an email attachment, or use some other method to carry it with you.

However, if you have multimedia content, such as video clips, those may not be embedded in the PowerPoint file: They may be *linked.* Linked content is not stored in the main data file, but rather a link is created from the clip to your PowerPoint file, so that when the presentation plays, the content from the linked file is accessed. That means if you copy the PowerPoint file, you won't automatically copy the linked content. If you didn't know that in advance, you could run into a situation where you arrive at the site where you're going to give your speech only to find out that you didn't have all the presentation available!

There are other little gotchas, as well, about showing a presentation on a PC other than the one it was created on. For example, any fonts that the presentation uses must be available on the PC on which you're showing it. If those fonts aren't available, PowerPoint will try to substitute a similar font, but its definition of "similar" and yours might not be the same!

You can get around these problems by allowing PowerPoint to "pack" and copy the presentation file to another location. When it does so, it automatically also copies all the fonts, linked files, and other associated content needed to ensure a trouble-free show. You can package it to a folder on your hard drive and then copy that folder anywhere you like, or you can burn the package directly to a CD.

Here's how to pack a presentation to a CD:

1. Choose File ➪ Export ➪ Package Presentation for CD ➪ Package for CD. The Package for CD dialog box opens. See **Figure 17-8**.
2. (Optional) If you want to put additional presentations on the same CD, click Add, select the presentation to include, and click Add to place it on the list. Use the up- and down-arrow buttons to the left of the list to reorder the presentations if needed.
3. In the Name the CD field, type the label you want to assign to the CD.

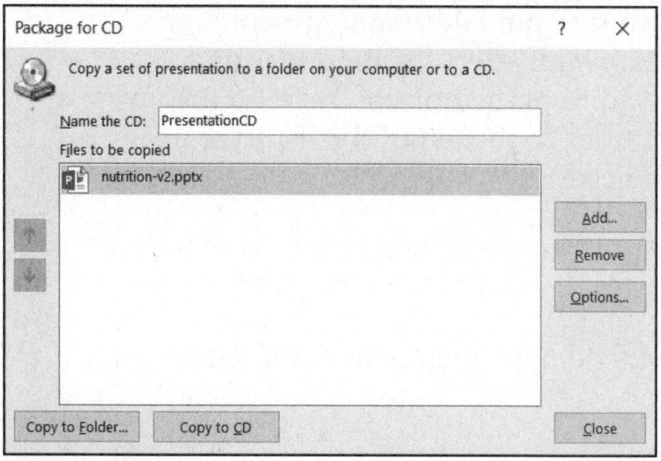

Figure 17-8

4. Insert a blank, writeable CD into your PC's CD drive.

5. Click the Copy to CD button. If a warning appears about linked files, click Yes.

6. Wait for PowerPoint to copy the presentation to the CD.

7. A message appears asking whether you want to copy the same files to another CD. If so, insert another CD and click Yes. Otherwise, click No.

8. Click Close to close the Package for CD dialog box.

When you make a CD or copy to a folder (coming up next), the PowerPoint Viewer utility is included. This utility allows the presentation to run without PowerPoint being installed on the computer.

Here's how to pack a PowerPoint presentation if you want to copy the files to a folder (for example, to transfer later to a flash drive or portable hard disk), rather than to a CD:

1. Choose File⇨Export⇨Package Presentation for CD⇨Package for CD. The Package for CD dialog box opens. Refer to Figure 17-8.

2. (Optional) If you want to put additional presentations on the same CD, click Add, select the presentation to include, and click Add to place it on the list. Use the up- and down-arrow buttons to the left of the list to reorder the presentations if needed.

3. Click the Copy to Folder button. The Copy to Folder dialog box opens.

4. In the Folder Name field, type the name of the folder you want to create.

5. In the Location field, type the path to the location where you want to store the new folder.

   Click Browse to select a location by browsing if you prefer.

6. Click OK to accept the location. The files are copied to that location.

7. Click Close to close the Package for CD dialog box.

Make a Video of the Presentation

You can save your presentation as a video, which you can then distribute using email, CD, or another method. You could, for example, create a PowerPoint presentation with pictures of your grandchildren and distribute it to your friends and family along with a holiday greeting.

By saving the presentation as a video, you lose the interactive capabilities; you can't choose how fast to advance the slides, for example, and you can't use a mouse to click on anything. Therefore, before making a video of the presentation, you should have it set up exactly the way you want it to self-run, including setting how long each slide is displayed onscreen. (Do this from the Transitions tab by setting a number of seconds in the After box, as Chapter 16 explains.) If you don't already have timings set, a default time will be spent on each slide (5 seconds, or whatever you specify when making the video).

When your presentation is exactly the way you want it, make the movie by following these steps:

1. Choose File ⇨ Export ⇨ Create a Video. The Create a Video options appear. See **Figure 17-9**.

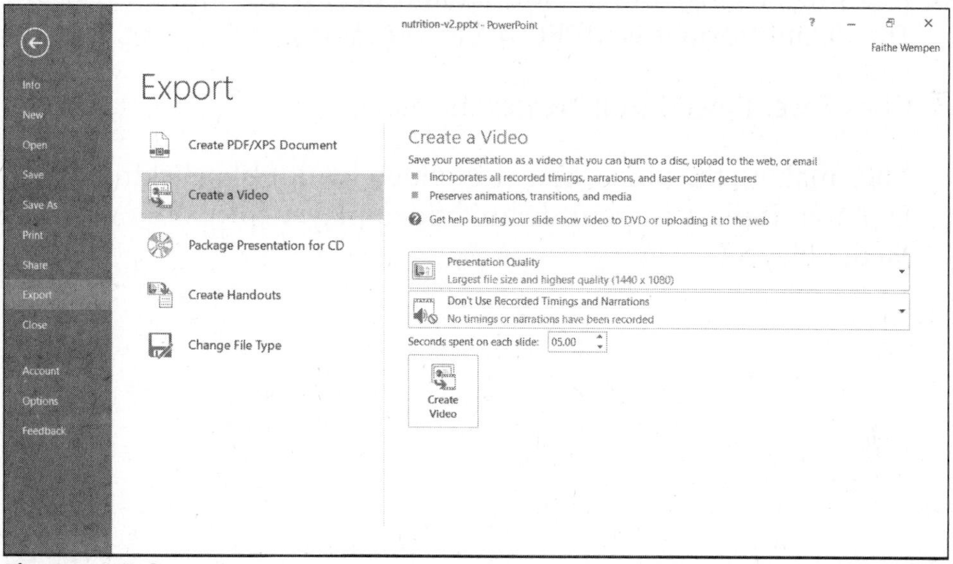

Figure 17-9

2. (Optional) The default resolution is Presentation Quality, the highest resolution available. If you want a lower resolution, click Presentation Quality and choose a different resolution from the menu (Internet Quality or Low Quality).

   Unless the presentation is so large that it won't fit on a single DVD at the default resolution, you should keep the resolution set to Presentation Quality.

3. (Optional) The default is to use any timings and narrations previously set up for the presentation. If you don't want to use these, click Use Recorded Timings and Narrations, and select Don't Use Recorded Timings and Narrations from the menu.

4. (Optional) Adjust the Seconds to Spend on Each Slide value if needed. The default is 5 seconds. This value will be used whenever a slide does not already have a timing set.

5. Click Create Video. The Save As dialog box appears.

6. If desired, change the file format and/or save location. The default format is MPEG-4 Video (`.mp4`).

7. Click Save. PowerPoint creates the video.

   After making the video, test your video by double-clicking it from File Explorer; it plays in your default video player (probably Windows Media Player).

Customizing Office Applications

Appendix A

Get ready to . . .

People have different ideas about what constitutes the "best" way for a program to operate. For every feature that one person finds ideal, someone else finds that same feature very annoying. That's why Microsoft Office 2016 has a variety of options you can customize to make the applications work more like you want.

In this appendix, I show you how to customize the Quick Access toolbar and the status bar in all the Office applications. (The process works basically the same in all of them.) Then I go through some of the most common program options in each application.

Customize the Quick Access Toolbar

The *Quick Access toolbar* is the small toolbar immediately above the File tab in each of the Office applications. By default, the Quick Access toolbar contains only a few buttons.

One of the handiest things about the Quick Access toolbar is that it's available no matter which tab you're on.

If you find yourself using a button frequently (other than one of the default buttons), consider placing it on the Quick Access toolbar so you don't have to switch tabs all the time.

Here's how to add a command to the Quick Access toolbar:

1. Right-click the button or other control. A shortcut menu opens.

2. Choose Add to Quick Access Toolbar.

Another use for the Quick Access toolbar is to add buttons for commands that don't appear on any of the tabs. (Yes, there are many such commands. Most of them are carryovers from previous versions of the software, but some are new features that are rather obscure.)

To browse the available commands and add any to the Quick Access toolbar (including commands not already on the Ribbon), follow these steps:

1. Choose File⇨Options. An Options dialog box appears for that application.

2. Click Quick Access Toolbar in the bar at the left. Two columns of commands appear in the middle of the window. The left column holds the commands you can add, and the right column holds the commands already on the Quick Access toolbar. See **Figure A-1**.

Choose commands to display

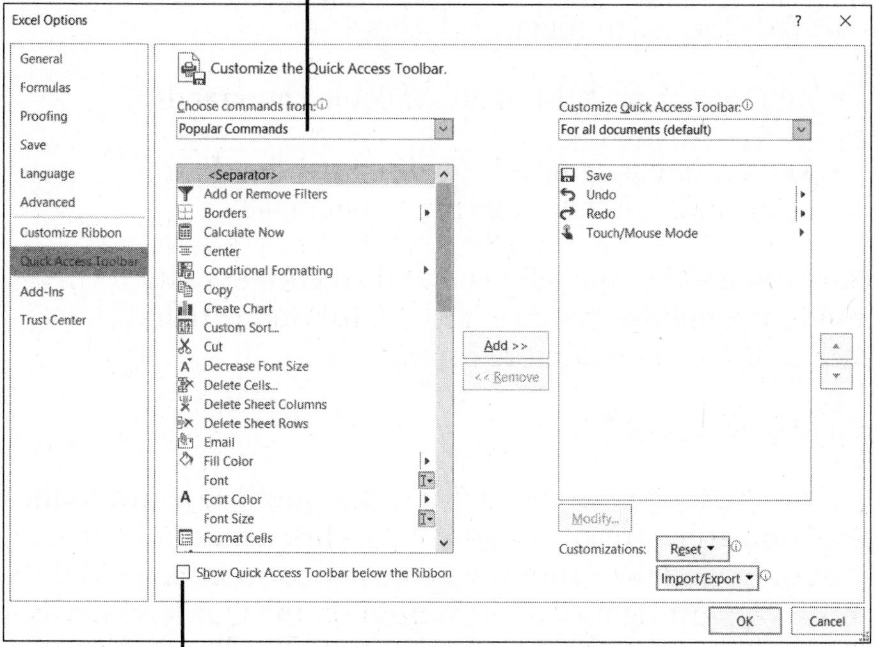

Relocate the QAT below the Ribbon if desired

Figure A-1

3. At the top of the left list, open the drop-down menu and choose what commands you want to see on the list:

- *Popular Commands:* A selection of the most commonly used commands
- *Commands Not in the Ribbon:* Commands that have no equivalent on any tab

Why would an application have a command that's not in the Ribbon? There are two main reasons. One is that the command was featured in an earlier version of the application but was removed in 2016, and it is available for those who still want to use it. Other commands may only be available several menu levels deep, or only in a dialog box; making them available to add to the QAT enables users to get faster access to them.

- *All Commands:* A list of all available commands
- *Macros:* Any *macros* (recorded scripts) that have been stored in the active file or template

4. Click a command in the left list and then click the Add button in the middle to move it to the list on the right. Repeat as desired to add more commands.
5. When finished, click OK.

To remove buttons from the Quick Access toolbar, return to the Quick Access Toolbar list (refer to Figure A-1), click a button's name in the *right* column, and then click the Remove button in the middle. Or take the easy way: Just right-click the button on the Quick Access toolbar and then choose Remove from Quick Access Toolbar from the menu that appears.

Customize the Status Bar

The *status bar* is the thin bar along the bottom of the application window. It contains *View buttons* (for switching between views), the Zoom slider, and perhaps a few other items, depending on the settings.

Just like the Quick Access toolbar, you can customize the status bar:

1. Right-click the status bar. On the shortcut menu that appears is a list of all the items that the status bar can contain. The ones with check marks next to them are already displayed.
2. Click an item to toggle it on or off. See **Figure A-2**.

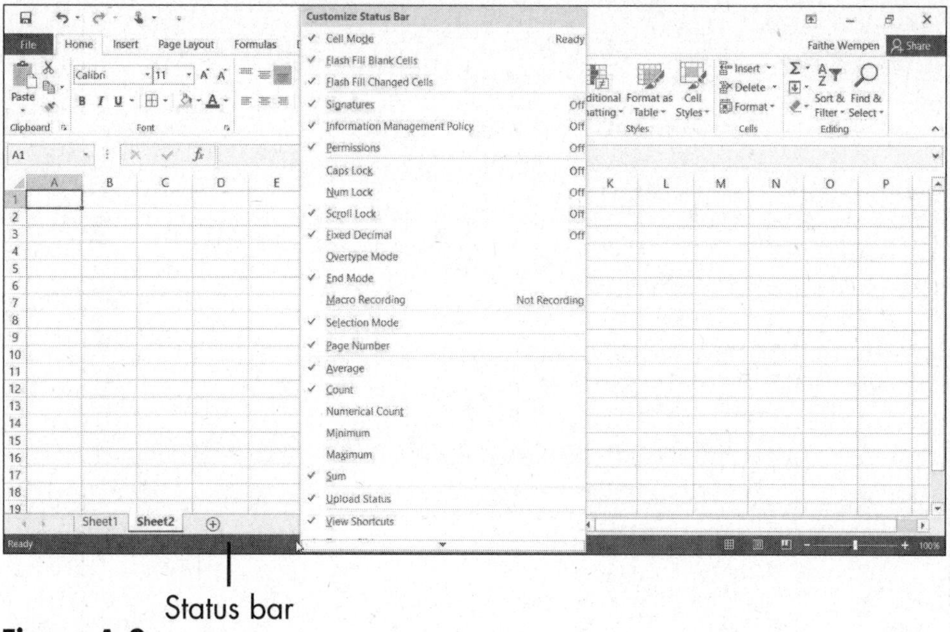

Figure A-2

Set Program Options

So many options are available in each application that it would take a much larger book to cover them all. In this appendix, I review a few of my favorite options in Word, Excel, Outlook, and PowerPoint. Outlook has many options that it doesn't share with the other applications, so I provide extra coverage of Outlook separately later in this appendix.

For each application, access the options by clicking the File button and then click the Options command. Then click a category at the left to display a page of options. See **Figure A-3**.

Use Table A-1 as a handy guide to customize Word, Excel, Outlook, and PowerPoint. Items marked with an asterisk (*) are not available in Outlook.

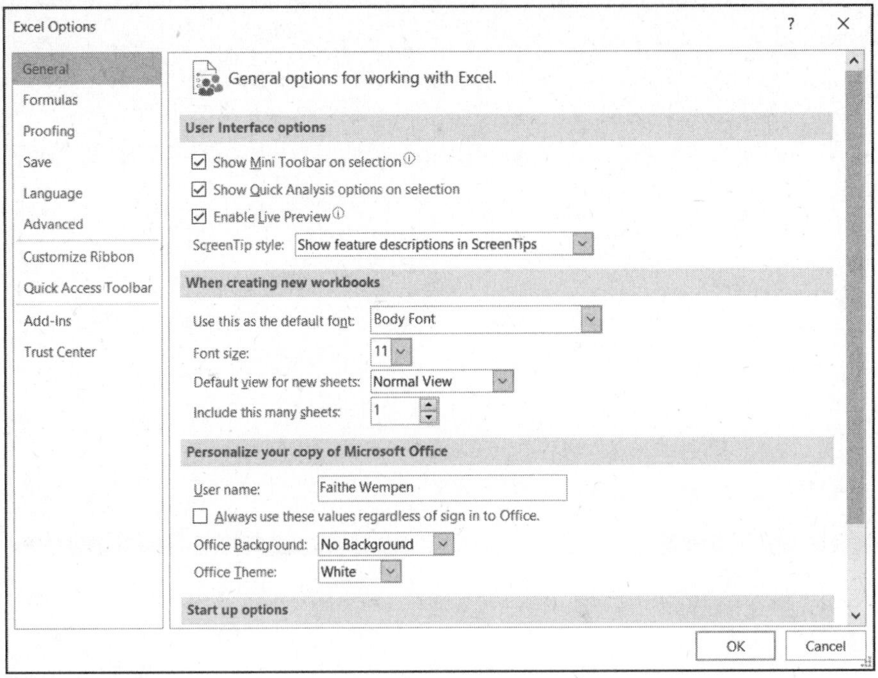

Figure A-3

Table A-1	**Common Options**
If You Want To . . .	***Choose This . . .***
Prevent the mini toolbar from popping up when you select text.	General ➪ Show Mini Toolbar on Selection
Change the color of the application window.	General ➪ Office Theme. Then choose a color from the drop-down list.
Turn off wavy red underlines of misspelled words.	(Word and PowerPoint only) Proofing ➪ Check Spelling as You Type
Save files in a format other than the application's standard format.	Save ➪ Save Files in This Format
Set the default local file location. (This determines the folder that appears by default in the Save As and Open dialog boxes when working with This PC.)	Save ➪ Default Local File Location

If You Want To . . .	Choose This . . .
Clear the Recent Documents list on the Office menu.	Advanced ➪ Display ➪ Show This Number of Recent (Documents/Workbooks/Presentations); then set the number to 0.
Turn on the Developer tab, which contains extra commands, such as those for templates.	Click Customize Ribbon and then mark the Developer check box in right column.
Change the default user name and initials.	General ➪ User Name General ➪ Initials (Word and PowerPoint only)
Set spelling options.	Proofing tab

Set Outlook Options

Outlook has many options that it doesn't share with the other Office applications, because its functionality is so different. To adjust those options, choose Office ➪ Options. Then, in the Outlook Options dialog box that opens, click a tab and select options on that tab.

Table A-2 lists some of the most common options you can set in Outlook.

Table A-2 Common Options in Outlook

If You Want To . . .	Choose This . . .
Turn off the envelope icon that pops up by the clock in Windows when mail is being sent and received.	Mail ➪ Message Arrival ➪ Show an Envelope Icon in the Taskbar Mail ➪ Message Arrival ➪ Display a Desktop Alert
Choose whether to save copies of messages you send to the Sent Items folder.	Mail ➪ Save Messages ➪ Save Copies of Messages in Sent Items Folder
Adjust the privacy and security of email handling.	Trust Center ➪ Trust Center Settings

(continued)

Table A-2 *(continued)*

If You Want To . . .	*Choose This . . .*
Adjust how frequently automatic sending/receiving occurs.	Advanced ➪ Send and Receive ➪ Send/Receive ➪ Schedule an Automatic Send/Receive Every ___ Minutes
Set the default text formatting for new e-mails.	Mail ➪ Compose Messages ➪ Compose Messages in This Format
Empty the Deleted Items folder each time you exit Outlook.	Advanced ➪ Outlook Start and Exit ➪ Empty Deleted Items Folders When Exiting Outlook
Bypass the confirmation prompt that appears when you permanently delete items (by pressing Shift+Delete).	Advanced ➪ Other ➪ Prompt for Confirmation Before Permanently Deleting Items
Choose which panes appear in Outlook.	Advanced ➪ Outlook Panes

Index

• A •

• B •

• D •

• *E* •

• F •

• I •

• L •

• M •

• N •

• O •

• p •

• S •

• T •

• U •

• V •

• W •

• X •

• Z •

About the Author

Faithe Wempen, MA, is a Microsoft Office Master Instructor and the author of more than 150 books on computer hardware and software, including *PowerPoint 2013 Bible* and *Office 2013 eLearning Kit For Dummies*. She is an adjunct instructor of Computer Information Technology at Purdue University, and her corporate training courses online have reached more than a quarter of a million students for clients such as Hewlett-Packard, Sony, and CNET.

Author's Acknowledgments

Thanks to the wonderful editorial staff at Wiley for another job well done. You guys are top notch!

Dedication

To Margaret.

Publisher's Acknowledgments

Acquisitions Editor: Andy Cummings

Project Editor: Christopher Morris

Copy Editor: Christopher Morris

Editorial Assistant: Claire Johnson

Sr. Editorial Assistant: Cherie Case

Project Coordinator: Suresh Srinivasan

Cover Image: Monkey Business Images/ Shutterstock